ACCA

PAPER F9

FINANCIAL MANAGEMENT

In this April 2007 new edition

- We discuss the **best strategies** for revising and taking your ACCA exams

- We show you how to be well prepared for the **December 2007 exam**

- We give you **lots of great guidance** on tackling questions

- We include **genuine student answers** with BPP commentary

- We show you how you can **build your own exams**

- We provide you with **three** mock exams including the **Pilot paper**

- We provide the **ACCA examiner's answers** as well as our own to key exam questions and the Pilot Paper as an additional revision aid

Our **i-Pass** product also supports this paper.

FOR EXAMS IN DECEMBER 2007

P
R
A
C
T
I
C
E

&

R
E
V
I
S
I
O
N

K
I
T

First edition April 2007

ISBN 9780 7517 3377 8

British Library Cataloguing-in-Publication Data
A catalogue record for this book
is available from the British Library

Published by

BPP Learning Media Ltd
BPP House, Aldine Place
London W12 8AA

www.bpp.com/learningmedia

Printed in Great Britain by
Antony Rowe Ltd
Bumpers Farm
Chippenham
Wiltshire
SN14 6LH

Your learning materials, published by BPP Learning
Media Ltd, are printed on paper sourced from
sustainable, managed forests.

We are grateful to the Association of Chartered Certified
Accountants for permission to reproduce past
examination questions. The answers to past examination
questions have been prepared by BPP Learning Media
Ltd.

Contents

Review form & free prize draw

Question index

The headings in this checklist/index indicate the main topics of questions, but questions often cover several different topics.

Questions set under the old syllabuses *Financial Management and Control (FMC)* are included because their style and content are similar to those that appear in the Paper F9 exam.

BPP
LEARNING MEDIA

Mock exam 1

Questions 51 to 54

Mock exam 2

Questions 55 to 58

Mock exam 3 (Pilot paper)

Questions 59 to 62

Planning your question practice

Our guidance from page 29 shows you how to organise your question practice, either by attempting questions from each syllabus area or **by building your own exams** – tackling questions as a series of practice exams.

Topic index

Listed below are the key Paper F9 syllabus topics and the numbers of the questions in this Kit covering those topics.

If you need to concentrate your practice and revision on certain topics or if you want to attempt all available questions that refer to a particular subject, you will find this index useful.

Syllabus topic	Question numbers
Asset replacement decisions	21
Behavioural finance	40
Business valuation	39, 40, 41, 42, 43
Capital rationing	20, 22, 23
CAPM	33, 34, 35, 38
Cash management	9, 10, 12, 31
Cash operating cycle	6
Competition policy	4, 14
Convertible loan stock	27, 28, 37
Corporate governance	1
Dividend policy	26
Exchange rate risk	45, 46, 47, 48
Financial intermediaries	5
Gearing	28, 29, 33
Inflation	6
Interest rate risk	49, 50
Interest rates	4
Inventory management	7, 8
Investment appraisal	14, 15, 16
IRR	15, 17
Leasing	19,20
Managerial reward schemes	2, 3
NPV	15. 16, 18, 19, 20, 21, 22, 23
Objectives	1, 2, 10
Overtrading	12
Payback	14, 18
Receivables management	11, 13, 45
Rights issue	24, 25, 27
Risk	18
Risk/return trade-off	5
Sensitivity analysis	17, 18
Shareholder ratios	3, 14, 25, 29, 30, 36
Shareholder wealth maximisation	2, 4
Sources of finance	24, 27, 30, 31, 32, 33, 37, 39, 44
Stakeholders	1, 10
Stock market efficiency	34, 40, 42, 43, 44
Value for money	4
WACC	32, 33, 35, 36, 37
Working capital financing	11, 12, 13, 24

Using your BPP Practice and Revision Kit

Tackling revision and the exam

You can significantly improve your chances of passing by tackling revision and the exam in the right ways. Our advice is based on feedback from ACCA examiners.

- We look at the dos and don'ts of revising for, and taking, ACCA exams
- We focus on Paper F9; we discuss revising the syllabus, what to do (and what not to do) in the exam, how to approach different types of question and ways of obtaining easy marks

Selecting questions

We provide signposts to help you plan your revision.

- A full **question index**
- A **topic index** listing all the questions that cover key topics, so that you can locate the questions that provide practice on these topics, and see the different ways in which they might be examined
- **BPP's question plan** highlighting the most important questions and explaining why you should attempt them
- **Build your own exams**, showing how you can practise questions in a series of exams

Making the most of question practice

At BPP we realise that you need more than just questions and model answers to get the most from your question practice.

- Our **Top tips** provide essential advice on tackling questions, presenting answers and the key points that answers need to include
- We show you how you can pick up **Easy marks** on questions, as we know that picking up all readily available marks often can make the difference between passing and failing
- We summarise **Examiner's comments**
- We include **marking guides** to show you what the examiner rewards
- We refer to the **2007 BPP Study Text** for detailed coverage of the topics covered in each question
- A number of questions include **Analysis** and **Helping hands** attached to show you how to approach them if you are struggling
- In a bank at the end of this Kit we include the **examiner's answers** to the Pilot paper and other questions. Used in conjunction with our answers they provide an indication of all possible points that could be made, issues that could be covered and approaches to adopt.

Attempting mock exams

There are three mock exams that provide practice at coping with the pressures of the exam day. We strongly recommend that you attempt them under exam conditions. **Mock exams 1 and 2** reflect the question styles and syllabus coverage of the exam; **Mock exam 3** is the Pilot paper. To help you get the most out of doing these exams, we not only provide help with each answer, but also guidance on how you should have approached the whole exam.

Passing ACCA exams

Revising and taking ACCA exams

To maximise your chances of passing your ACCA exams, you must make best use of your time, both before the exam during your revision, and when you are actually doing the exam.

- Making the most of your revision time can make a big, big difference to how well-prepared you are for the exam

- Time management is a core skill in the exam hall; all the work you've done can be wasted if you don't make the most of the three hours you have to attempt the exam

In this section we simply show you what to do and what not to do during your revision, and how to increase and decrease your prospects of passing your exams when you take them. Our advice is grounded in feedback we've had from ACCA examiners. You may be surprised to know that much examiner advice is the same whatever the exam, and the reasons why many students fail don't vary much between subjects and exam levels. So if you follow the advice we give you over the next few pages, you will **significantly** enhance your chances of passing **all** your ACCA exams.

How to revise

☑ Plan your revision

At the start of your revision period, you should draw up a **timetable** to plan how long you will spend on each subject and how you will revise each area. You need to consider the total time you have available and also the time that will be required to revise for other exams you're taking.

☑ Practise Practise Practise

The **more exam-standard questions** you do, the **more likely you are to pass** the exam. Practising full questions will mean that you'll get used to the time pressure of the exam. When the time is up, you should note where you've got to and then try to complete the question, giving yourself practice at everything the question tests.

☑ Revise enough

Make sure that your revision covers the breadth of the syllabus, as most or all topics could be examined in a compulsory question. However it is true that some topics are **key** – they often appear or are a particular interest of the examiner – and you need to spend sufficient time revising these. Make sure you also know the **basics** – the fundamental calculations, proformas and report layouts.

☑ Deal with your difficulties

Difficult areas are topics you find dull and pointless, or subjects that you found problematic when you were studying them. You mustn't become negative about these topics; instead you should build up your knowledge by reading the **Passcards** and using the **Quick Quiz** questions in the Study Text to test yourself. When practising questions in the Kit, go back to the Text if you're struggling.

☑ Learn from your mistakes

Having completed a question you must try to look at your answer critically. Always read the **Top tips guidance** in the answers; it's there to help you. Look at **Easy marks** to see how you could have quickly gained credit on the questions that you've done. As you go through the Kit, it's worth noting any traps you've fallen into, and key points in the **Top tips** or **Examiner's comments** sections, and referring to these notes in the days before the exam. Aim to learn at least one new point from each question you attempt, a technical point perhaps or a point on style or approach.

☑ Read the examiners' guidance

We refer throughout this Kit to **Examiner's comments**. As well as highlighting weaknesses, examiners' reports often provide clues to future questions, as many examiners will test areas where problems are likely to arise. ACCA's website also contains articles by examiners which you **must** read, as they may form the basis of questions on any paper after they've been published.

Read through the examiner's answers to exam questions included at the back of the Kit. In general these are far longer and more comprehensive than any answer you could hope to produce in the exam, but used in conjunction with our more realistic solutions, they provide a useful revision tool, covering all possible points and approaches.

☑ Complete all three mock exams

You should attempt the **Mock exams** at the end of the Kit under **strict exam conditions**, to gain experience of selecting questions, managing your time and producing answers.

How NOT to revise

☒ Revise selectively

Examiners are well aware that some students try to forecast the contents of exams, and only revise those areas that they think will be examined. Examiners try to prevent this by doing the unexpected, for example setting the same topic in successive sittings.

☒ Spend all the revision period reading

You cannot pass the exam just by learning the contents of Passcards, Course Notes or Study Texts. You have to develop your **application skills** by practising questions.

☒ Audit the answers

This means reading the answers and guidance without having attempted the questions. Auditing the answers gives you **false reassurance** that you would have tackled the questions in the best way and made the points that our answers do. The feedback we give in our answers will mean more to you if you've attempted the questions and thought through the issues.

☒ Practise some types of question, but not others

Although you may find the numerical parts of certain papers challenging, you shouldn't just practise calculations. These papers will also contain written elements, and you therefore need to spend time practising written question parts.

☒ Get bogged down

Don't spend a lot of time worrying about all the minute detail of certain topic areas, and leave yourself insufficient time to cover the rest of the syllabus. Remember that a key skill in the exam is the ability to **concentrate on what's important** and this applies to your revision as well.

☒ Overdo studying

Studying for too long without interruption will mean your studying becomes less effective. A five minute break each hour will help. You should also make sure that you are leading a **healthy lifestyle** (proper meals, good sleep and some times when you're not studying).

How to PASS your exams

☑ Prepare for the day

Make sure you set at least one alarm (or get an alarm call), and allow plenty of time to get to the exam hall. You should have your route planned in advance and should listen on the radio for potential travel problems. You should check the night before to see that you have pens, pencils, erasers, watch, calculator with spare batteries, also exam documentation and evidence of identity.

☑ Select the right questions

You should select the optional questions you feel you can answer **best**, basing your selection on the topics covered, the requirements of the question, how easy it will be to apply the requirements and the availability of easy marks.

☑ Plan your three hours

You need to make sure that you will be answering the correct number of questions, and that you spend the right length of time on each question – this will be determined by the number of marks available. Each mark carries with it a **time allocation** of **1.8 minutes**. A 25 mark question therefore should be selected, completed and checked in 45 minutes. With some papers, it's better to do certain types of question first or last.

☑ Read the questions carefully

To score well, you must follow the requirements of the question, understanding what aspects of the subject area are being covered, and the tasks you will have to carry out. The requirements will also determine what information and examples you should provide. Reading the question scenarios carefully will help you decide what **issues** to discuss, **techniques** to use, **information** and **examples** to include and how to **organise** your answer.

☑ Plan your answers

Five minutes of planning plus twenty-five minutes of writing is certain to earn you more marks than thirty minutes of writing. Consider when you're planning how your answer should be **structured, w**hat the **format** should be and **how long** each part should take.

Confirm before you start writing that your plan makes **sense,** covers **all relevant points** and does not include **irrelevant material.**

☑ Show evidence of judgement

Remember that examiners aren't just looking for a display of knowledge; they want to see how well you can **apply** the knowledge you have. Evidence of application and judgement will include writing answers that only contain **relevant** material, using the material in scenarios to **support** what you say, **criticising** the **limitations** and **assumptions** of the techniques you use and making **reasonable recommendations** that follow from your discussion.

☑ Stay until the end of the exam

Use any spare time to **check and recheck** your script. This includes checking you have filled out the candidate details correctly, you have labelled question parts and workings clearly, you have used headers and underlining effectively and spelling, grammar and arithmetic are correct.

How to FAIL your exams

☒ Don't do enough questions

If you don't attempt sufficient questions on the paper, you are making it harder for yourself to pass the questions that you do attempt. If for example you don't do a 20 mark question, then you will have to score 50 marks out of 80 marks on the rest of the paper, and therefore have to obtain 63% of the marks on the questions you do attempt. Failing to attempt all of the paper is symptomatic of poor time management or poor question selection.

☒ Include irrelevant material

Markers are given detailed mark guides and will not give credit for irrelevant content. Therefore you should **NOT** braindump all you know about a broad subject area; the markers will only give credit for what is **relevant**, and you will also be showing that you lack the ability to **judge what's important.** Similarly forcing irrelevant theory into every answer won't gain you marks, nor will providing uncalled for features such as situation analyses, executive summaries and background information.

☒ Fail to use the details in the scenario

General answers or reproductions of Kit answers that don't refer to what is in the scenario in **this** question won't score enough marks to pass.

☒ Copy out the scenario details

Examiners see **selective** use of the right information as a key skill. If you copy out chunks of the scenario which aren't relevant to the question, or don't use the information to support your own judgements, you won't achieve good marks.

☒ Don't do what the question asks

Failing to provide all the examiner asks for will limit the marks you score. You will also decrease your chances by not providing an answer with enough **depth** – producing a single line bullet point list when the examiner asks for a discussion.

☒ Present your work poorly

Markers will only be able to give you credit if they can read your writing. There are also plenty of other things that will make it more difficult for markers to reward you. Examples include:

- Not using black or blue ink
- Not showing clearly which question you're attempting
- Scattering question parts from the same question throughout your answer booklet
- Not showing clearly workings or the results of your calculations

Paragraphs that are too long or which lack headers also won't help markers and hence won't help you.

Using your BPP products

This Kit gives you the question practice and guidance you need in the exam. Our other products can also help you pass:

- **Learning to Learn Accountancy** gives further valuable advice on revision

- **Passcards** provide you with clear topic summaries and exam tips

- **Success CDs** help you revise on the move

- **i-Pass CDs** offer tests of knowledge against the clock

- **Learn Online** is an e-learning resource delivered via the Internet, offering comprehensive tutor support and featuring areas such as study, practice, email service, revision and useful resources

You can purchase these products by visiting www.bpp.com/mybpp.

Visit our website www.bpp.com/acca/learnonline to sample aspects of Learn Online free of charge. Learn Online is hosted by BPP Professional Education.

Passing F9

Revising F9

Topics to revise

The exam consists of four questions, all of which are compulsory. No one section in the syllabus is more important than another so there are **no** short-cuts. You will have to be able to answer questions on the **entire syllabus**.

Question practice

You need to practise exam standard and exam style questions on a regular basis.

As you get closer to the exam, try to do complete questions in 45 minutes so that you are able to work at an appropriate speed.

Make sure you practise written sections as well as the calculations.

Passing the F9 exam

Displaying the right qualities

The aim of Paper F9 is to develop the knowledge and skills expected of a finance manager in relation to investment, financing and dividend decisions.

You need to be able to communicate your understanding clearly in an exam context. Calculations and discussions are equally important so do not concentrate on the numbers and ignore the written parts.

You need to be able to:

- Discuss the role and purpose of the financial management function
- Assess and discuss the impact of the economic environment on financial management
- Discuss and apply working capital management techniques
- Carry out effective investment appraisal
- Identify and evaluate alternative sources of business finance
- Explain and calculate cost of capital and the factors that affect it
- Explain and apply risk management techniques in business

Avoiding weaknesses

Do not avoid any syllabus areas, they are all equally examinable. Make sure you can discuss techniques as well as apply them, you will not pass this exam with calculations alone.

Plan your answers to ensure you do not run out of time and miss out on easy marks.

Reading time

You will have 15 minutes reading time for Paper F9. Here are some helpful tips on how best to utilise this time.

- Speed read through the question paper, jotting down any ideas that come to you about any of the questions.

- Decide the order which you're likely to tackle the questions (probably easiest questions first, most difficult questions last).

- Spend the remainder of the reading time reading the question(s) you will do first in detail, jotting down proformas and plans (any proformas or plans written on the question paper should be reproduced in the answer booklet).

- When you can start writing, get straight on with the question(s) you have planned in detail. If you have looked at all the questions during the reading time, this should hopefully mean that you will find it easier to answer the more difficult questions when you come to them, as you will have been generating ideas and remembering facts while answering the easier questions.

Choosing which questions to answer first

You can use the planning time in the exam to choose the order in which to attempt the questions. You may prefer to attempt the questions that you are more confident about first. However, make sure you watch the time carefully and do not spend too long on any one question.

Alternatively, you could answer the questions in strict order. This will force you to spend an equal time on each question but make sure you leave plenty of space if you decide to move on and finish a question later.

Tackling questions

Write a short plan for each question containing bullet points per mark and **use** it to write your answer when the writing time begins.

If you get stuck, make an assumption, write it down and **move on**.

Make sure your answers are **focused** and **specific** to the organisation in the question. Show clear workings for your calculations and write full sentences in your explanations.

Never overrun on any question and once the 45 minutes is up, move on to the next.

Gaining the easy marks

Easy marks in this paper tend to fall into two categories.

Calculations

The calculations within a question will get progressively harder and easy marks will be available in the easy stages. Set our your calculations clearly and show all your workings in a clear format. Use a proforma, for example in complex NPV questions and slot the simpler figures into the proforma straight away before you concentrate on the figures that need a lot of adjustment.

Discussions

Discussions that are focused on the specific organisation in the question will gain more marks than regurgitation of knowledge. Read the question carefully and more than once, to ensure you are actually answering the specific requirements.

Pick out key words such as 'describe', 'evaluate' and 'discuss'. These all mean something specific.

- 'Describe' means to communicate the key features of

- 'Evaluate' means to assess the value of

- 'Discuss' means to examine in detail by argument

Clearly label the points you make in discussions so that the marker can identify them all rather than getting lost in the detail. Provide answers in the form requested, particularly using report format if asked for and giving recommendations if required.

Formulae

Set out below are the formulae which you will be given in the exam, and formulae which you should learn. If you are not sure what the symbols mean, or how the formulae are used, you should go back to the Study Text. Study Text page references (2007 edition) are given for each formula.

Exam formulae

Page ref

Economic Order Quantity

129

$$= \sqrt{\frac{2C_0 D}{C_H}}$$

Miller-Orr Model

166

Return point = Lower limit + (1/3 × spread)

$$\text{Spread} = 3 \left[\frac{\frac{3}{4} \times \text{transaction cost} \times \text{variance of cash flows}}{\text{interest rate}} \right]^{\frac{1}{3}}$$

The Capital Asset Pricing Model

330

$$E(r_i) = R_f + \beta_i (E(r_m) - R_f)$$

The Asset Beta Formula

354

$$\beta_a = \left[\frac{V_e}{(V_e + V_d(1-T))} \beta_e \right] + \left[\frac{V_d(1-T)}{(V_e + V_d(1-T))} \beta_d \right]$$

The Growth Model

374

$$P_0 = \frac{D_0(1+g)}{(K_e - g)}$$

Gordon's Growth Approximation

327

$$g = br$$

The weighted average cost of capital

339

$$\text{WACC} = \left[\frac{V_e}{V_e + V_d} \right] k_e + \left[\frac{V_d}{V_e + V_d} \right] k_d (1-T)$$

The Fisher formula

216

$$(1 + i) = (1 + r)(1 + h)$$

Purchasing Power Parity and Interest Rate Parity

$$S_1 = S_0 \times \frac{(1+h_c)}{(1+h_b)}$$

408

$$F_0 = S_0 \times \frac{(1+i_c)}{(1+i_b)}$$

407

Formulae to learn

Profitability ratios include:

$$ROCE = \frac{\text{Profit from operations}}{\text{Capital employed}} \%$$

$$ROCE = \frac{\text{Profit from operations}}{\text{Revenue}} \times \frac{\text{Revenue}}{\text{Capital employed}}$$

$$\text{Profit margin} \times \text{Asset turnover}$$

Debt ratios include:

$$\text{Gearing} = \frac{\text{Book value of debt}}{\text{Book value of equity}}$$

$$\text{Interest coverage} = \frac{\text{Profit from operations}}{\text{Interest}}$$

Liquidity ratios include:

Current ratio = Current assets : Current liabilities

Acid Test ratio = Current assets : Current liabilities (less inventory)

Shareholder investor ratios include:

$$\text{Dividend yield} = \frac{\text{Dividend per share}}{\text{Market price per share}} \times 100$$

$$\text{Earnings per share} = \frac{\text{Profits distributable to ordinary shareholders}}{\text{Number of ordinary shares issued}}$$

$$\text{Price-earnings ratio} = \frac{\text{Market price per share}}{\text{EPS}}$$

Av. collection period $\dfrac{\text{Receivables}}{\text{(credit) sales}} \times 365$ days

Inventory days

(a) Finished goods: $\dfrac{\text{Finished goods}}{\text{Cost of sales}} \times 365$ days

(b) WIP: $\dfrac{\text{WIP}}{\text{Cost of production}} \times 365$ days

(c) Raw material: $\dfrac{\text{Raw material}}{\text{Raw material purchases}} \times 365$ days

Av. payables period $\dfrac{\text{Payables}}{\text{(credit) purchases}} \times 365$ days

$$\text{IRR} = a + \frac{NPV_a}{NPV_a - NPV_b}(b-a)$$

$$\text{Equivalent annual cost} = \frac{\text{NPV of costs}}{\text{Annuity factor for the life of the project}}$$

Cost of equity $= K_e = \dfrac{D_1}{P_0} + g$

Cost of debt $= K_d = \dfrac{i(1-T)}{P_0}$

Cost of preference shares $= K_{pref} = \dfrac{\text{Preference Dividend}}{\text{Market Value}_{(ex\,div)}} = \dfrac{d}{P_0}$

Profitability index $= \dfrac{\text{NPV of cash inflows}}{\text{Cash outflow}}$

Exam information

The exam is a three-hour paper containing **four** compulsory 25 mark questions. There will be a mixture of calculations and discussion and the examiner's aim is to cover as much of the syllabus as possible.

Additional information

The Study Guide provides more detailed guidance on the syllabus.

Pilot paper

1   Weighted average cost of capital: Calculation; discussion; ratio analysis

2   Foreign currency: Risk; forecasts; forward market; money market hedge; futures contract

3   Working capital: Evaluation of credit policy; Miller-Orr; accounts receivable management; funding policy

4   Investment appraisal: Calculations of NPV and ROCE; strengths and weaknesses of IRR

The Pilot paper is Mock exam 3 in this Kit.

Useful websites

The websites below provide additional sources of information of relevance to your studies for *Performance Management.*

- www.accaglobal.com

  ACCA's website. Includes student section.

- www.bpp.com

  Our website provides information about BPP products and services, with a link to the ACCA website.

- www.ft.com

  This website provides information about current international business. You can search for information and articles on specific industry groups as well as individual companies.

- www.economist.com

  Here you can search for business information on a week-by-week basis, search articles by business subject and use the resources of the Economist Intelligence Unit to research sectors, companies or countries.

- www.invweek.co.uk

  This site carries business news and articles on markets from Investment Week and International Investment.

- www.pweglobal.com/uk

  The PricewaterhouseCoopers website includes UK Economic Outlook

- www.bbc.co.uk

  The website of the BBC carries general business information as well as programme-related content.

BPP LEARNING MEDIA

Planning your question practice

Planning your question practice

We have already stressed that question practice should be right at the centre of your revision. Whilst you will spend some time looking at your notes and Paper F9 Passcards, you should spend the majority of your revision time practising questions.

We recommend two ways in which you can practise questions.

- Use **BPP's question plan** to work systematically through the syllabus and attempt key and other questions on a section-by-section basis

- **Build your own exams** – attempt questions as a series of practice exams

These ways are suggestions and simply following them is no guarantee of success. You or your college may prefer an alternative but equally valid approach.

BPP's question plan

The BPP plan below requires you to devote a **minimum of 40 hours** to revision of Paper F9. Any time you can spend over and above this should only increase your chances of success.

Step 1 **Review your notes** and the chapter summaries in the Paper F9 **Passcards** for each section of the syllabus.

Step 2 **Answer the key questions** for that section. These questions have boxes round the question number in the table below and you should answer them in full. Even if you are short of time you must attempt these questions if you want to pass the exam. You should complete your answers without referring to our solutions.

Step 3 **Attempt the other questions** in that section. For some questions we have suggested that you prepare **answer plans or do the calculations** rather than full solutions. Planning an answer means that you should spend about 40% of the time allowance for the questions brainstorming the question and drawing up a list of points to be included in the answer.

Step 4 Attempt **Mock exams 1, 2 and 3** under strict exam conditions.

Syllabus section	2007 Passcards chapters	Questions in this Kit	Comments	Done ☑
Revision period 1				
Financial management	1–3	1	Prepare an answer plan to this question. Either part could be combined with calculations in your exam.	☐
		3	Answer in full. This question shows how ratio calculations can be combined with discussion.	☐
		4	Prepare an answer plan as this question covers a number of important areas.	☐
Revision period 2				
Working capital management	4	6	Answer in full. This is a good example of how exam questions may cover a number of different areas of the syllabus.	☐
Inventory management	5	8	Answer in full. An excellent example of an inventory management question written by the F9 examiner.	☐
		9	Answer in full. Excellent practice at calculations and discussion applied to a specific organisation.	☐
Revision period 3				
Cash management	6	10	Do the calculations and prepare an answer plan for the written sections for this wide ranging question.	☐
		11	Answer in full. There are a number of working capital management issues to discuss.	☐
		13	Answer in full. This question provides practice on a wide range of working capital issues and is in the style that you can expect in the F9 exam.	☐
Revision period 4				
Investment appraisal	7–10	14	Do the calculations and prepare an answer plan for the written sections as this question covers a number of areas of the syllabus.	☐
		15	Answer in full. This question is a good example of how the examiner might test investment appraisal.	☐
		18	Answer in full. This question provides excellent practice at using investment appraisal techniques.	☐
		19	Answer in full. A classic lease v buy question.	☐

Syllabus section	2007 Passcards chapters	Questions in this Kit	Comments	Done ☑
Revision period 5 Specific investment decisions	11	20	Answer in full. Another leasing question to practise which also covers capital rationing.	☐
		21	Answer in full. This question provides practice at asset replacement calculations and also a detailed discussion on the limitations of NPV.	☐
		23	Answer in full. A good test of your knowledge of capital rationing combining calculations and discussion.	☐
Revision period 6 Sources of finance	12–13	24	Do the calculations and prepare an answer plan for the written parts. This question makes you think about the links between the working capital and sources of finance parts of the syllabus.	☐
		25	Answer this Paper 2.4 question in full. It provides good practice of some important calculations.	☐
		26	Prepare an answer plan for this question on dividend policy.	☐
		27	Answer in full. This question covers a wide range of calculations from this area of the syllabus.	☐
Revision period 7 Sources of finance	12–14	29	Answer in full. This question gives you valuable practice at doing ratio calculations and understanding their meaning.	☐
		30	Do the calculations and prepare answer plans for the written sections of this wide ranging sources of finance question.	☐
		31	Answer in full. This question covers a range of syllabus areas and would be very useful to do under timed conditions.	☐

Syllabus section	2007 Passcards chapters	Questions in this Kit	Comments	Done ☑
Revision period 8 Cost of capital	15	32	Do the calculations in parts (a) and (b) as they are essential techniques. Prepare answer plans for parts (c) and (d).	☐
		33	Answer in full. This question gives you practice at these essential calculations as well as 13 marks for explanations.	☐
		34	Do the CAPM calculations in parts (a) and (b).	☐
		35	Answer in full. More WACC calculation practice and a discussion question that you will need to plan carefully.	☐
Revision period 9 Cost of capital	15–16	36	Do the calculations in parts (a) and (c) and write brief answers to the written parts.	☐
		37	Answer in full. This question provides practice in a number of areas of the syllabus and shows they can be linked into one question.	☐
		38	Answer in full. A good test of various aspects of CAPM.	☐
Revision period 10 Business valuations	17–18	39	Answer in full. This is a lengthy question which combines business valuation with sources of finance.	☐
		40	Do the tricky calculations in full as far as you can. Do some brief notes for part (d) on behavioural finance.	☐
		41	Answer in full. Another useful business valuation question that also looks at venture capital.	☐
Revision period 11 Business valuations	17–18	42	Do the calculations in part (a), prepare brief notes on part (b) and prepare a full answer for part (c) on how share markets work.	☐
		43	Answer in full. A question requiring you to demonstrate your understanding of EMH and earnings valuation.	☐
		44	Answer in full. A wide ranging question on market efficiency and sources of finance.	☐

Syllabus section	2007 Passcards chapters	Questions in this Kit	Comments	Done ☑
Revision period 12 Exchange rate risk management	19	45	Answer in full. This question tests your knowledge of foreign currency risk as well as working capital management.	☐
		46	Answer in full. An excellent test of various aspects of foreign currency risk management.	☐
		47	Do the calculations in parts (a) to (c) and prepare answer plans for the written parts (d) and (e).	☐
		48	Do the calculations in part (a) and prepare answer plans for the written parts of the question.	☐
Revision period 13 Interest rates	20	49	Answer in full. This question gives you practice at explaining various aspects of interest rates.	☐
		50	Answer in full. Another discussion question covering a range of interest rate topics.	☐

Build your own exams

Having revised your notes and the BPP Passcards, you can attempt the questions in the Kit as a series of practice exams.

	Practice exams					
	1	2	3	4	5	6
1	1	3	4	6	8	9
2	10	11	13	15	18	19
3	20	21	23	25	27	29
4	33	37	38	45	46	44

Whichever practice exams you use, you must attempt **Mock exams 1, 2 and 3** at the end of your revision.

Questions

FINANCIAL MANAGEMENT FUNCTION

Questions 1 to 3 cover Financial Management Function, the subject of Part A of the BPP Study Text for Paper F9.

1 Private sector companies (FMC, 12/02)   45 mins

Private sector companies have multiple stakeholders who are likely to have divergent interests.

Required

(a)   Identify five stakeholder groups and briefly discuss their financial and other objectives.   **(12 marks)**

(b)   Examine the extent to which good corporate governance procedures can help manage the problems arising from the divergent interests of multiple stakeholder groups in private sector companies.   **(13 marks)**

(Total = 25 marks)

2 Goals   45 mins

(a)   Assume you are Finance Director of a large multinational company, listed on a number of international stock markets. The company is reviewing its corporate plan. At present, the company focuses on maximising shareholder wealth as its major goal. The Managing Director thinks this single goal is inappropriate and asks his co-directors for their views on giving greater emphasis to the following:

   (i)   Cash flow generation

   (ii)   Profitability as measured by profits after tax and return on investment

   (iii)   Risk-adjusted returns to shareholders

   (iv)   Performance improvement in a number of areas such as concern for the environment, employees' remuneration and quality of working conditions and customer satisfaction

Required

Provide the Managing Director with a report for presentation at the next board meeting which:

   (i)   Discusses the argument that maximisation of shareholder wealth should be the only true objective of a company, and

   (ii)   Discusses the advantages and disadvantages of the MD's suggestions about alternative goals

(15 marks)

(b)   The company is already considering improving the methods of remuneration for its senior employees. As a member of the executive board, you are asked to give your opinions on the following suggestions:

   (i)   A high basic salary with usual 'perks' such as company car, pension scheme etc but no performance-related bonuses

   (ii)   A lower basic salary with usual 'perks' plus a bonus related to their division's profit before tax

   (iii)   A lower basic salary with usual 'perks' plus a share option scheme which allows senior employees to buy a given number of shares in the company at a fixed price at the end of each financial year

Required

Discuss the arguments for and against *each* of the *three* options from the point of view of both the company and its employees. Detailed comments on the taxation implications are *not* required.   **(10 marks)**

(Total = 25 marks)

3 RZP Co (FMC, 6/05)

45 mins

As assistant to the Finance Director of RZP Co, a company that has been listed on the London Stock Market for several years, you are reviewing the draft Annual Report of the company, which contains the following statement made by the chairman:

'This company has consistently delivered above-average performance in fulfilment of our declared objective of creating value for our shareholders. Apart from 20X2, when our overall performance was hampered by a general market downturn, this company has delivered growth in dividends, earnings and ordinary share price. Our shareholders can rest assured that my directors and I will continue to deliver this performance in the future'.

The five-year summary in the draft Annual Report contains the following information:

Year	20X4	20X3	20X2	20X1	20X0
Dividend per share	2.8p	2.3p	2.2p	2.2p	1.7p
Earnings per share	19.04p	14.95p	11.22p	15.84p	13.43p
Price/earnings ratio	22.0	33.5	25.5	17.2	15.2
General price index	117	113	110	105	100

A recent article in the financial press reported the following information for the last five years for the business sector within which RZP Co operates:

Share price growth	average increase per year of 20%
Earnings growth	average increase per year of 10%
Nominal dividend growth	average increase per year of 10%
Real dividend growth	average increase per year of 9%

You may assume that the number of shares issued by RZP Co has been constant over the five-year period. All price/earnings ratios are based on end-of-year share prices.

Required

(a) Analyse the information provided and comment on the views expressed by the chairman in terms of:

   (i)   growth in dividends per share;
   (ii) share price growth;
   (iii) growth in earnings per share.

   Your analysis should consider both arithmetic mean and equivalent annual growth rates.   **(13 marks)**

(b) Calculate the total shareholder return (dividend yield plus capital growth) for 20X4 and comment on your findings.   **(3 marks)**

(c) Discuss the factors that should be considered when deciding on a management remuneration package that will encourage the directors of RZP Co to maximise the wealth of shareholders, giving examples of management remuneration packages that might be appropriate for RZP Co.   **(9 marks)**

(Total = 25 marks)

FINANCIAL MANAGEMENT ENVIRONMENT

Questions 4 to 5 cover Financial Management Environment, the subject of Part B of the BPP Study Text for Paper F9.

4 Tagna (FMC 6/03, amended)   45 mins

Tagna is a medium-sized company that manufactures luxury goods for several well-known chain stores. In real terms, the company has experienced only a small growth in turnover in recent years, but it has managed to maintain a constant, if low, level of reported profits by careful control of costs. It has paid a constant nominal (money terms) dividend for several years and its managing director has publicly stated that the primary objective of the company is to increase the wealth of shareholders. Tagna is financed as follows:

	$m
Overdraft	1.0
10 year fixed interest bank loan	2.0
Share capital and reserves	4.5
	7.5

Tagna has the agreement of its existing shareholders to make a new issue of shares on the stock market but has been informed by its bank that current circumstances are unsuitable. The bank has stated that if new shares were to be issued now they would be significantly under-priced by the stock market, causing Tagna to issue many more shares than necessary in order to raise the amount of finance it requires. The bank recommends that the company waits for at least six months before issuing new shares, by which time it expects the stock market to have become strong-form efficient.

The financial press has reported that it expects the Central Bank to make a substantial increase in interest rate in the near future in response to rapidly increasing consumer demand and a sharp rise in inflation. The financial press has also reported that the rapid increase in consumer demand has been associated with an increase in consumer credit to record levels.

Required

(a)   On the assumption that the Central Bank makes a substantial interest rate increase, discuss the possible consequences for Tagna in the following areas:

    (i)   sales;
    (ii)   operating costs; and,
    (iii)   earnings (profit after tax).   **(10 marks)**

(b)   Explain and compare the public sector objective of 'value for money' and the private sector objective of 'maximisation of shareholder wealth'.   **(6 marks)**

(c)   Outline the economic problems caused by monopoly and explain the role of government in maintaining competition between companies.   **(9 marks)**

(Total = 25 marks)

5 Investment

45 mins

Write a report to a private client covering the topics outlined below.

(a)   Discussion of the factors that should be taken into account by the private investor when considering the purchase of different types of traded investments.   **(7 marks)**

(b)   Explanation of the 'risk/return trade-off'.   **(5 marks)**

(c)   Explanation of the role of financial intermediaries and their usefulness to the private investor.   **(8 marks)**

(d)   Identification of the effects on private sector businesses of a significant public sector budget deficit.

(5 marks)

(Total = 25 marks)

WORKING CAPITAL MANAGEMENT

Questions 6 to 13 cover Working Capital Management, the subject of Part C of the BPP Study Text for Paper F9.

6 East Meets West Co   45 mins

You are an accounting technician working at East Meets West Co, a company that manufactures and distributes clothing. You have estimated the following figures for the coming year:

Sales	$5,600,000
Average receivables	$506,000
Gross profit margin	25% on sales
Average inventories	
Finished goods	$350,000
Work in progress (80% complete)	$550,000
Raw materials	$220,000
Average payables	$210,000

Material costs represent 50% of the total cost of sales.

East Meets West Co imports most of its materials from overseas countries, especially Pernisia. The high inflation rates in Pernisia have meant that the company's cost of materials has risen rapidly over recent years. This has led to a significant deterioration in the company's margins, which, coupled with its increasing liquidity problems, is making the shareholders nervous.

Required

(a) Calculate the cash operating cycle, to the nearest day.   **(6 marks)**

(b) Suggest four methods of reducing the length of the cash operating cycle.   **(4 marks)**

(c) Discuss:

    (i)   The significance of trade payables in a firm's working capital cycle; and   **(4 marks)**

    (ii) The dangers of over-reliance on trade credit as a source of finance.   **(4 marks)**

(d) Explain the general problems associated with inflation.   **(7 marks)**

(Total = 25 marks)

7 JIT and EOQ   45 mins

PS Co has an opportunity to engage in a just-in-time stock delivery arrangement with its main customer, which normally takes 90 days to settle accounts with PS Co. The customer accounts for 20% of PS Co's annual turnover of $20 million. This involves borrowing $0.5m on overdraft to invest in dedicated handling and transport equipment. This would be depreciated over five years on a straight-line basis. The customer is uninterested in the early payment discount but would be prepared to settle after 60 days and to pay a premium of 5% over the present price in exchange for guarantees regarding product quality and delivery. PS Co judges the probability of failing to meet these guarantees in any one year at 5%. Failure would trigger a penalty payment of 10% of the value of total sales to this customer (including the premium). PS Co borrows from the bank at 13%.

Required

(a) Calculate the improvement in *profits before tax* to be expected in the first trading year after entering into the JIT arrangement. Comment on your results.   **(8 marks)**

(b) Suggest the benefits PS Co might expect to derive from a JIT agreement in addition to the benefits specified in the question.   **(6 marks)**

(c) SP Co purchases many hundreds of components each year from external suppliers for assembling into products. It uses 40,000 units pa of one particular component. It is considering converting its purchasing, delivery and stock control of this item to a just-in-time system. This will raise the number of orders placed but lower the administrative and other costs of placing and receiving orders. If successful, this will provide the model for switching most of its inwards supplies on to this system. Details of actual and expected ordering and carrying costs are given in the table below.

	Actual	Proposed
Ordering cost per order (O)	$100	$25
Purchase cost per item (P)	$2.50	$2.50
Inventory holding cost (as a percentage of the purchase cost) (I)	20%	20%

To implement the new arrangements will require 'one-off' reorganisation costs estimated at $4,000 which will be treated as a revenue item for tax purposes. The rate of corporation tax is 30% and SP can obtain finance at 12%. The effective life span of the new system can be assumed to be eight years.

Required

(i) Determine the effect of the new system on the Economic Order Quantity (EOQ).
(ii) Determine whether the new system is worthwhile in financial terms.

Note. EOQ is given by EOQ = $\sqrt{\dfrac{2C_0 D}{C_H}}$.

(11 marks)

(Total = 25 marks)

8 TNG Co (FMC, 6/05)

45 mins

TNG Co expects annual demand for product X to be 255,380 units. Product X has a selling price of $19 per unit and is purchased for $11 per unit from a supplier, MKR Co. TNG places an order for 50,000 units of product X at regular intervals throughout the year. Because the demand for product X is to some degree uncertain, TNG maintains a safety (buffer) stock of product X which is sufficient to meet demand for 28 working days. The cost of placing an order is $25 and the storage cost for Product X is 10 cents per unit per year.

TNG normally pays trade suppliers after 60 days but MKR has offered a discount of 1% for cash settlement within 20 days.

TNG Co has a short-term cost of debt of 8% and uses a working year consisting of 365 days.

Required

(a) Calculate the annual cost of the current ordering policy. Ignore financing costs in this part of the question.

(4 marks)

(b) Calculate the annual saving if the economic order quantity model is used to determine an optimal ordering policy. Ignore financing costs in this part of the question.

(5 marks)

(c) Determine whether the discount offered by the supplier is financially acceptable to TNG Co.

(4 marks)

(d) Critically discuss the limitations of the Economic Order Quantity model as a way of managing stock.

(4 marks)

(e) Discuss the advantages and disadvantages of using just-in-time stock management methods.

(8 marks)

(Total = 25 marks)

9 Question with answer plan: Thorne Co (FMC, 12/05) 45 mins

Thorne Co values, advertises and sells residential property on behalf of its customers. The company has been in business for only a short time and is preparing a cash budget for the first four months of 20X6. Expected sales of residential properties are as follows.

	20X5	20X6	20X6	20X6	20X6
Month	December	January	February	March	April
Units sold	10	10	15	25	30

The average price of each property is $180,000 and Thorne Co charges a fee of 3% of the value of each property sold. Thorne Co receives 1% in the month of sale and the remaining 2% in the month after sale. The company has nine employees who are paid on a monthly basis. The average salary per employee is $35,000 per year. If more than 20 properties are sold in a given month, each employee is paid in that month a bonus of $140 for each additional property sold.

Variable expenses are incurred at the rate of 0.5% of the value of each property sold and these expenses are paid in the month of sale. Fixed overheads of $4,300 per month are paid in the month in which they arise. Thorne Co pays interest every three months on a loan of $200,000 at a rate of 6% per year. The last interest payment in each year is paid in December.

An outstanding tax liability of $95,800 is due to be paid in April. In the same month Thorne Co intends to dispose of surplus vehicles, with a net book value of $15,000, for $20,000. The cash balance at the start of January 20X6 is expected to be a deficit of $40,000.

Required

(a) Prepare a monthly cash budget for the period from January to April 20X6. Your budget must clearly indicate each item of income and expenditure, and the opening and closing monthly cash balances.   **(10 marks)**

(b) Discuss the factors to be considered by Thorne Co when planning ways to invest any cash surplus forecast by its cash budgets.   **(5 marks)**

(c) Discuss the advantages and disadvantages to Thorne Co of using overdraft finance to fund any cash shortages forecast by its cash budgets.   **(5 marks)**

(d) Explain how the Baumol model can be employed to reduce the costs of cash management and discuss whether the Baumol cash management model may be of assistance to Thorne Co for this purpose.   **(5 marks)**

(Total = 25 marks)

10 Plankers Co   45 mins

You are in charge of developing long term plans for your business, Plankers Co. Plans are developed on the basis that the business has a single objective and seeks to maximise its profits as measured by profit after tax.

The company has a loan facility from its bank of $8m at 8% annually. The outstanding liability at 31 May 20X2 is $7m. It is possible to extend the facility up to $12m but only at an interest cost of 9% on the whole outstanding balance. The condition attached to this loan is that interest cover should at least be equal to 3: that is, profit before interest and tax (PBIT) should be at least three times the interest. If the condition is breached then the loan becomes repayable immediately. Interest charges in the income statements are calculated on year end balances (at 31 May each year). For example, interest charges in the year-end 31 May 20X1 income statements were based on year end balances at 31 May 20X1.

Targets set by the directors of Plankers are as follows:

1. Cash balances must not fall below $1m, and

2. It is desirable that Basic Earnings per Share should not fall below 20c per share. The company has in issue 4m $1 ordinary shares.

The constraint set by the bank and the targets set by the directors are measured and assessed at each year end. The summary income statement for the year just ended (31 May 20X2) and a summary balance sheet are shown below along with forecasts for the next two years:

	31 May 20X2 $m	31 May 20X3 $m	31 May 20X4 $m
PBIT	1.71	1.80	1.89
Interest charges	(0.56)	(0.56)	(0.56)
Profit before tax	1.15	1.24	1.33
Tax	(0.35)	(0.37)	(0.40)
Profit after tax	0.80	0.87	0.93
Dividends	(0.40)	(0.44)	(0.47)
Retained	0.40	0.43	0.46
Non cash net assets	5.25	5.57	5.91
Cash	8.25	8.36	8.48
Loan liabilities	(7.00)	(7.00)	(7.00)
Shareholders' funds	6.50	6.93	7.39

Forecasts are based on the assumption that PBIT is likely to grow at a rate of 5% per annum. The forecasts of PBIT growth include the effect of the building programme and the depreciation on it. The corporation tax rate is 30%.

The company is planning a major building programme on 1 June 20X4 at which time a cash outflow of $12m would have to be paid. 50% of this expenditure will be depreciated at the rate of 15% per annum (the company has no other depreciable assets). This depreciation has been agreed as allowable for tax purposes with the tax authorities. The directors of Plankers are considering utilising the loan facility to help meet the funding requirements of the building programme but are wondering whether their targets will be met or whether the loan conditions will be breached. They have asked you to conduct an analysis of the company's financial position at 31 May 20X5 assuming the building programme begins on 1 June 20X4. For 20X5 only, the company will not pay any dividends to minimise its refinancing needs.

Required

(a) (i) Prepare a forecast summary income statement for the year to 31 May 20X5 assuming that the building programme is undertaken at 1 June 20X4 and that any additional funds are provided by an extension of the bank loan.

Assume that tax is paid in the year in which incurred.

Work to 3 decimal places of $m in your answer. **(5 marks)**

(ii) Assess whether, at 31 May 20X5 and based on the scenario in (i) above, the loan condition would be breached and whether the directors' targets would be achieved.

Work to 3 decimal places of $m in your answer. **(3 marks)**

(iii) Identify five options the company could use, assuming it faced a cash shortfall, to ease any cash shortage. **(5 marks)**

(iv) Explain, without further computations, whether each of the options in (a)(iii) is likely to meet Planker's requirements for additional capital and also the constraint set by the bank. **(3 marks)**

(b) Whilst the financial plans of the business are based on a single objective, it faces a number of constraints that put pressure on the company to address more than one objective simultaneously.

Required

What types of constraints might the company face when assessing its long-term plans? Specifically refer in your answer to:

(i)	responding to various stakeholder groups; and	**(4 marks)**
(ii)	the difficulties associated with managing organisations with multiple objectives.	**(5 marks)**

(Total = 25 marks)

11 Velm Co (FMC,6/03)   45 mins

Velm Co sells stationery and office supplies on a wholesale basis and has an annual turnover of $4,000,000. The company employs four people in its sales ledger and credit control department at an annual salary of $12,000 each. All sales are on 40 days' credit with no discount for early payment. Bad debts represent 3% of turnover and Velm Co pays annual interest of 9% on its overdraft. The most recent accounts of the company offer the following financial information:

Velm Co: Balance sheet as at 31 December 20X2

	$'000	$'000
Non-current assets		17,500
Current assets		
Inventory of goods for resale	900	
Receivables	550	
Cash	120	
		1,570
		19,070
Equity and liabilities		
Ordinary shares	3,500	
Reserves	11,640	
		15,140
Non-current liabilities		
12% Debenture due 20Y0		2,400
Current liabilities		
Trade payables	330	
Overdraft	1,200	
		1,530
		19,070

Velm Co is considering offering a discount of 1% to customers paying within 14 days, which it believes will reduce bad debts to 2.4% of turnover. The company also expects that offering a discount for early payment will reduce the average credit period taken by its customers to 26 days. The consequent reduction in the time spent chasing customers where payments are overdue will allow one member of the credit control team to take early retirement. Two-thirds of customers are expected to take advantage of the discount.

Required

(a)	Using the information provided, determine whether a discount for early payment of 1 per cent will lead to an increase in profitability for Velm Co.	**(5 marks)**
(b)	Discuss the relative merits of short-term and long-term debt sources for the financing of working capital.	**(6 marks)**
(c)	Discuss the different policies that may be adopted by a company towards the financing of working capital needs and indicate which policy has been adopted by Velm Co.	**(7 marks)**
(d)	Outline the advantages to a company of taking steps to improve its working capital management, giving examples of steps that might be taken.	**(7 marks)**

(Total = 25 marks)

11 Question with analysis: Velm Co (FMC, 6/03) 45 mins

| Receivable |

Velm Co sells stationery and office supplies on a wholesale basis and has an annual turnover of $4,000,000. The company employs four people in its sales ledger and credit control department at an annual salary of $12,000 each. **All sales are on 40 days' credit** with no discount for early payment. **Bad debts represent 3% of turnover** and Velm Co **pays annual interest of 9% on its overdraft**. The most recent accounts of the company offer the following financial information:

| Overdraft rate | | Bad debt cost |

Velm Co: Balance sheet as at 31 December 20X2

	$'000	$'000
Non-current assets		17,500
Current assets		
Inventory of goods for resale	900	
Receivables	550	
Cash	120	
		1,570
		19,070
Equity and liabilities		
Ordinary shares	3,500	
Reserves	11,640	
		15,140
Non-current liabilities		
12% Debenture due 20Y0		2,400
Current liabilities		
Trade payables	330	
Overdraft	1,200	
		1,530
		19,070

| Receivable | (points to Receivables)

| Bad debt cost |

Velm Co is considering offering a discount of 1% to customers paying within 14 days, which it believes will **reduce bad debts to 2.4% of turnover**. The company also expects that offering a discount for early payment will reduce the average credit period taken by its customers to 26 days. The consequent reduction in the time spent chasing customers where payments are overdue will allow one member of the credit control team to take early retirement. **Two-thirds of customers** are expected to take advantage of the discount.

| Saving |

| Discount |

Required

| So work out the savings and extra costs from this policy |

(a) Using the information provided, determine whether a discount for early payment of 1 per cent will lead to **an increase in profitability** for Velm Co. **(5 marks)**

| Requirements: discuss so write about and comment on |

(b) **Discuss** the relative merits of short-term and long-term debt sources for the financing of working capital. **(6 marks)**

(c) **Discuss** the different policies that may be adopted by a company towards the financing of working capital needs and indicate which policy has been adopted by Velm Co. **(7 marks)**

(d) **Outline the advantages** to a company of taking steps to improve its working capital management, giving examples of steps that might be taken. **(7 marks)**

| At least four to five points here and try to write a sentence or so about each. |

(Total = 25 marks)

12 PCB Co

45 mins

PCB Co manufacture printed circuit boards for use in pocket calculators. It is now December 20X8. Since the year 20X5 business has been expanding very rapidly and the company has now encountered a liquidity problem, as illustrated by the most recent balance sheets reproduced below.

PCB company balance sheet extracts

	As at 30 November 20X8	As at 30 November 20X7
	$	$
Non-current assets	308,000	264,000
Current assets		
Inventory	220,000	95,000
Receivables	210,000	108,000
Cash	Nil	1,750
	430,000	204,750
Current liabilities		
Bank	158,000	41,250
Trade payables	205,000	82,500
Net current assets	67,000	81,000
Capital and reserves		
Issued share capital	18,000	18,000
Reserves	357,000	327,000
Equity		
Shareholders' funds	375,000	345,000

Other information

(a)   Sales for the year to 30 November 20X7 were $1.7 million, yielding a gross profit of $330,000, and a net profit before tax of $82,000.

(b)   The tax rate on company profits is 30%.

(c)   For the year ending 30 November 20X7 dividends of $35,000 were paid out.

(d)   At the beginning of the year to 30 November 20X8 the company bought some new manufacturing equipment and recruited six more sales staff.

(e)   Sales for the year to 30 November 20X8 were $3 million, with a gross profit of $450,000, and net profit before tax of $60,000.

(f)   Dividends payable for the year to 30 November 20X8 amounted to $12,000.

Required

(a)   Illustrating your answer with figures taken from the question, explain why it is not unusual for manufacturing companies to face a cash shortage when sales are expanding very rapidly.   **(7 marks)**

(b)   Explain why PCB Co has not increased its net profit, despite the large increase in sales between 20X7 and 20X8.   **(5 marks)**

(c)   How has the mix of funding used by PCB changed between the two years, and what are the implications of such changes in terms of investor and payable risks?   **(7 marks)**

(d)   Suggest ways in which PCB might seek to resolve its current funding problems, and avoid the risks associated with overtrading.   **(6 marks)**

(Total = 25 marks)

13 Special gift suppliers (FMC, 12/01)

45 mins

Special Gift Suppliers Co is a wholesale distributor of a variety of imported goods to a range of retail outlets. The company specialises in supplying ornaments, small works of art, high value furnishing (rugs, etc) and other items that the chief buyer for the company feels would have a market. In seeking to improve working capital management, the financial controller has gathered the following information.

	Months
Average period for which items are held in inventory	3.5
Average receivables collection period	2.5
Average payables payment period	2.0

Required

(a)   Calculate Special Gift Suppliers' funding requirement for working capital measured in terms of months.

(2 marks)

In looking to reduce the working capital funding requirement, the financial controller of Special Gift Suppliers is considering factoring credit sales. The company's annual turnover is $2.5m of which 90% are credit sales. Bad debts are typically 3% of credit sales. The offer from the factor is conditional on the following.

1   The factor will take over the sales ledger of Special Gift Suppliers completely.

2   80% of the value of credit sales will be advanced immediately (as soon as sales are made to the customer) to Special Gift Suppliers, the remaining 20% will be paid to the company one month later. The factor charges 15% per annum on credit sales for advancing funds in the manner suggested. The factor is normally able to reduce the receivables' collection period to one month.

3   The factor offers a 'no recourse' facility whereby they take on the responsibility for dealing with bad debts. The factor is normally able to reduce bad debts to 2% of credit sales.

4   A charge for factoring services of 4% of credit sales will be made.

5   A one-off payment of $25,000 is payable to the factor.

The salary of the Sales Ledger Administrator ($12,500) would be saved under the proposals and overhead costs of the credit control department, amounting to $2,000 per annum, would have to be reallocated. Special Gift Suppliers' cost of overdraft finance is 12% per annum. Special Gift Suppliers pays its sales force on a commission only basis. The cost of this is 5% of credit sales and is payable immediately the sales are made. There is no intention to alter this arrangement under the factoring proposals.

Required

(b)   Evaluate the proposal to factor the sales ledger by comparing Special Gift Suppliers' existing receivable collection costs with those that would result from using the factor (assuming that the factor can reduce the receivables collection period to one month).

(8 marks)

(c)   As an adviser to Special Gift Suppliers Co, write a report to the financial controller that outlines:

(i)   How a credit control department might function

(ii)   The benefits of factoring

(iii)   How the financing of working capital can be arranged in terms of short and long term sources of finance

In particular, make reference to:

(1)   The financing of working capital or net current assets when short term sources of finance are exhausted

(2)   The distinction between fluctuating and permanent current assets.

(15 marks)

(Total = 25 marks)

INVESTMENT APPRAISAL

Questions 14 to 23 cover Investment Appraisal, the subject of Part D of the BPP Study Text for Paper F9.

---

14 Chromex Co

45 mins

It is now June 20X8. Chromex Co manufactures bicycles for the UK and European markets, and has made a bid of $150 million to take over Bexell Co, their main UK competitor, which is also active in the German market. Chromex currently supplies 24% of the UK market and Bexell has a 10% share of the same market.

Chromex anticipates labour savings of $700,000 per year, created by more efficient production and distribution facilities, if the takeover is completed. In addition, the company intends to sell off surplus land and buildings with a balance sheet value of $15 million, acquired in the course of the takeover.

Total UK bicycle sales for 20X7 were $400 million. For the year ended 31 December 20X7, Bexell reported an operating profit of $10 million, compared with a figure of $55 million for Chromex. In calculating profits, Bexell included a depreciation charge of $0.5 million.

Note. The takeover is regarded by Chromex in the same way as any other investment, and is appraised accordingly.

Required

(a) 'Despite the theoretical limitations of the payback method of investment appraisal, it is the method most used in practice.'

Required

Discuss this statement briefly. **(5 marks)**

(b) Assuming that the bid is accepted by Bexell, calculate the payback period (pre-tax) for the investment, if the land and buildings are immediately sold for $5 million less than the balance sheet valuation, and Bexell's sales figures remain static. **(3 marks)**

(c) Chromex has also appraised the investment in Bexell by calculating the present value of the company's future expected cash flows. What additional information to that required in (b) would have been necessary? **(5 marks)**

(d) Explain how and why the UK Government might seek to intervene in the takeover bid for Bexell. **(6 marks)**

(e) Suggest four ratios, which Chromex might usefully compute in order to compare the financial performance of Bexell with that of companies in the same manufacturing sector. You should include in your answer a justification of your choice of ratios. Briefly explain why it is important to base a comparison on companies in the same sector. **(6 marks)**

(Total = 25 marks)

15 Charm Co (FMC, 6/06)

45 mins

Charm Co, a software company, has developed a new game, 'Fingo', which it plans to launch in the near future. Sales of the new game are expected to be very strong, following a favourable review by a popular PC magazine. Charm Co has been informed that the review will give the game a 'Best Buy' recommendation. Sales volumes, production volumes and selling prices for 'Fingo' over its four-year life are expected to be as follows.

Year	1	2	3	4
Sales and production (units)	150,000	70,000	60,000	60,000
Selling price ($ per game)	$25	$24	$23	$22

Financial information on 'Fingo' for the first year of production is as follows:

Direct material cost	$5.40 per game
Other variable production cost	$6.00 per game
Fixed costs	$4.00 per game

Advertising costs to stimulate demand are expected to be $650,000 in the first year of production and $100,000 in the second year of production. No advertising costs are expected in the third and fourth years of production. Fixed costs represent incremental cash fixed production overheads. 'Fingo' will be produced on a new production machine costing $800,000. Although this production machine is expected to have a useful life of up to ten years, government legislation allows Charm Co to claim the capital cost of the machine against the manufacture of a single product. Capital allowances will therefore be claimed on a straight-line basis over four years.

Charm Co pays tax on profit at a rate of 30% per year and tax liabilities are settled in the year in which they arise. Charm Co uses an after-tax discount rate of 10% when appraising new capital investments. Ignore inflation.

Required

(a) Calculate the net present value of the proposed investment and comment on your findings. **(11 marks)**

(b) Calculate the internal rate of return of the proposed investment and comment on your findings. **(5 marks)**

(c) Discuss the reasons why the net present value investment appraisal method is preferred to other investment appraisal methods such as payback, return on capital employed and internal rate of return. **(9 marks)**

(Total = 25 marks)

16 Zedland Postal Services   45 mins

The general manager of the nationalised postal service of a small country, Zedland, wishes to introduce a new service. This service would offer same-day delivery of letters and parcels posted before 10am within a distance of 150km. The service would require 100 new vans costing $8,000 each and 20 trucks costing $18,000 each. 180 new workers would be employed at an average annual wage of $13,000 and five managers at average annual salaries of $20,000 would be moved from their existing duties, where they would not be replaced.

Two postal rates are proposed. In the first year of operation letters will cost $0.525 and parcels $5.25. Market research undertaken at a cost of $50,000 forecasts that demand will average 15,000 letters each working day and 500 parcels each working day during the first year, and 20,000 letters a day and 750 parcels a day thereafter. There is a five day working week and a 52 week year. Annual running and maintenance costs on similar new vans and trucks are estimated in the first year of operation to be $2,000 a van and $1,000 a truck. These costs will increase by 25% a year. Vehicles are depreciated over a five year period on a straight line basis. Depreciation is tax allowable and the vehicles will have negligible scrap value at the end of five years. Advertising in year one will cost $1,300,000 and year two $263,000. There will be no advertising after year two. Existing premises will be used for the new service but additional costs of $150,000 a year will be incurred in year 1.

All the above data are based on price levels in the first year and exclude any inflation effects. Staff and premises costs are expected to rise because of inflation by approximately 5% a year during the five year planning horizon of the postal service. The government of Zedland will not allow the prices charged by nationalised industries to increase by more than 5%.

Nationalised industries are normally required by the government to earn at least an annual after tax return of 5% on average investment and to achieve, on average, at least zero net present value on their investments.

The new service would be financed half with internally generated funds and half by borrowing on the capital market at an interest rate of 12% a year. The opportunity cost of capital for the postal service is estimated to be 14% a year. Corporate taxes in Zedland, to which the postal service is subject, are at the rate of 30% for annual profits of up to $500,000 and 40% for the balance in excess of $500,000. Tax is payable one year in arrears. The postal service's taxable profits from existing activities exceed $10,000,000 a year. All transactions may be assumed to be on a cash basis and to occur at the end of the year with the exception of the initial investment which would be required almost immediately.

Required

(a) Calculate the average return on investment (ROCE) for each year. **(10 marks)**
(b) Calculate the net present value of the project. **(8 marks)**
(c) Discuss whether the new service should be introduced. What other factors would need to be considered? **(7 marks)**

(Total = 25 marks)

17 Preparation question: Sensitivity analysis

A company is considering investing in a new manufacturing facility with the following characteristics.

A Initial investment $350,000, scrap value nil
B Expected life ten years
C Sales volume 20,000 units a year
D Selling price $20 a unit
E Variable direct costs $15 a unit
F Fixed costs excluding depreciation $25,000 a year.

The project shows an internal rate of return (IRR) of 17%. The managing director is concerned about the viability of the investment as the return is close to the company's hurdle rate of 15%. He has requested a sensitivity analysis.

Required

(a) Recalculate the internal rate of return (IRR) assuming each of the characteristics A to F above, in isolation, varies adversely by 10%.

(b) Advise the managing director of the most vulnerable area likely to prevent the project meeting the company's hurdle rate.

(c) Explain what further work might be undertaken to improve the value of the sensitivity analysis undertaken in (a).

(d) Re-evaluate the situation if another company, already manufacturing a similar product, offered to supply the units at $18 each. This would reduce the investment required to $25,000 and the fixed costs to $10,000.

Helping hand

1 Set up and complete a table with the characteristics as columns and investment, annual cash flow and DCF index (investment divided by annual cash flow) as rows, taking account of the adverse variation of 10%. Look up the DCF index in cumulative tables to find an approximate IRR for each characteristic (part (a)).

2 Consider what a ranking of the IRR for each altered characteristic shows about the vulnerability of each area (part (b)).

3 Think about, for example, different types of change in characteristics (part (c)).

4 Calculate the cash inflow under the supply situation and consider whether it would be a successful project (part (d)).

18 Umunat Co (FMC, 12/04)   45 mins

Umunat Co is considering investing $50,000 in a new machine with an expected life of five years. The machine will have no scrap value at the end of five years. It is expected that 20,000 units will be sold each year at a selling price of $3.00 per unit. Variable production costs are expected to be $1.65 per unit, while incremental fixed costs, mainly the wages of a maintenance engineer, are expected to be $10,000 per year. Umunat Co uses a discount rate of 12% for investment appraisal purposes and expects investment projects to recover their initial investment within two years.

Required

(a)   Explain why risk and uncertainty should be considered in the investment appraisal process.   **(5 marks)**

(b)   Calculate and comment on the payback period of the project   **(4 marks)**

(c)   Evaluate the sensitivity of the project's net present value to a change in the following project variables:

   (i)   sales volume;
   (ii)   sales price;
   (iii)   variable cost;

   and discuss the use of sensitivity analysis as a way of evaluating project risk.   **(10 marks)**

(d)   Upon further investigation it is found that there is a significant chance that the expected sales volume of 20,000 units per year will not be achieved. The sales manager of Umunat Co suggests that sales volumes could depend on expected economic states that could be assigned the following probabilities:

Economic state	Poor	Normal	Good
Probability	0.3	0.6	0.1
Annual sales volume (units)	17,500	20,000	22,500

   Calculate and comment on the expected net present value of the project.   **(6 marks)**

(Total = 25 marks)

18 Question with analysis: Umunat Co (12/04)   45 mins

note | Umunat Co is considering investing $50,000 in a new machine with an **expected life of five years**. The | Project life

machine will have **no scrap value at the end of five years**. It is expected that 20,000 units will be sold each year at a selling price of $3.00 per unit. Variable production costs are expected to be $1.65 per unit, while incremental fixed costs, mainly the wages of a maintenance engineer, are expected to be $10,000 per year.

Discount rate | Umunat Co uses a **discount rate of 12%** for investment appraisal purposes and expects investment projects to **recover their initial investment within two years**.

Define each as well as discuss | *Required* — Timing of payback

(a)   **Explain why risk and uncertainty** should be considered in the investment appraisal process.

(5 marks)

Define each as well as discuss | (b)   Calculate and comment on the payback period of the project   **(4 marks)**

(c)   **Evaluate the sensitivity of the project's net present value** to a change in the following project variables: — Sensitivity analysis

   (i)   sales volume;
   (ii)   sales price;
Comment here | (iii)   variable cost;

   and **discuss** the use of sensitivity analysis as a way of evaluating project risk.   **(10 marks)**

(d) Upon further investigation it is found that there is a significant chance that the expected sales volume of 20,000 units per year will not be achieved. The sales manager of Umunat Co suggests that sales volumes could depend on expected economic states that could be assigned the following probabilities:

Economic state	Poor	Normal	Good
Probability	0.3	0.6	0.1
Annual sales volume (units)	17,500	20,000	22,500

Calculate and comment on the expected net present value of the project. **(6 marks)**

(Total = 25 marks)

Two requirements

19 AGD Co (FMC, 12/05)   45 mins

AGD Co is a profitable company which is considering the purchase of a machine costing $320,000. If purchased, AGD Co would incur annual maintenance costs of $25,000. The machine would be used for three years and at the end of this period would be sold for $50,000. Alternatively, the machine could be obtained under an operating lease for an annual lease rental of $120,000 per year, payable in advance.

AGD Co can claim capital allowances on a 25% reducing balance basis. The company pays tax on profits at an annual rate of 30% and all tax liabilities are paid one year in arrears. AGD Co has an accounting year that ends on 31 December. If the machine is purchased, payment will be made in January of the first year of operation. If leased, annual lease rentals will be paid in January of each year of operation.

Required

(a) Using an after-tax borrowing rate of 7%, evaluate whether AGD Co should purchase or lease the new machine. **(12 marks)**

(b) Explain and discuss the key differences between an operating lease and a finance lease. **(8 marks)**

(c) The after-tax borrowing rate of 7% was used in the evaluation because a bank had offered to lend AGD Co $320,000 for a period of five years at a before-tax rate of 10% per year with interest payable every six months.

Required

(i) Calculate the annual percentage rate (APR) implied by the bank's offer to lend at 10% per year with interest payable every six months. **(2 marks)**

(ii) Calculate the amount to be repaid at the end of each six-month period if the offered loan is to be repaid in equal instalments. **(3 marks)**

(Total = 25 marks)

20 Leaminger Co (FMC, 12/02)   45 mins

Leaminger Co has decided it must replace its major turbine machine on 31 December 20X2. The machine is essential to the operations of the company. The company is, however, considering whether to purchase the machine outright or to use lease financing.

Purchasing the machine outright

The machine is expected to cost $360,000 if it is purchased outright, payable on 31 December 20X2. After four years the company expects new technology to make the machine redundant and it will be sold on 31 December 20X6 generating proceeds of $20,000. Capital allowances for tax purposes are available on the cost of the machine at the rate of 25% per annum reducing balance. A full year's allowance is given in the year of acquisition but no writing down allowance is available in the year of disposal. The difference between the proceeds and the tax written down value in the year of disposal is allowable or chargeable for tax as appropriate.

Leasing

The company has approached its bank with a view to arranging a lease to finance the machine acquisition. The bank has offered two options with respect to leasing which are as follows:

	Finance lease	Operating lease
Contract length (years)	4	1
Annual rental	$135,000	$140,000
First rent payable	31 December 20X3	31 December 20X2

General

For both the purchasing and the finance lease option, maintenance costs of $15,000 per year are payable at the end of each year. All lease rentals (for both finance and operating options) can be assumed to be allowable for tax purposes in full in the year of payment. Assume that tax is payable one year after the end of the accounting year in which the transaction occurs. For the operating lease only, contracts are renewable annually at the discretion of either party. Leaminger Co has adequate taxable profits to relieve all its costs. The rate of tax on profits can be assumed to be 30%. The company's accounting year-end is 31 December. The company's annual after tax cost of capital is 10%.

Required

(a)   Calculate the net present value at 31 December 20X2, using the after tax cost of capital, for

(i)   purchasing the machine outright;
(ii)   using the finance lease to acquire the machine; and
(iii)   using the operating lease to acquire the machine.

Recommend the optimal method.   **(12 marks)**

(b)   Assume now that the company is facing capital rationing up until 30 December 20X3 when it expects to make a share issue. During this time the most marginal investment project, which is perfectly divisible, requires an outlay of $500,000 and would generate a net present value of $100,000. Investment in the turbine would reduce funds available for this project. Investments cannot be delayed.

Calculate the revised net present values of the three options for the turbine given capital rationing. Advise whether your recommendation in (a) would change.   **(5 marks)**

(c)   As their business advisor, prepare a report for the directors of Leaminger Co that assesses the issues that need to be considered in acquiring the turbine with respect to capital rationing.   **(8 marks)**

(Total = 25 marks)

21 Bread Products Co (FMC, Pilot paper)   45 mins

Bread Products Co is considering the replacement policy for its industrial size ovens which are used as part of a production line that bakes bread. Given its heavy usage each oven has to be replaced frequently. The choice is between replacing every two years or every three years. Only one type of oven is used, each of which costs $24,500. Maintenance costs and resale values are as follows.

Year	Maintenance per annum	Resale value
	$	$
1	500	
2	800	15,600
3	1,500	11,200

Original cost, maintenance costs and resale values are expressed in current prices. That is, for example, maintenance for a two year old oven would cost $800 for maintenance undertaken now. It is expected that maintenance costs will increase at 10% per annum and oven replacement cost and resale values at 5% per annum. The money discount rate is 15%.

Required

(a) Calculate the preferred replacement policy for the ovens in a choice between a two year or three year replacement cycle. **(12 marks)**

(b) Identify the limitations of net present value techniques when applied generally to investment appraisal.
(13 marks)

(Total = 25 marks)

22 Filtrex Co
45 mins

(a) Explain how cash shortages can restrict the investment opportunities of a business. **(5 marks)**

(b) Distinguish between 'hard' and 'soft' capital rationing, explaining why a company may deliberately choose to restrict its capital expenditure. **(5 marks)**

(c) Filtrex Co is a medium-sized, all equity-financed, unquoted company which specialises in the development and production of water- and air-filtering devices to reduce the emission of effluents. Its small but ingenious R & D team has recently made a technological breakthrough which has revealed a number of attractive investment opportunities. It has applied for patents to protect its rights in all these areas. However, it lacks the financial resources required to exploit all of these projects, whose required outlays and post-tax NPVs are listed in the table below. Filtrex's managers consider that delaying any of these projects would seriously undermine their profitability, as competitors bring forward their own new developments. All projects are thought to have a similar degree of risk.

Project	Required outlay	NPV
	$	$
A	150,000	65,000
B	120,000	50,000
C	200,000	80,000
D	80,000	30,000
E	400,000	120,000

The NPVs have been calculated using as a discount rate the 18% post-tax rate of return which Filtrex requires for risky R & D ventures. The maximum amount available for this type of investment is $400,000, corresponding to Filtrex's present cash balances, built up over several years' profitable trading. Projects A and C are mutually exclusive and no project can be sub-divided. Any unused capital will either remain invested in short-term deposits or used to purchase marketable securities, both of which offer a return well below 18% post-tax.

Required

(i) Advise Filtrex Co, using suitable supporting calculations, which combination of projects should be undertaken in the best interests of shareholders; and

(ii) Suggest what further information might be obtained to assist a fuller analysis. **(9 marks)**

(d) Explain how, apart from delaying projects, Filtrex Co could manage to exploit more of these opportunities.
(6 marks)

(Total = 25 marks)

23 Basril Co (FMC, 12/03)

45 mins

Basril Co is reviewing investment proposals that have been submitted by divisional managers. The investment funds of the company are limited to $800,000 in the current year. Details of three possible investments, none of which can be delayed, are given below.

Project 1

An investment of $300,000 in work station assessments. Each assessment would be on an individual employee basis and would lead to savings in labour costs from increased efficiency and from reduced absenteeism due to work-related illness. Savings in labour costs from these assessments in money terms are expected to be as follows:

Year	1	2	3	4	5
Cash flows ($'000)	85	90	95	100	95

Project 2

An investment of $450,000 in individual workstations for staff that is expected to reduce administration costs by $140,800 per annum in money terms for the next five years.

Project 3

An investment of $400,000 in new ticket machines. Net cash savings of $120,000 per annum are expected in current price terms and these are expected to increase by 3.6% per annum due to inflation during the five-year life of the machines.

Basril Co has a money cost of capital of 12% and taxation should be ignored.

Required

(a)   Determine the best way for Basril Co to invest the available funds and calculate the resultant NPV:

    (i)   on the assumption that each of the three projects is divisible;

    (ii)   on the assumption that none of the projects are divisible.   **(10 marks)**

(b)   Explain how the NPV investment appraisal method is applied in situations where capital is rationed.

    (3 marks)

(c)   Discuss the reasons why capital rationing may arise.   **(7 marks)**

(d)   Discuss the meaning of the term 'relevant cash flows' in the context of investment appraisal, giving examples to illustrate your discussion.   **(5 marks)**

(Total = 25 marks)

BUSINESS FINANCE

Questions 24 to 31 cover Business Finance, the subject of Part E of the BPP Study Text for Paper F9.

24 Burnsall Co

45 mins

Burnsall Co is a listed company which manufactures and distributes leisurewear under the brand name Paraffin. It made sales of 10 million units world-wide at an average wholesale price of $10 per unit during its last financial year ending 30 June 20X5. In 20X5-X6, it is planning to introduce a new brand, Meths, which will be sold at a lower unit price to more price-sensitive market segments. Allowing for negative effects on existing sales of Paraffin, the introduction of the new brand is expected to raise total sales value by 20%.

To support greater sales activity, it is expected that additional financing, both capital and working, will be required. Burnsall expects to make capital expenditures of $20m in 20X5-X6, partly to replace worn-out equipment but largely to support sales expansion. You may assume that, except for taxation, all current assets and current liabilities will vary directly in line with sales.

Burnsall's summarised balance sheet for the financial year ending 30 June 20X5 shows the following.

	$m	$m
Non-current assets (net)		120
Current assets:		
Inventories	16	
Receivables	23	
Cash	6	
		45
		165
Ordinary shares (50c par value)		60
Reserves		62
Long-term debt at 12%		20
Current liabilities:		
Tax payable		
Trade payables	5	
	18	23
		165

Burnsall's profit before interest and tax in 20X4-X5 was 16% of sales, after deducting depreciation of $5m. The depreciation charge for 20X5-X6 is expected to rise to $9m. Tax on profits is levied at 30%, paid with a one-year delay. Burnsall has an established distribution policy of raising dividends by 10% pa. In 20X4-X5, it paid dividends of $5m net.

You have been approached to advise on the extra financing required to support the sales expansion. Company policy is to avoid cash balances falling below 6% of sales.

Required

(a)   By projecting its financial statements, calculate how much additional *external* finance Burnsall must raise. You may assume that all depreciation provisions qualify for tax relief. **(9 marks)**

(b)   Discuss the main factors which a company should consider when determining the appropriate mix of long-term and short-term debt in its capital structure. **(7 marks)**

Armada Leisure Industries Co is already highly geared by industry standards, but wishes to raise external capital to finance the development of a new bowling alley in Plymouth. The stock market has recently reached a record level but economic forecasters are expressing doubts about the future prospects for the home economy.

Required

(c)   Assess the arguments for and against a rights issue by Armada. **(9 marks)**

(Total = 25 marks)

25 Question with answer plan: Tirwen Co (FMC, 12/04) 45 mins

Tirwen Co is a medium-sized manufacturing company which is considering a 1 for 5 rights issue at a 15% discount to the current market price of $4.00 per share. Issue costs are expected to be $220,000 and these costs will be paid out of the funds raised. It is proposed that the rights issue funds raised will be used to redeem some of the existing loan stock at par. Financial information relating to Tirwen Co is as follows:

Current balance sheet

	$'000	$'000
Non-current assets		6,550
Current assets		
Inventory	2,000	
Receivables	1,500	
Cash	300	
		3,800
		10,350
Ordinary shares (par value 50c)		2,000
Reserves		1,500
12% loan notes 2X12		4,500
Current liabilities		
Trade payables	1,100	
Overdraft	1,250	
		2,350
		10,350

Other information:

Price/earnings ratio of Tirwen Co:	15.24
Overdraft interest rate:	7%
Tax rate:	30%
Sector averages: debt/equity ratio (book value):	100%
interest cover:	6 times

Required

(a)   Ignoring issue costs and any use that may be made of the funds raised by the rights issue, calculate:

   (i)   the theoretical ex rights price per share;
   (ii)   the value of rights per existing share.   **(3 marks)**

(b)   What alternative actions are open to the owner of 1,000 shares in Tirwen Co as regards the rights issue? Determine the effect of each of these actions on the wealth of the investor.   **(6 marks)**

(c)   Calculate the current earnings per share and the revised earnings per share if the rights issue funds are used to redeem some of the existing loan stock.   **(6 marks)**

(d)   Evaluate whether the proposal to redeem some of the loan notes would increase the wealth of the shareholders of Tirwen Co. Assume that the price/earnings ratio of Tirwen Co remains constant.   **(3 marks)**

(e)   Discuss the reasons why a rights issue could be an attractive source of finance for Tirwen Co. Your discussion should include an evaluation of the effect of the rights issue on the debt/equity ratio and interest cover.   **(7 marks)**

(Total = 25 marks)

26 RG

45 mins

The following financial data relate to RG.

Year	Earnings per share Cents	Net dividend per share Cents	Share price Cents
20X1	42	17	252
20X2	46	18	184
20X3	51	20	255
20X4	55	22	275
20X5	62	25	372

A firm of market analysts which specialises in the industry in which RG operates has recently re-evaluated the company's future prospects. The analysts estimate that RG's earnings and dividends will grow at 25% for the next two years. Thereafter, earnings are likely to increase at a lower annual rate of 10%. If this reduction in earnings growth occurs, the analysts consider that the dividend payout ratio will be increased to 50%.

RG is all equity financed and has one million ordinary shares in issue.

The tax rate of 30% is not expected to change in the foreseeable future.

Required

(a) Discuss whether the dividend policy being considered by the analysts would be appropriate for the company in the following two sets of circumstances.

    (i) The company's shareholders are mainly financial institutions.

    (ii) The company's shareholders are mainly small private investors. **(7 marks)**

DV is a large international company with widespread interests in advertising, media and various consultancy activities associated with sales promotion and marketing. In recent years the company's earnings and dividend payments, in real terms, have grown on average by 15% and 12% per year respectively. The company is likely to have substantial cash surpluses in the coming year, but a number of investment opportunities are being considered for the subsequent two years. The senior managers of the company are reviewing their likely funding requirements for the next two to three years and the possible consequences for dividend policy.

At present the company has a debt:equity ratio of 1:5, measured in market value terms. It does not want to increase this ratio at the present time but might need to borrow to pay a maintained dividend in the future.

The senior managers of the company are discussing a range of issues concerning financial strategy in general and dividend policy in particular.

Required

Assume you are an independent financial adviser to the Board of DV. Write a report to the board which discusses the following issues.

(b) The repurchase of some of the company's shares in the coming year using the forecast surplus cash, the aim being to reduce the amount of cash needed to pay dividends in subsequent years. Other implications of share repurchase for the company's financial strategy should also be considered. **(8 marks)**

(c) The advisability of borrowing money to pay dividends in years 2 and 3. **(6 marks)**

(d) The likely effect on the company's cost of equity if the company decides on share repurchase and/or further borrowing. **(4 marks)**

(Total = 25 marks)

27 PG
45 mins

(a) PG Co has a paid-up ordinary share capital of $4,500,000 represented by 6 million shares of 75c each. It has no loan capital. Earnings after tax in the most recent year were $3,600,000. The P/E ratio of the company is 15.

The company is planning to make a large new investment which will cost $10,500,000, and is considering raising the necessary finance through a rights issue at 800c.

Required

(i) Calculate the current market price of PG Co's ordinary shares. **(2 marks)**

(ii) Calculate the theoretical ex-rights price, and state what factors in practice might invalidate your calculation. **(6 marks)**

(iii) Briefly explain what is meant by a deep-discounted rights issue, identifying the main reasons why a company might raise finance by this method. **(3 marks)**

(b) As an alternative to a rights issue, PG Co might raise the $10,500,000 required by means of an issue of convertible loan notes at par, with a coupon rate of 6%. The loan notes would be redeemable in seven years' time. Prior to redemption, the loan notes may be converted at a rate of 11 ordinary shares per $100 nominal loan notes.

Required

(i) Explain the term *conversion premium* and calculate the conversion premium at the date of issue implicit in the data given. **(4 marks)**

(ii) Identify the advantages to PG Co of issuing convertible loan notes instead of the rights issue to raise the necessary finance. **(5 marks)**

(iii) Explain why the market value of convertible loan notes is likely to be affected by the dividend policy of the issuing company. **(5 marks)**

(Total = 25 marks)

28 Newsam Co
45 mins

It is now December 20X4. Newsam Co is a quoted company which produces a range of branded products all of which are well-established in their respective markets, although overall sales have grown by an average of only 2% per annum over the past decade. The board of directors is currently concerned about the company's level of financial gearing, which although not high by industry standards, is near to breaching the covenants attaching to its 15% debenture issue, made in 20W2 at a time of high market interest rates. Issued in order to finance the acquisition of the premises on which it is secured, the debenture is repayable at par value of $100 per unit at any time during the period 20X4-X7.

There are two covenants attaching to the debenture, which state:

'At no time shall the ratio of debt capital to shareholders' fund exceed 50%. The company shall also maintain a prudent level of liquidity, defined as a current ratio at no time outside the range of the industry average (as published by the corporate credit analysts, Creditex), plus or minus 20%.'

Newsam's most recent set of accounts is shown in summarised form below. The buildings have been depreciated since 20W2 at 4% per annum, and most of the machinery is only two or three years old, having been purchased mainly via a bank overdraft. The interest rate payable on the bank overdraft is currently 9%. The finance director argues that Newsam should take advantage of historically low interest rates on the European money markets by issuing a medium-term Eurodollar bond at 5%. The dollar is currently selling at a premium of about 1% on the three-month forward market.

Newsam's ordinary shares currently sell at a P/E ratio of 14, and look unattractive compared to comparable companies in the sector which exhibit an average P/E ratio of 18. According to the latest published credit assessment by Creditex, the average current ratio for the industry is 1.35. The loan stock currently sell in the market at $15 above par.

Summarised financial accounts for Newsam Co for the year ended 30 June 20X4

BALANCE SHEET AS AT 30 JUNE 20X4

	$m	$m
Assets employed		
Non-current (net):		
Land		5.0
Premises		4.0
Machinery and vehicles		11.0
		20.0
Current:		
Inventory	2.5	
Receivables	4.0	
Cash	0.5	
		7.0
		27.0
Financed by:		
Ordinary shares (25c par value)		5.0
Reserves		10.0
Long-term payables:		
15% Loan notes 20X4-X7		5.0
Current liabilities:		
Payables	4.0	
Bank overdraft	3.0	
		7.0
		27.0

INCOME STATEMENT EXTRACTS FOR THE YEAR ENDED 30 JUNE 20X4

	$m
Sales	28.00
Operating profit	3.00
Interest payable	(1.00)
Profit before tax	2.00
Taxation	(0.66)
Profit after tax	1.34
Dividend	(0.70)
Retained profit	0.64

Required

(a) Calculate appropriate gearing ratios for Newsam Co using:

    (i)   book values; and

    (ii)   market values. **(3 marks)**

(b) Assess how close Newsam Co is to breaching the debenture covenants. **(3 marks)**

(c) Discuss whether Newsam Co's gearing is in any sense 'dangerous'. **(6 marks)**

(d)   Discuss what financial policies Newsam Co might adopt:

      (i)   in order to lower its capital gearing; and

      (ii)   to improve its interest cover.   **(9 marks)**

(e)   Explain what strategy a company might be pursuing when raising capital in the form of convertible debt as distinct from raising straight debt or straight equity.   **(4 marks)**

        (Total = 25 marks)

29 Arwin (FMC, 6/04)   45 mins

Arwin plans to raise $5m in order to expand its existing chain of retail outlets. It can raise the finance by issuing 10% loan notes redeemable in 2X15, or by a rights issue at $4.00 per share. The current financial statements of Arwin are as follows.

Income statement for the last year	$'000
Sales	50,000
Cost of sales	30,000
Gross profit	20,000
Administration costs	14,000
Profit before interest and tax	6,000
Interest	300
Profit before tax	5,700
Taxation at 30%	1,710
Profit after tax	3,990
Dividends	2,394
Retained earnings	1,596

Balance sheet extract	$'000
Net non-current assets	20,100
Net current assets	4,960
12% loan notes 2X10	2,500
	22,560
Ordinary shares, par value 25c	2,500
Retained profit	20,060
	22,560

The expansion of business is expected to increase sales revenue by 12% in the first year. Variable cost of sales makes up 85% of cost of sales. Administration costs will increase by 5% due to new staff appointments. Arwin has a policy of paying out 60% of profit after tax as dividends and has no overdraft.

Required

(a)   For each financing proposal, prepare the forecast income statement after one additional year of operation.

        (5 marks)

(b)   Evaluate and comment on the effects of each financing proposal on the following:

      (i)   Financial gearing;

      (ii)   Operational gearing;

      (iii) Interest cover;

      (iv) Earnings per share.   **(12 marks)**

(c) Discuss the dangers to a company of a high level of gearing, including in your answer an explanation of the following terms:

(i) Business risk;
(ii) Financial risk. **(8 marks)**

(Total = 25 marks)

29 Question with analysis: Arwin (FMC, 6/04)

2 sources of finance

Arwin plans to raise $5m in order to expand its existing chain of retail outlets. It can raise the finance by issuing 10% loan notes redeemable in 2X15, or by a rights issue at $4.00 per share. The current financial statements of Arwin are as follows.

Income statement for the last year	$'000
Sales	50,000
Cost of sales	30,000
Gross profit	20,000
Administration costs	14,000
Profit before interest and tax	6,000
Interest	300
Profit before tax	5,700
Taxation at 30%	1,710
Profit after tax	3,990
Dividends	2,394
Retained earnings	1,596

Balance sheet extract	$'000
Net non-current assets	20,100
Net current assets	4,960
12% loan notes 2X10	2,500
	22,560

Ordinary shares, par value 25c	2,500
Retained profit	20,060
	22,560

The expansion of business is expected to increase sales revenue by 12% in the first year. Variable cost of sales makes up 85% of cost of sales. Administration costs will increase by 5% due to new staff

Remember distributions from Post Tax profits

ing out 60% of profit after tax as dividends and has no overdraft.

See 1st paragraph for 2 sources

So based on next year's forecast

Required

(a) For **each financing proposal**, prepare the forecast income statement after **one additional year** of operation. **(5 marks)**

(b) **Evaluate** and comment on the effects of each financing proposal on the following:

Calculate

So 2 x ratios based on each financing proposal

(i) Financial gearing;
(ii) Operational gearing;
(iii) Interest cover;
(iv) Earnings per share.

Comment on your calculation

(12 marks)

(c)   **Discuss** the dangers to a company of a high level of gearing, including in your answer an explanation of the following terms:

Comment on

(i)   Business risk;

(ii)   Financial risk.   **(8 marks)**

(Total = 25 marks)

30 Food retailers   45 mins

Food Retailers: Ordinary Shares, Key Stock Market Statistics

Company	Current	Share price (cents) 52 week high	52 week low	Dividend Yield (%)	P/E ratio
Ply	63	112	54	1.8	14.2
Axis	291	317	187	2.1	13.0
Spin	187	201	151	2.3	21.1

Required

(a)   Illustrating your answer by use of data in the table above, define and explain the term P/E ratio, and comment on the way it may be used by an investor to appraise a possible share purchase.   **(7 marks)**

(b)   Using data in the above table, calculate the dividend cover for Spin and Axis, and explain the meaning and significance of the measure from the point of view of equity investors.   **(8 marks)**

(c)   Under what circumstances might a company be tempted to pay dividends which are in excess of earnings, and what are the dangers associated with such an approach?

You should ignore tax in answering this question.   **(6 marks)**

(d)   The directors of AXIS Co are currently considering whether to raise finance by means of a debenture issue or an issue of preference shares.

Describe the reasons why the directors might choose to issue loan notes rather than preference shares to raise the required finance.   **(4 marks)**

(Total = 25 marks)

31 CF Co   45 mins

CF Co is about to commence trading as a wholesaler of hats. CF's only shareholders, Mr and Mrs Topper, worked as employees of a hat retailer for many years, but have recently been made redundant. They intend to subscribe $200,000 as the initial share capital.

Sales in 20X2 are expected to be as follows.

	Units
January	2,400
February	3,600
March	4,800
Thereafter	9,600 each month

The average selling price of each hat is to be $10. All sales will be made on credit terms, requiring settlement two months after the date of sale. However, if settlement is made by customers within one month, a 2.5% cash discount will be given. Of the total sales, 60% are expected to be settled two months after the date of sale and 40% (before any discount is deducted) are expected to be settled one month after the date of sale.

The average purchase price for each hat will be $7. CF intends to make purchases at the end of each month in order to maintain inventories at a sufficient level to cover the following month's sales. Initially, therefore, purchases of 2,400 hats will be made in December 20X1. Payment for purchases will be made one month in arrears.

Non-current assets are expected to cost $250,000, payable on 1 January 20X2. Depreciation on these assets will be $5,000 each month, commencing January 20X2. These assets are likely to have a low net realisable value.

Annual rent is expected to be $24,000 and will be payable quarterly in advance, commencing January 20X2.

Monthly wages are expected to be $4,000 and are payable in the month they are incurred. Other overheads are expected to be $6,000 each month, half of which are payable in the month they are incurred and half are payable one month later.

Required

(a) Prepare a monthly cash budget for CF Co for the period January 20X2 to May 20X2 inclusive. It should show the expected net cash flow for each month and the cumulative budgeted cash surplus or deficit at the end of each month. Assume for the purposes of this cash budget that the bank has not provided any loan finance. Ignore interest charges and taxation payments. **(8 marks)**

(b) Discuss the finance needs of CF. **(5 marks)**

(c) Explain and evaluate the sources of finance available to small businesses for non-current assets. **(8 marks)**

(d) Describe four circumstances in which a business might seek venture capital finance. **(4 marks)**

(Total = 25 marks)

COST OF CAPITAL

Questions 32 to 38 cover Cost of Capital, the subject of Part F of the BPP Study Text for Paper F9.

32 XYZ Co

45 mins

XYZ Co is a large company whose 200 million $1 shares are listed on a major international stock exchange. It manufactures a variety of concrete and clay building materials. It has decided to replace 100 of its grinding machines with 100 of a new type of machine that has just been launched. The company is unable to issue any further equity and is therefore considering alternative methods of financing the new machines.

The company's accounting year end is 31 December.

Option 1 – Issue debt to purchase the machines

The machines are expected to cost $720,000 each on 31 December 20X1 and on average are expected to have a useful economic life of 10 years. After this time, the company expects to scrap the machines, but it has no idea what proceeds would be generated from the sale.

If XYZ Co issues debt, it would do so on 31 December 20X1 for the full purchase price of the machines in order to finance the investment. The debt would be issued at a discount of 10% of par value (that is, at $90 per $100 nominal) being redeemable at par on 31 December 20Y1 (in ten years' time) and carrying a coupon annual interest rate of 6%. Debt interest is tax allowable and the corporation tax rate can be assumed to be 30% (ignore any tax on the redemption). If this option is chosen, the share price on 31 December 20X1 is expected to be $1.50, and the cost of equity 10%.

The debt would be secured by fixed and floating charges.

Option 2 – Long-term lease

The machines can be leased with equal annual rentals payable in arrears. The lease term would be eight years, but this can be extended indefinitely at the option of the company at a nominal rent. The lease cannot be cancelled within the minimum lease term of eight years. The company would need to pay its own maintenance costs.

Option 3 – Short-term leases

The machines can be leased using a series of separate annual contracts. Maintenance costs would be paid by the lessor under these contracts but, even so, the average lease rentals would be much higher than under option 2. There is no obligation on either party to sign a new annual contract on the termination for the previous lease contract.

Required

(a) Calculate the after tax cost of debt at 31 December 20X1 to be used in option 1. **(8 marks)**

(b) Calculate the weighted average cost of capital for Option 1. **(4 marks)**

(c) Discuss the appropriateness of using the after tax cost of debt or the weighted average cost of capital to evaluate XYZ Co's investment in grinding machines. **(5 marks)**

(d) Write a memorandum to the directors of XYZ Co which identifies the factors that should be considered when deciding which of the three methods of financing the grinding machines is the most appropriate. **(8 marks)**

(Total = 25 marks)

33 D Co

45 mins

The summarised balance sheet of D Co at 30 June 20X9 was as follows.

	$'000	$'000
Non-current assets		15,350
Current assets	5,900	
Creditors falling due within one year	(2,600)	
Net current assets		3,300
9% loan notes		(8,000)
		10,650
Ordinary share capital (25c shares)		2,000
7% preference shares ($1 shares)		1,000
Share premium account		1,100
Retained earnings		6,550
		10,650

The current price of the ordinary shares is 135c ex dividend. The dividend of 10c is payable during the next few days. The expected rate of growth of the dividend is 9% per annum. The current price of the preference shares is 77c and the dividend has recently been paid. The loan notes interest has also been paid recently and the loan notes are currently trading at $80 per $100 nominal. Assume that D Co issued the loan notes one year ago to finance a new investment. Company income tax is at the rate of 30%.

Required

(a) Calculate the gearing ratio for D Co using:

    (i)   Book values

    (ii)   Market values   **(5 marks)**

(b) Calculate the company's weighted average cost of capital (WACC), using the respective market values as weighting factors.   **(7 marks)**

(c) Explain how the capital asset pricing model would be used as an alternative method of estimating the cost of equity, indicating what information would be required and how it would be obtained.   **(8 marks)**

(d) Discuss the reasons why D Co may have issued loan notes rather than preference shares to raise the required finance.   **(5 marks)**

    (Total = 25 marks)

34 IML Co

45 mins

IML Co is an all equity financed listed company. It develops customised software for clients which are mainly large civil engineering companies. Nearly all its shares are held by financial institutions.

IML Co's chairman has been dissatisfied with the company's performance for some time. Some directors were also concerned about the way in which the company is perceived by financial markets. In response, the company recently appointed a new finance director who advocated using the capital asset pricing model as a means of evaluating risk and interpreting the stock market's reaction to the company.

The following initial information was put forward by the finance director for two rival companies operating in the same industry:

	Beta
AZT Co	0.7
BOR Co	1.4

The *finance director* notes that the risk-free rate is 5% each year and the expected rate of return on the market portfolio is 15% each year.

The *chairman* set out his concerns at a meeting of the board of directors: 'I fail to understand these calculations. AZT Co operates largely in overseas markets with all the risk which that involves, yet you seem to be arguing that it is a lower risk company than BOR Co, whose income is mainly derived from long-term contracts in our domestic building industry. I am very concerned that we can take too much notice of the stock market. Take last year for instance, we had to announce a loss and the share price went up.'

Required

(a)   Calculate, using the capital asset pricing model, the required rate of return on equity of:

(i)   AZT Co
(ii)   BOR Co   **(4 marks)**

(b)   Calculate the beta of IML Co, assuming its required annual rate of return on equity is 17% and the stock market uses the capital asset pricing model to calculate the beta, and explain the significance of the beta factor.   **(6 marks)**

(c)   As the new finance director, write a memorandum to the chairman which explains, in language understandable to a non-financial manager, the following:

(i)   The assumptions and limitations of the capital asset pricing model; and
(ii)   An explanation of why IML Co's share price could rise following the announcement of a loss.

In so doing, discuss the observations and concerns expressed by the chairman. You may refer, where appropriate, to your calculations in (a) and (b) above.   **(15 marks)**

(Total = 25 marks)

35 DEA Co   **45 mins**

DEA Co is a listed company which manufactures quality cut-glass products. The company's sole manufacturing site and 95% of its sales are in the Country A. The company is, however, currently considering entering into a contract to sell a specialist range of glass ware to a Japanese retailer. The revenues from the Japanese contract are expected to amount to 25% of all future sales and 15% of future profit. It will require a significant initial investment, but it is expected that the money could be borrowed from the company's bank.

The Deaton family and other directors own the majority of the equity share capital, the remainder being held by employees and small shareholders. The total share capital amounts to 12 million $1 ordinary shares and has been unchanged for many years. Dividends per share paid on 31 May each year have been

20X2	20X3	20X4	20X5
35.64 cents	37.78 cents	40.05 cents	42.45 cents

The dividend on 31 May 20X6 will be 45.00 cents per share.

The company also has $12.5 million of 8% loan notes to be redeemed at par on 31 May 20X7. Interest is payable annually in arrears on 31 May.

At 31 May 20X6 the company's ordinary shares were quoted at $5.50 (cum div) and the loan notes at $98 per $10 nominal (ex interest).

The company income tax rate can be assumed to be 30% for the foreseeable future.

Interest is allowable for tax purposes.

Ignore any taxation of dividends.

The directors' meeting

The directors of DEA Co were uncertain whether to proceed with the Japanese contract and in particular they were concerned about the discount rate that should be used for assessing the project.

The *marketing director* argued: 'We should use the weighted average cost of capital. This is the rate we have used in the past and it reflects the average cost of acquiring funds.'

The *production director* disagreed: 'If we are going to borrow to finance this project, then we have to pay interest. So long as the cash flows from the project cover the interest payments, we will make a profit on the contract. Common sense dictates that we should therefore simply use the interest rate charged to us by the bank as the discount rate.'

The *chairman* commented: 'My son is studying accountancy and I recollect from talking to him that you should use the capital asset pricing model to determine the weighted average cost of capital. I don't know though what information you need to use the capital asset pricing model and how the information can be obtained.'

The *finance director* argued: 'The real issue in deciding the relevant discount rate is the finance that we use. I suggest that instead of paying more and more dividends each year, largely to ourselves as individual shareholders, we should reduce dividends and use the cash saved to decrease the company's debt. If the company can earn a better rate of return than individual shareholders then the cash should be retained in the company. As it is, the company is in effect borrowing to pay a dividend. Also this project is high risk and therefore demands a high-risk premium in the discount rate.'

Required

(a) Calculate DEA Co's weighted average cost of capital at 31 May 20X6. **(8 marks)**

(b) As a member of the treasury team, write a memorandum to the directors of DEA Co which discusses the views expressed by the directors. In so doing, and so far as the information permits, describe the factors to be considered in determining a discount rate for the Japanese project. **(17 marks)**

(Total = 25 marks)

36 KJI
45 mins

The following financial information is available for KJI.

	20X6	20X7	20X8	20X9
Earnings attributed to ordinary shareholders	$200m	$225m	$205m	$230m
Number of ordinary shares	2,000m	2,100m	2,100m	1,900m
Price per share	220c	305c	290c	260c
Dividend per share	5c	7c	8c	8c

Assume that share prices are as at the last day of each year.

Required

(a) Calculate KJI's earnings per share, dividend yield, dividend cover and price/ earnings ratio. Explain the meaning of each of these terms and why investors use them, and what limitations they may have.
(8 marks)

(b) Explain why the changes that occurred in the figures calculated in (a) above over the past four years might have happened. **(6 marks)**

The following is an extract from the balance sheet of LI Co, a company in the same industry as KJI, at 31 December 20X9.

	$'000
Ordinary shares of 50c each	5,200
Reserves	4,850
9% preference shares of $1 each	4,500
14% loan notes	5,000
Total long-term funds	19,550

The ordinary shares are quoted at 80c. Assume the market estimate of the next ordinary dividend is 4c, growing thereafter at 12% per annum indefinitely. The preference shares which are irredeemable are quoted at 72c and the loan notes are quoted at par. Tax on profits is 33%.

Required

(c)   Use the relevant data above to calculate the company's weighted average cost of capital (WACC), ie the return required by the providers of the three types of capital, using the respective market values as weighting factors. **(6 marks)**

(d)   Assume that the loan notes have recently been issued specifically to fund the company's expansion programme under which a number of projects are being considered. It has been suggested at a project appraisal meeting that because these projects are to be financed by the loan notes, the cutoff rate for project acceptance should be the after-tax interest rate on the loan notes rather than the WACC. Discuss this suggestion. **(5 marks)**

(Total = 25 marks)

37 WEB Co   45 mins

WEB Co operates a low-cost airline and is a listed company. By comparison to its major competitors it is relatively small, but it has expanded significantly in recent years. The shares are held mainly by large financial institutions.

The following are extracts from WEB Co's budgeted balance sheet at 31 May 20X2.

	$m
Ordinary shares of $1	100
Reserves	50
9% loan notes 20X5 (at nominal value)	200
	350

Dividends have grown in the past at 3% a year, resulting in an expected dividend of $1 per share to be declared on 31 May 20X2. (Assume for simplicity that the dividend will also be paid on this date.) Due to expansion, dividends are expected to grow at 4% a year from 1 June 20X2 for the foreseeable future. The price per share is currently $10.40 ex div, and this is not expected to change before 31 May 20X2.

The existing loan notes are due to be redeemed at par on 31 May 20X5. The market value of these loan notes at 1 June 20X2 is expected to be $100.84 (ex interest) per $100 nominal. Interest is payable annually in arrears on 31 May and is allowable for tax purposes. Tax is payable on profits at a rate for of 30%. Assume taxation is payable at the end of the year in which the taxable profits arise.

New finance

The company has now decided to purchase three additional aircraft at a cost of $10 million each. The board has decided that the new aircraft will be financed in full by an 8% bank loan on 1 June 20X2.

Required

(a)   Calculate the expected weighted average cost of capital of WEB Co at 31 May 20X2.   **(8 marks)**

(b)   Without further calculations, explain the impact of the new bank loan on WEB Co's

    (i)   Cost of equity
    (ii)   Cost of debt
    (iii)   Weighted average cost of capital (using the traditional model).   **(8 marks)**

(c)   Explain and distinguish

    (i)   A bank loan
    (ii)   Loan notes

    In so doing, explain why, in the circumstances of WEB Co, the cost of debt may be different for the two types of security.   **(4 marks)**

(d)   Explain why WEB might decide to raise capital in the form of a convertible debt issue rather than straight equity or debt.   **(5 marks)**

(Total = 25 marks)

38 CAP Co

CAP Co is a listed company that owns and operates a large number of farms throughout the world. A variety of crops are grown.

Financing structure

The following is an extract from the balance sheet of CAP Co at 30 September 20X2.

	$ million
Ordinary shares of $1 each	200
Reserves	100
9% irredeemable $1 preference shares	50
8% loan notes 20X3	250
	600

The ordinary shares were quoted at $3 per share ex div on 30 September 20X2. The beta of CAP Co's equity shares is 0.8, the annual yield on treasury bills is 5%, and financial markets expect an average annual return of 15% on the market index.

The market price per preference share was $0.90 ex div on 30 September 20X2.

Loan notes interest is paid annually in arrears and is allowable for tax at a rate of 30%. The loan notes were priced at $100.57 ex interest per $100 nominal on 30 September 20X2. Loan notes are redeemable on 30 September 20X3.

Assume that taxation is payable at the end of the year in which taxable profits arise.

A new project

Difficult trading conditions in European farming have caused CAP Co to decide to convert a number of its farms in Southern Europe into camping sites with effect from the 20X3 holiday season. Providing the necessary facilities for campers will require major investment, and this will be financed by a new issue of loan notes. The returns on the new campsite business are likely to have a very low correlation with those of the existing farming business.

Required

(a)   Using the capital asset pricing model, calculate the required rate of return on equity of CAP Co at 30 September 20X2. Ignore any impact from the new campsite project. Briefly explain the implications of a Beta of less than 1, such as that for CAP Co.   **(5 marks)**

71

(b)   Calculate the weighted average cost of capital of CAP Co at 30 September 20X2 (use your calculation in answer to requirement (a) above for the cost of equity). Ignore any impact from the new campsite project.

(10 marks)

(c)   Without further calculations, identify and explain the factors that may change CAP Co's equity beta during the year ending 30 September 20X3.

(5 marks)

(d)   Explain the limitations of the capital asset pricing model.

(5 marks)

(Total = 25 marks)

39 Question with student answer: MC   45 mins

MC provides a range of services to the medical and healthcare industry. These services include providing locum (temporary) cover for healthcare professionals (mainly doctors and nurses), emergency call-out and consultancy/advisory services to government-funded health organisations. The company also operates a research division that has been successful in recent years in attracting funding from various sources. Some of the employees in this division are considered to be leading experts in their field and are very highly paid.

A consortium of doctors and redundant health-service managers started the company some years ago. It is still owned by the same people, but has since grown into an organisation employing over 100 full-time staff throughout the UK. In addition, the company uses specialist staff employed in state-run organisations on a part-time contract basis. The owners of the company are now interested in either obtaining a stock market quotation, or selling the company if the price accurately reflects what they believe to be the true worth of the business.

Summary financial statistics for MC and a competitor company, which is listed on the UK Stock Exchange, are shown below. The competitor company is broadly similar to MC but uses a higher proportion of part-time to full-time staff and has no research capability.

	MC Last year end: 31.3.20X0	Competitor Last year end: 31.3.20X0
Shares in issue (m)	10.1	20
Earnings per share (pence)	75	60
Dividend per share (pence)	55	50
Net asset value (£m)	60	75
Debt ratio (outstanding debt as % of total financing)	10	20
Share price (pence)	N/A	980
Beta coefficient	N/A	1.25
Forecasts:		
Growth rate in earnings and dividends (% per annum)	8	7
After tax cash flow for 20X0/20X1 (£m)	9.2	N/A

Notes

1   The expected post-tax return on the market for the next twelve months is 12 per cent and the post-tax risk-free rate is 5 per cent.

2   The treasurer of the company has provided the forecast growth rate for MC. The forecast for the competitor is based on published information.

3   The net assets of MC are the net book values of land, buildings, equipment and vehicles plus net working capital.

4   Sixty per cent of the shares in the competitor company are owned by the directors and their relatives or associates.

5   MC uses a 'rule-of-thumb' discount rate of 15 per cent to evaluate its investments.

6   Assume that growth rates in earnings and dividends are constant per annum.

7   Debt is assumed to be risk-free.

8   The tax rate is 30%.

Required

Assume that you are an independent consultant retained by MC to advise on the valuation of the company and on the relative advantages of a public flotation versus outright sale.

Prepare a report for the directors that:

(a)   Produces a range of share prices at which shares in MC might be issued. Use whatever information is available. Explain the methods of valuation that you have used and discuss their suitability for providing an appropriate valuation of the company.   **(16 marks)**

(b)   Discusses the relative advantages of flotation and direct sale of shares.   **(6 marks)**

(c)   Recommends a course of action that the company should take.   **(3 marks)**

(Total = 25 marks)

40 OA & ML

45 mins

It is 20X8. OA, a company quoted on the London Stock Exchange, has cash balances of £23 million which are currently invested in short-term money market deposits. The cash is intended to be used primarily for strategic acquisitions, and the company has formed an acquisition committee with a remit to identify possible acquisition targets. The committee has suggested the purchase of ML, a company in a different industry that is quoted on the AIM (Alternative Investment Market). Although ML is quoted, approximately 50% of its shares are still owned by three directors. These directors have stated that they might be prepared to recommend the sale of ML, but they consider that its shares are worth £22 million in total.

Summarised financial data

	OA	ML
	£'000	£'000
Revenue	480,000	38,000
Pre tax operating cash flow	51,000	5,300
Taxation (33%)	16,830	1,749
Post tax operating cash flow	34,170	3,551
Dividend	11,000	842
Non-current assets	168,000	8,400
Current assets	135,000	4,700
Current liabilities	99,680	3,900
	203,320	9,200

	OA		ML
	£'000		£'000
Long-term finance			
Ordinary shares (25 pence par)	10,000	(ML 10 pence par)	500
Reserves	158,320		5,200
12% Debentures 20Y6	20,000		–
10% Bank term loan	15,000		
		Recent 11% bank loan	3,500
	203,320		9,200

	OA	ML
	£'000	£'000
Current share price	785 pence	370 pence
Earnings yield	10.9%	19.2%
Average dividend growth during the last five years	7% pa	8% pa
Equity beta	0.95	0.8
Industry data:		
Average P/E ratio	10:1	6:1
Average P/E of companies recently taken over, based upon the offer price	12:1	7:1

The risk free rate of return is 6% per annum and the market return 14% per annum.

The rate of inflation is 2.4% per annum and is expected to remain at approximately this level.

Expected effects of the acquisition:

(i) 50 employees of ML would immediately be made redundant at an after tax cost of £1.2 million. Pre-tax annual wage savings are expected to be £750,000 (at current prices) for the foreseeable future.

(ii) Some land and buildings of ML would be sold for £800,000 (after tax).

(iii) Pre-tax advertising and distribution savings of £150,000 per year (at current prices) would be possible.

(iv) The three existing directors of ML would each be paid £100,000 per year for three years for consultancy services. This amount would not increase with inflation.

Required

(a) Calculate the value of ML based upon:

    (i) The use of comparative P/E ratios **(5 marks)**

    (ii) The dividend valuation model **(6 marks)**

    (iii) The present value of relevant operating cash flows over a 10 year period and discuss the advantages and disadvantages of *each* of the three valuation methods. **(8 marks)**

    (iv) Recommend whether OA should go ahead with the offer for ML. **(2 marks)**

(b) Explain what is meant by behavioural finance. **(4 marks)**

(Total = 25 marks)

41 BiOs

45 mins

BiOs is an unquoted company that provides consultancy services to the biotechnology industry. It has been trading for 4 years. It has an excellent reputation for providing innovative and technologically advanced solutions to clients' problems. The company employs 18 consultants plus a number of self employed contract staff and is planning to recruit additional consultants to handle a large new contract. The company 'outsources' most administrative and accounting functions. A problem is recruiting well qualified experienced consultants and BiOs has had to turn down work in the past because of lack of appropriate staff.

The company's two owners/directors have been approached by the marketing department of an investment bank and asked if they have considered using venture capital financing to expand the business. No detailed proposal has been made but the bank has implied that a venture capital company would require a substantial percentage of the equity in return for a large injection of capital. The venture capitalist would want to exit from the investment in 4-5 years' time.

The company is all-equity financed and neither of the directors is wholly convinced that such a large injection of capital is appropriate for the company at the present time.

Financial information

Revenue in year to 31 December 20X3	$3,600,000
Shares in issue (ordinary $1 shares)	100,000
Earnings per share	756c
Dividend per share	0
Net asset value	$395,000 (Note 1)

Note. The net assets of BiOs are the net book values of purchased and/or leased buildings, equipment and vehicles plus net working capital. The book valuations are considered to reflect current realisable values.

Forecast

- Sales revenue for the year to 31 December 20X4 – $4,250,000. This is heavily dependent on whether or not the company obtains the new contract.

- Operating costs, inclusive of depreciation, are expected to average 50% of revenue in the year to 31 December 20X4.

- Tax is expected to be payable at 30%.

- Assume book depreciation equals capital allowances for tax purposes. Also assume, for simplicity, that profit after tax equals cash flow.

Growth in earnings in the years to 31 December 20X5 and 20X6 is expected to be 30% per annum, falling to 10% per annum after that. This assumes that no new long-term capital is raised. If the firm is to grow at a faster rate then new financing will be needed.

This is a niche market and there are relatively few listed companies doing precisely what BiOs does. However, if the definition of the industry is broadened the following figures are relevant:

P/E Ratios

Industry Average:	18
Range (individual companies)	12 to 90

Cost of Equity

Industry average	12%
Individual companies	Not available

BiOs does not know what its cost of equity is.

Required

(a) Calculate a range of values for the company that could be used in negotiation with a venture capitalist, using whatever information is currently available and relevant. Make and state whatever assumptions you think are necessary. Explain, briefly, the relevance of each method to a company such as BiOs. **(15 marks)**

(b) Discuss the advantages and disadvantages of using either venture capital financing to assist with expansion or alternatively a flotation on the stock market in 2-3 years' time. Include in your discussion likely exit routes for the venture capital company. **(10 marks)**

(Total = 25 marks)

42 BST

45 mins

BST Motors Co (BST) is a long-established listed company. Its main business is the retailing of new and used motor cars and the provision of after-sales service. It has sales outlets in most of the major towns and cities in the country. It also owns a substantial amount of land and property that it has acquired over the years, much of which it rents or leases on medium-long term agreements. Approximately 80% of its net current asset value is land and buildings.

The company has grown organically for the last few years but is now considering expanding by acquisition.

SM owns a number of car showrooms in wealthy, semi-rural locations. All of these showrooms operate the franchise of a well-known major motor manufacturer. SM is a long-established private company with the majority of shares owned by the founding family, many of whom still work for the company. The major shareholders are now considering selling the business if a suitable price can be agreed. The Managing Director of SM, who is a major shareholder, has approached BST to see if they would be interested in buying SM. He has implied that holders of up to 50% of SM's shares might be willing to accept BST shares as part of the deal.

The forecast earnings of BST for the next financial year are $35 million. According to the Managing Director of SM, his company's earnings are expected to be $4 million for the next financial year.

Financial statistics and other information on BST and SM are shown below:

	BST	SM
Shares in issue (millions)	25	1.5
Earnings per share (cents)	112.5	153
Dividend per share (cents)	50.6	100
Share price (cents)	1237	N/A
Net asset value attributable to equity ($m)	350	45
Debt ratio (outstanding debt as percentage of total market value of company)	20	0
Forecast growth rate percentage (constant, annualised)	4	5
Cost of equity	9%	N/A

SM does not calculate a cost of equity, but the industry average for similar companies is 10%

Required

Assume you are a financial manager working with BST. Advise the BST Board on the following issues in connection with a possible bid for SM:

(a) Methods of valuation that might be appropriate and a range of valuations for SM within which BST should be prepared to negotiate. **(10 marks)**

(b) The financial factors relating to both companies that might affect the bid. **(5 marks)**

(c) Explain the practical considerations in the valuation of shares and businesses. **(10 marks)**

(Total = 25 marks)

43 COE

45 mins

COE plc is an all-equity financed, listed company in the pharmaceutical industry which produces a small, specialist range of drugs that treat heart disorders. The drugs are protected by international patent as soon as new research and development has progressed sufficiently.

On 1 March 20X2, following many years of testing, a new drug, kryothin, was given government approval in the United Kingdom. It was approved for use in most other countries during April and May 20X2. Sales of kryothin will commence on 1 January 20X3. The company's accounting year end is 31 December.

Including the earnings generated by sales of kryothin, the company could pay a total annual dividend of £32.2 million in each of the years ending 31 December 20X3 to 31 December 20X7. Thereafter it is expected that competitors will develop similar drugs and most of the excess profits will disappear, in which case the company could pay a total annual dividend of £19 million from 31 December 20X8 onwards. (Assume for simplicity that dividends are declared and paid on 31 December each year.)

In order to manufacture kryothin, it will be necessary to raise £80 million of new capital on 1 January 20X3 to finance the purchase of equipment.

The financing options being considered are:

Option (1)   An offer for sale at the market price per share on 1 January 20X3.

Option (2)   An issue at par of 7% irredeemable corporate bonds. In this case, the interest could reduce the amount otherwise available to pay dividends.

The directors of COE plc assume that the annual cost of equity will remain at its current level of 10%. The company currently has in issue a share capital of 20 million £1 ordinary shares.

Required

(a)   Assuming a semi-strong efficient market, explain the nature and timing of the share price reaction to the new drug kryothin at each stage of its development. Calculations are not required. **(7 Marks)**

(b)   Calculate COE plc's price per share at 2 January 20X3 under each of the following options for raising the £80 million of new finance:

Option (1)   An offer for sale
Option (2)   An issue at par of 7% irredeemable corporate bonds

Assume that the directors are correct in assuming that the annual cost of equity will remain at 10%, and that financial markets believe the directors' forecasts of future dividends.

Ignore taxation.   **(13 Marks)**

(c)   Explain the main assumptions of the model you have used in part (b).   **(5 Marks)**

(Total = 25 marks)

44 Collingham Co   45 mins

It is currently June 20X5. Collingham Co produces electronic measuring instruments for medical research. It has recorded strong and consistent growth during the past 10 years since its present team of managers bought it out from a large multinational corporation. They are now contemplating obtaining a stock market listing.

Collingham's accounting statements for the last financial year are summarised below. Non-current assets, including freehold land and premises, are shown at historic cost net of depreciation. The debenture is redeemable in two years although early redemption without penalty is permissible.

Income statement for the year ended 31 December 20X4

	$m
Revenue	80.0
Cost of sales	(70.0)
Operating profit	10.0
Interest charges	(3.0)
Pre-tax profit	7.0
Tax (after tax-allowable depreciation)	(1.0)
Profits attributable to ordinary shareholders	6.0
Dividends	(0.5)
Retained earnings	5.5

Balance sheet as at 31 December 20X4

	$m	$m
Assets employed		
Non-current assets		
Land and premises	10.0	
Machinery	20.0	
		30.0
Current assets		
Inventories	10.0	
Receivables	10.0	
Cash	3.0	
		23.0
		53.0
Issued share capital (par value 50c)		
Voting shares		2.0
Non-voting 'A' shares		2.0
Retained earnings		24.0
14% debenture		5.0
Current liabilities		
Trade payables	15.0	
Bank overdraft	5.0	20.0
		53.0

The following information is also available regarding key financial indicators for Collingham's industry.

Return on (long-term) capital employed	22% (pre-tax)
Return on equity	14% (post-tax)
Operating profit margin	10%
Current ratio	1.8:1
Acid test	1.1:1
Gearing (total debt equity)	18%
Interest coverage	5.2
Dividend cover	2.6
P/E ratio	13:1

Required

(a) Briefly explain why companies like Collingham seek stock market listings. **(4 marks)**

(b) Discuss the performance and financial health of Collingham in relation to that of the industry as a whole. **(8 marks)**

(c) In what ways would you advise Collingham:

    (i) to restructure its balance sheet *prior* to flotation **(5 marks)**

    (ii) to change its financial policy *following* flotation? **(3 marks)**

(d) If the stock market is believed to operate with a strong level of efficiency, what effect might this have on the directors of publicly-quoted companies? **(5 marks)**

(Total = 25 marks)

RISK MANAGEMENT

Questions 45 to 50 cover Risk Management, the subject of Part H of the BPP Study Text for Paper F9.

45 Marton Co

45 mins

Marton Co produces a range of specialised components, supplying a wide range of UK and overseas customers, all on credit terms. 20% of UK turnover is sold to one firm. Having used generous credit policies to encourage past growth, Marton now has to finance a substantial overdraft and is concerned about its liquidity. Marton borrows from its bank at 13% per annum interest. No further sales growth in volume or value terms is planned for the next year.

In order to speed up collection from UK customers, Marton is considering two alternative policies.

Option one

Factoring on a with-recourse, service only basis, the factor administering and collecting payment from Marton's UK customers. This is expected to generate administrative savings of £200,000 per annum and to lower the average receivable collection period by 15 days. The factor will make a service charge of 1% of Marton's UK turnover and also provide credit insurance facilities for an annual premium of £80,000.

Option two

Offering discounts to UK customers who settle their accounts early. The amount of the discount will depend on speed of payment as follows.

Payment within 10 days of despatch of invoices: 3%

Payment within 20 days of despatch of invoices: 1.5%

It is estimated that UK customers representing 20% and 30% of Marton's sales respectively will take up these offers, the remainder continuing to take their present credit period.

In addition, Marton is concerned about the risk of its overseas earnings. All overseas customers pay in US dollars and Marton does not hedge currency risk, invoicing at the prevailing spot rate, which is currently US$1.45:£1. It is considering the use of an overseas factor and also hedging its US dollar income on the forward market. Its bank has offered to buy all of its dollar earnings at a fixed rate of US$1.55:£1. Marton's advisers estimate the following chances of various dollar/sterling rates of exchange:

US Dollars per £	Probability
1.60	0.1
1.50	0.2
1.45	0.4
1.40	0.2
1.30	0.1

Extracts from Marton's most recent accounts are given below.

	£'000	£'000
Sales (all on credit)		
Home	20,000	
Export	5,000	
		25,000
Cost of sales		(17,000)
Operating profit		8,000
Current assets		
Inventory	2,500	
Receivables*	4,500	
Cash	–	

*There are no overseas receivables at the year end.

Note. Taxes and inflation can be ignored in this question.

Required

(a) Calculate the relative costs and benefits *in terms of annual profit before tax* of each of the two proposed methods of reducing domestic receivables, and recommend the most financially advantageous policy. Comment on your results. **(13 marks)**

(b) Briefly outline the services provided by an overseas factor. **(4 marks)**

(c) (i) Calculate the maximum loss which Marton can sustain through movements in the dollar/sterling exchange rate if it does not hedge overseas sales. **(2 marks)**

   (ii) Calculate the maximum opportunity cost of selling dollar earnings forward at US$1.55:$1. **(2 marks)**

   (iii) Briefly discuss whether Marton should hedge its foreign currency risk. **(4 marks)**

   (Total = 25 marks)

46 SDT
45 mins

SDT plc is a UK based manufacturer of a wide range of printed circuit boards (PCBs) that are used in a variety of electrical products. SDT exports over 90% of its production to assembly plants owned by large multinational electronics companies all around the world. Two companies (A and B) require SDT to invoice them in a single currency, regardless of the export destination of the PCBs. The chosen currencies are the Japanese Yen (Company A) and the US$ (Company B) respectively. The remaining export sales all go to European customers and are invoiced in Euros.

The variable cost and export price per unit PCB are shown below.

Market	Unit variable cost (£)	Unit export sales price
Company A	2.75	Yen 632.50
Company B	4.80	US$ 10.2678
Europe	6.25	Euro 12.033

Goods are supplied on 60 day credit terms.

The following receipts for export sales are due in 60 days:

Company A	Yen 9,487,500
Company B	US$ 82,142
Europe	Euro 66,181

The foreign exchange rates to be used by SDT in evaluating its revenue from the export sales are as follows.

	Yen/£	US$/£	Euro/£
Spot market	198.987 – 200.787	1.7620 – 1.7826	1.4603 – 1.4813
2 months forward	197.667 – 200.032	1.7550 – 1.7775	1.4504 – 1.4784
3 months forward	196.028 – 198.432	1.7440 – 1.7677	1.4410 – 1.4721
1 year forward	188.158 – 190.992	1.6950 – 1.7311	1.4076 – 1.4426

The Managing Director of SDT believes that the foreign exchange markets are efficient and so the likelihood that SDT will make foreign exchange gains is the same as the likelihood that it will make foreign exchange losses. Furthermore, any exchange risk is already diversified across three currencies, each from countries in very different economic regions of the world. The Managing Director has therefore recommended that the Treasury Department should not hedge any foreign exchange risks arising from export sales.

Required

(a) Critically comment on the validity of the views and recommendations expressed by the Managing Director and explain how currency hedging might nevertheless be beneficial to SDT. **(6 marks)**

(b) (i) Calculate the sterling value of the contribution earned from exports to each of the customers (A, B and Europe) assuming that SDT:

   (1) Hedges the risk in the forward market; **(3 marks)**

   (2) Does not hedge the risk and the relevant spot exchange rates in two months' time are as follows:

   Two month spot
   Yen/£ 200.18 – 202.63
   US$/£ 1.7650 – 1.7750
   Euro/£ 1.4600 – 1.4680

   (3 marks)

   (ii) Calculate the average contribution to sales ratio in each of the above scenarios and advise SDT accordingly on whether to hedge its foreign exchange exposure. **(3 marks)**

(c) Comment on why (based on relative risk analysis) a company might seek to generate higher rates of return from export sales compared to domestic sales. **(6 marks)**

(d) If the payment from Company B is received late, briefly explain what risk SDT is taking in hedging B's payment in the forward market, and how this risk could be avoided. **(4 marks)**

(Total = 25 marks)

47 RET   45 mins

RET Inc is a medium sized US company that trades with companies in several European countries. Trade deals over the next three months are shown below. Assume that it is now 20 April.

	Two months time		*Three months time*	
	Receipts	*Payments*	*Receipts*	*Payments*
France	–	€393,265	€491,011	€60,505
Germany	–	–	€890,217	€1,997,651
Denmark	–	–	Kr 8.6m	–

Foreign exchange rates:

	Dkroner/$	*Euro €/$*
Spot	10.68 – 10.71	1.439 – 1.465
Two months forward	10.74 – 10.77	1.433 – 1.459
Three months forward	10.78 – 10.83	1.431 – 1.456

Annual interest rates (valid for 2 months or 3 months)

	Borrowing	*Investing*
	%	%
USA	7.50	5.50
France	5.75	3.50
Germany	5.75	3.50
Denmark	8.00	6.00

Required

(a) State the values of the net receipts and payments the company may need to hedge. **(2 marks)**

(b) Calculate the expected $ values of the receipt and payments using the forward market.

   (3 marks)

(c) Calculate the expected $ values of the receipt and payments using a money market hedge.

   (6 marks)

(d)   Discuss the advantages and disadvantages of forward contracts and currency futures for hedging against foreign exchange risk.   **(6 marks)**

(e)   Briefly explain four other traditional and basic methods of foreign currency risk management.   **(8 marks)**

(Total = 25 marks)

48 BS   45 mins

BS is an importer/exporter of heavy machinery for a variety of industries. It is based in the UK but trades extensively with the USA. Assume that you are a newly appointed management accountant with BS. The company does not have a separate treasury function and it is part of your duties to assess and manage currency risks. You are concerned about the recent fluctuations in the exchange rate between US$ and sterling and are considering various methods of hedging the exchange risk involved. Assume it is now the end of March. The following transactions are expected on 30 June.

Sales receipts $450,000
Purchases payable $250,000

Economic data

*   The spot rate of exchange is US$1.6540-1.6590 to the £.
*   The three-month forward rate that will apply for this contract is $1.6513/£
*   Annual interest rates for three months' borrowing are: USA 6 per cent; UK 9 per cent.
*   Annual interest rates for three months' lending are: USA 4 per cent; UK 6.5 per cent.

Required

(a)   Calculate the net sterling receipts that BS can expect from its transactions if the company hedges the exchange risk using each of the following alternatives:

(i)   The forward foreign exchange market
(ii)   The money market

Accompany your calculations with brief explanations of your approach and recommend the most financially advantageous alternative for BS. Assume transaction costs would be 0.2 per cent of the US$ transaction value under either method, paid at the beginning of the transaction (ie now).   **(10 marks)**

(b)   Explain the factors the company should consider before deciding to hedge the risk using the foreign currency markets, and identify any alternative actions available to minimise risk.   **(5 marks)**

(c)   Discuss the causes of exchange rate fluctuations.   **(10 marks)**

(Total = 25 marks)

49 Interest rates

45 mins

(a)   The following table of London money rates shows the relationship between maturity and interest rates for four types of short-term investment, as published in the financial press.

	One month	Three months	Six months	One year
Sterling certificates of deposit	$9^7/_8$	$10^1/_{16}$	$10^3/_{16}$	$10^5/_{16}$
Local authority bonds	$9^7/_8$	10	$10^1/_4$	$10^1/_2$
Finance house deposits	10	$10^1/_8$	$10^3/_8$	$10^9/_{16}$
Treasury bills (buy)	$9^{11}/_{16}$	$9^3/_4$	–	–

Required

Explain:

(i)   The nature of the instruments listed, and

(ii)   The main reasons for the differences in interest rate between the instruments and over time

(11 marks)

(b)   Describe the likely implications to a typical company of lower interest rates.   **(6 marks)**

(c)   If you were the Financial Director of a company with a large investment programme and no capital gearing, explain what changes might result to both the investment programme and its financing as a result of falling interest rates.   **(8 marks)**

(Total = 25 marks)

50 QW

45 mins

Assume that you are treasurer of QW, a company with diversified, international interests. The company wishes to borrow £10 million for a period of three years. Your company's credit rating is good and current market data suggests that you could borrow at a fixed rate of interest at 8 per cent per annum or at a floating rate of LIBOR + 0.2 per cent per annum. You believe that interest rates are likely to fall over the next three years, and favour borrowing at a floating rate.

You have been in the post for twelve months, having been recruited from a large financial institution. You have a keen interest in using financial derivatives (such as futures and options) to both manage risk and generate revenue. Some board members have expressed concern that your activities may be involving the company in unnecessary risk.

Required

(a)   Describe and discuss different types of interest rate risk.   **(8 marks)**

(b)   Explain the meaning and use of financial derivatives, in general terms, and the advantages and disadvantages of their use for companies such as QW.   **(8 marks)**

(c)   Describe the characteristics and benefits of interest rate swaps compared with other forms of interest-rate-risk management, such as forward rate agreements and interest rate futures.   **(9 marks)**

(Total = 25 marks)

Answers

1 Private sector companies

> **Text references.** Stakeholders and corporate governance are covered in Chapter 1.
>
> **Top tips.** Only five groups are required, so there are no marks to be gained for listing more. We do so here for illustration only. In part (b), a good answer should refer to the corporate governance procedures and how these may assist in managing potential conflicts.

(a)   The various stakeholder groups in a private sector company may include the following.

Internal	Employees and pensioners
	Managers
Connected	Shareholders
	Debtholders
	Customers
	Bankers
	Suppliers
	Competitors
External	Government
	Pressure groups
	Local and national communities
	Professional and regulatory bodies

Objectives of stakeholder groups

The various groups of stakeholders in a firm will have different objectives which will depend in part on the particular situation of the enterprise. Some of the more important aspects of these different goals are as follows.

(i)   **Ordinary (equity) shareholders**

Ordinary (equity) shareholders are the providers of the risk capital of a company. Usually their goal will be to **maximise the wealth which they have** as a result of the ownership of the shares in the company.

(ii)   **Directors and management**

Management has, like other employees (and managers who are not directors will normally be employees), the objective of **maximising** their **own rewards**. Directors and the managers to whom they delegate responsibilities must manage the company for the benefit of shareholders. It may be argued that the objective of reward maximisation might conflict with the exercise of this duty.

(iii)   **Employees**

Employees will usually want to **maximise their rewards** paid to them in salaries and benefits, according to the particular skills and the rewards available in alternative employment. Most employees will also want **continuity of employment**.

(iv)   **Long-term payables**

Long-term payables, which will often be banks, have the objective of **receiving payments of interest and capital** on the loan by the due date for the repayments. Where the loan is secured on assets of the company, the payable will be able to appoint a receiver to dispose of the company's assets if the company defaults on the repayments. To avoid the possibility that this may result in a loss to the lender if the assets are not sufficient to cover the loan, the lender will wish to **minimise the risk of default** and will not wish to lend more than is prudent.

(v) **Trade payables**

Trade payables have supplied goods or services to the firm. Trade payables will generally be profit-maximising firms themselves and have the objective of **being paid the full amount due by the date agreed**. On the other hand, they usually wish to ensure that they continue their trading relationship with the firm and may sometimes be prepared to accept later payment to avoid jeopardising that relationship.

(vi) **Customers**

The customers' objectives will be customer satisfaction, in terms of good service, quality, price, delivery and a range of other variables.

(vii) **Government**

Government has objectives which can be formulated in political terms. Government agencies impinge on the firm's activities in different ways including through taxation of the firm's profits, the provision of grants, health and safety legislation, training initiatives and so on. Government policies will often be related to macroeconomic objectives such as **sustained economic growth** and **high levels of employment**.

The actions of stakeholder groups in pursuit of their various goals can exert influence on strategy. The greater the power of the stakeholder, the greater his influence will be. Each stakeholder group will have different expectations about what it wants, and the **expectations of the various groups may conflict**. Each group, however, will influence strategic decision-making.

(b) **Corporate governance** is the system by which organisations are directed and controlled.

Those directors who have the power to direct and control the organisation also have the duty of accountability to the organisation's stakeholders.

Although the directors' role is a key one in deciding how the divergent interests of the various stakeholders should be promoted, the directors primary duty is to **enhance the value of shareholders' investment** over time.

Corporate governance regulation aims to control the ability of the directors to promote their own interests and ensure adequate disclosure of their activities.

There are a number of key elements in corporate governance:

(i) The management and **reduction of risk** is a fundamental issue in all definitions of good governance; whether explicitly stated or merely implied.

(ii) The notion that **overall performance enhanced** by **good supervision** and **management** within set best practice guidelines underpins most definitions.

(iii) Good governance provides a **framework** for an organisation to pursue its strategy in an **ethical and effective** way from the perspective of all stakeholder groups affected, and offers safeguards against misuse of resources, physical or intellectual.

(iv) Good governance is not just about externally established codes, it also requires a willingness to **apply the spirit** as well as the letter of the law.

(v) **Accountability** is generally a major theme in all governance frameworks.

Corporate governance codes of good practice generally cover the following areas:

(i) The board should be responsible for taking major **policy** and **strategic** decisions.

(ii) Directors should have a **mix of skills** and their **performance** should be assessed regularly.

(iii) Appointments should be conducted by formal procedures administered by a **nomination committee**.

(iv) **Division of responsibilities** at the head of an organisation is most simply achieved by separating the roles of chairman and chief executive.

(v) **Independent non-executive directors** have a key role in governance. Their number and status should mean that their views carry significant weight.

(vi) Directors' remuneration should be set by a **remuneration committee** consisting of independent non-executive directors.

(vii) Remuneration should be dependent upon **organisation** and **individual performance**.

(viii) Accounts should disclose **remuneration policy** and (in detail) the **packages of individual directors.**

(ix) Boards should regularly review **risk management** and **internal control**, and carry out a wider review annually, the results of which should be disclosed in the accounts.

(xi) Audit committees of independent non-executive directors should liaise with external audit, supervise internal audit, and review the annual accounts and internal controls.

(xii) The board should maintain a regular dialogue with shareholders, particularly institutional shareholders. The annual general meeting is the most significant forum for communication.

(xiii) Annual reports must **convey** a **fair and balanced view** of the organisation. They should state whether the organisation has complied with governance regulations and codes, and give specific disclosures about the board, internal control reviews, going concern status and relations with stakeholders.

2 Goals

Text references. Chapter 1 looks at objectives of organisations.

Top tips. You are given some very strong hints about answer structure in (a). You should start off with the main idea of maximisation of shareholder wealth, and then discuss two problems; how do we measure whether wealth has been maximised, and what about other stakeholders. These provide the framework for the rest of the answer. When discussing measurement of success, you need to include limitations of measurement; timescale is an important problem here.

In (b) setting out the criteria against which each policy will be judged at the start of your answer makes it easy for the marker to see that you have appreciated the main issues. Although detailed analysis of the tax position is not required, you can mention fiscal implications briefly.

Easy marks. Generally a fairly reasonable question. If you struggled to discuss the other methods suggested in (a), remember these may need to be considered in the discussion part of a question.

(a)   REPORT

    To: Managing Director
    From: Finance Director
    Date: 17 November 20X5
    Subject: Definition of corporate objectives

Introduction

1   This report has been drafted for use as a discussion document at the forthcoming board meeting. It deals with the validity of continuing to operate with the single major goal of **shareholder wealth maximisation**. The remaining sections of the report contain an analysis of the advantages and disadvantages of some of the alternative objectives that have been put forward in recent discussions.

Maximisation of shareholder wealth

2   The concept that the **primary financial objective** of the firm is to **maximise** the **wealth** of shareholders, by which is meant the **net present value** of estimated future cash flows, underpins much of modern financial theory.

3   While the relevance of the wealth maximisation goal is under discussion, it might also be useful to consider the way in which this type of objective is defined, since this will impact upon both parallel and subsidiary objectives. A widely adopted approach is to seek to **maximise the present value of the projected cash flows**. In this way, the objective is both made measurable and can be translated into a yardstick for financial decision making. It cannot be defined as a single attainable target but rather as a criterion for the continuing allocation of the company's resources.

4   There has been some recent debate as to whether wealth maximisation should or can be the only true objective, particularly in the context of the multinational company. The **stakeholder view** of corporate objectives is that **many groups** of people have a stake in what the company does. Each of these groups, which include suppliers, workers, manager, customers and governments as well as shareholders, has its own objectives, and this means that a compromise is required. For example, in the case of the multinational firm with a facility in a politically unstable third world economy, the directors may at times need to place the **interests of local government and economy** ahead of those of its shareholders, in part at least to ensure its own continued stability there.

Cash flow generation

5   The validity of **cash flow generation** as a major corporate objective depends on the timescale over which performance is measured. If the business maximises the net present value of the cash flows generated in the medium to long term, then this objective is effectively the same as that discussed above. However, if the aim is to **maximise all cash flows**, then decisions are likely to be disproportionately focused on **short-term performance**, and this can work against the long-term health of the business. Defining objectives in terms of long-term cash flow generation makes the shareholder wealth maximisation goal more clearly definable and measurable.

Profitability

6   Many companies use **return on investment (ROI)** targets to **assess performance** and **control the business**. This is useful for the comparison of widely differing divisions within a diverse multinational company, and can provide something approaching a 'level playing field' when setting targets for the different parts of the business. It is important that the **measurement techniques** to be used in respect of both profits and the asset base are very clearly defined, and that there is a clear and consistent approach to accounting for inflation. As with the cash flow generation targets discussed above, the selection of the time frame is also important in ensuring that the selected objectives do work for the long-term health of the business.

Risk adjusted returns

7   It is assumed that the use of **risk adjusted returns** relates to the criteria used for investment appraisal, rather than to the performance of the group as a whole. As such, risk adjusted returns cannot be used in defining the top level major **corporate goals**; however they can be one way in which corporate goals are made **congruent** with operating decisions. At the same time, they do provide a **useful input** to the goal setting process in that they focus attention on the company's policy with regard to making risky investments. Once the overall corporate approach to risk has been decided, this can be made effective in operating decisions, for example by **specifying the amount** by which the **cost of capital** is to be **augmented** to allow for risk in various types of investment decisions.

Performance improvement in non-financial areas

8   As discussed in the first section of this report, recent work on corporate objectives suggests that firms should take specific account of those areas which impact only indirectly, if at all, on **financial performance**. The firm has responsibilities towards many groups in addition to the shareholders, including:

(i)   **Employees:** to provide good working conditions and remuneration, the opportunity for personal development, outplacement help in the event of redundancy and so on

(ii)   **Customers:** to provide a product of good and consistent quality, good service and communication, and open and fair commercial practice

(iii)   **The public:** to ensure responsible disposal of waste products.

9   There are many **other interest groups** that should also be included in the discussion process. Non-financial objectives may often work indirectly to the financial benefit of the firm in the long term, but in the short term they do often appear to compromise the primary financial objectives.

Conclusions

10   It is very difficult to find a comprehensive and appropriate alternative primary financial objective to that of **shareholder wealth maximisation**. However, achievement of this goal can be pursued, at least in part, through the setting of specific **subsidiary targets** in terms of items such as return on investment and risk adjusted returns. The definition of non-financial objectives should also be addressed in the context of the overall review of the corporate plan.

Signed: Finance Director

(b)   **Factors affecting remuneration policy**

(i)   **Cost:** the extent to which the package provides value for money.

(ii)   **Motivation:** the extent to which the package motivates employees both to stay with the company and to work to their full potential.

(iii)   **Fiscal effects:** government tax incentives may promote different types of pay. At present there are tax benefits in offering some types of share option schemes. At times of wage control and high taxation this can act as an incentive to make the 'perks' a more significant part of the package.

(iv)   **Goal congruence:** the extent to which the package encourages employees to work in such a way as to achieve the objectives of the firm – perhaps to maximise rather than to satisfice.

Option (i)

In this context, Option (i) is likely to be **relatively expensive** with no payback to the firm in times of low profitability. It is unlikely to encourage staff to maximise their efforts, although the extent to which it acts as a motivator will depend on the individual psychological make-up of the employees concerned. Many staff prefer this type of package however, since they know where they are financially. In the same way the company is also able to budget accurately for its staff costs.

Option (ii)

The costs of this scheme will be **lower**, though not proportionately so, during a time of low profits. The effect on motivation will vary with the **individual** concerned, and will also depend on whether it is an **individual** or a **group performance calculation**. There is a further risk that figures and performance may be manipulated by managers in such a way as to maximise their bonus to the detriment of the overall longer term company benefit.

Option (iii)

A share option scheme (Option (iii)) carries **fiscal benefits** in the same way as the performance related pay above. It also **minimises the cost to the firm** since this is effectively borne by the existing shareholders through the dilution of their holdings. Depending on how pricing is determined, it may assist in **achieving goal congruence**. However, since the share price depends on many factors which are external to the firm, it is possible for the scheme to operate in a way which is unrelated to the individual's performance. Thus such a scheme is **unlikely to motivate directly** through links with performance. Staff will continue to obtain the vast majority of their income from salary and perks and are thus likely to be more concerned with maximising these elements of their income than with working to raise the share price.

3 RZP Co

Top tips. It is important to read the question clearly. Thus, in part (a) the question states exactly what you are required to calculate. So for instance, share price growth for each year and then the arithmetic mean and equivalent annual growth rates.

Easy marks. Set out your workings to part (a) in a table such as that in our answer. It helps the marker and allows you to pick out key figures for calculating means and growth rates.

Examiner's comments. Part (a) required candidates to analyse information provided, and comment on views expressed by a chairman on dividend growth, share price growth, and earnings growth. Candidates who commented on the chairman's views without analysing the information provided gained little credit.

The requirement in part (b) was to calculate total shareholder return and comment on the result. The question explained that total shareholder return was dividend yield plus capital growth. Most candidates were unable to calculate dividend yield.

Part (c) asked for a discussion of the factors to be considered when deciding on a management remuneration package that would encourage shareholder wealth maximisation. The key to answering this part was an awareness of how the actions of managers might lead to an increase or decrease in shareholder wealth.

Marking scheme

			Marks
(a)	Growth in dividends per share: analysis/discussion	4–5	
	Share price growth: analysis/discussion	4–5	
	Growth in earnings per share: analysis/discussion	4–5	
		Maximum	13
(b)	Calculation of total shareholder return	2	
	Comment	1	
			3
(c)	Discussion of factors	5–6	
	Examples of appropriate remuneration packages	4–5	
		Maximum	9
			25

Year	20X4	20X3	20X2	20X1	20X0
Dividend per share	2.8p	2.3p	2.2p	2.2p	1.7p
Annual dividend growth	21.7%	4.5%	nil	29.4%	
General price index	117	113	110	105	100
Real dividend per share	2.4p	2.0p	2.0p	2.1p	1.7p
Annual dividend growth	20.0%	nil	(4.8)%	23.5%	
Earnings per share	19.04p	14.95p	11.22p	15.84p	13.43p
Annual earnings growth	27.3%	33.2%	(29.2)%	17.9%	
Price/earnings ratio	22.0	33.5	25.5	17.2	15.2
Share price	418.9p	500.8p	286.1p	272.4p	204.1p
Annual share price growth	(16.3)%	75.0%	5.0%	33.5%	

(i) Average dividend growth:
Arithmetic mean = (21.7 + 4.5 + 0 + 29.4)/4 = 55.6/4 = 13.9%
Equivalent annual growth rate = $[(2.8/1.7)^{0.25} - 1] \times 100 = 13.3\%$

Average real dividend growth:
Arithmetic mean = (20.0 + 0 – 4.8 + 23.5)/4 = 38.7/4 = 9.7%
Equivalent annual growth rate = $[(2.4/1.7)^{0.25} - 1] \times 100 = 9.0\%$

(ii) Average share price growth:
Arithmetic mean = (–16.3 + 75.0 + 5.0 + 33.5)/4 = 97.2/4 = 24.3%
Equivalent annual growth rate = $[(418.9/204.1)^{0.25} - 1] \times 100 = 19.7\%$

(iii) Average earnings per share growth:
Arithmetic mean = (27.3 + 33.2 – 29.2 + 17.9)/4 = 49.2/4 =12.3%
Equivalent annual growth rate = $[(19.04/13.43)^{0.25} - 1] \times 100 = 9.1\%$

The claim that the company has delivered growth every year in dividends, earnings and ordinary share price (apart from 20X2), is largely borne out by the above figures, with a couple of exceptions. No growth in real dividends occurred in 20X3, and the company's share price fell by 16.3% in 20X4. In fact, the statement should try to explain the reasons for the decline in share price in order to reassure shareholders, rather than gloss over it.

The statement also claims that RZP Co has consistently delivered above-average performance. Without information on sector averages for individual years, it is not possible to comment authoritatively here. The average growth rates for the sector cannot be used to comment on performance in individual years. If the company has consistently delivered above-average performance, however, the company's average annual growth rates should be greater than the sector averages.

Comparison of growth rates:

	Arithmetic mean	Equivalent annual rate	Sector
Nominal dividends	13.9%	13.3%	10%
Real dividends	9.7%	9.0%	9%
Earnings per share	12.3%	9.1%	10%
Share price	24.3%	19.7%	20%

If the sector average growth rates are arithmetic mean growth rates, the chairman's statement is technically correct. The basis on which the sector average growth rates have been prepared should therefore be clarified, in order to determine whether the chairman's statement is correct. Overall however, the company looks to be performing in line with the sector average, whatever method of calculation is used.

(b)   The dividend yield and capital growth for 20X4 are calculated by reference to the 20X3 end-of-year share price.

The dividend yield is 0.56% (100 × 2.8/500.8) and the capital growth is –16.35% (100 × (418.9 – 500.8)/500.8). The total shareholder return is therefore –15.8% (0.56 – 16.35).

This negative total shareholder return conflicts with the chairman's claim to have delivered growth in dividends and share price in 20X4. Share prices may be affected by other factors than corporate activity, however, and it is possible that the negative return may represent a good performance when compared to the sector as a whole.

(c)   The objectives of managers may conflict with the objectives of shareholders, so management remuneration package are often designed to encourage goal congruence. It is also interesting to note that in recent years there has been a tendency to remove managerial remuneration packages from the control of the very managers who benefit. Remuneration committees exist in listed companies aim to reduce managerial self-interest and encourage remuneration packages that support the achievement of shareholder wealth rather than purely managerial goals.

Packages need to motivate managers while supporting the achievement of shareholder wealth maximisation. The following factors need to be considered.

Performance measure

The managerial performance measure selected for use in the remuneration package should support the achievement of the primary objective of shareholder wealth maximisation. It could be linked to share price changes.

The managerial performance measure should be quantitative, and the manner in which it is to be calculated should be specified. The managerial performance measure might be linked to industry best practice, and should not be capable of being manipulated or influenced by the manager concerned.

Clear and fair

The terms of the remuneration package should be clear, so that directors and shareholders know when rewards have been earned and how they have been calculated.

Timescale

The remuneration package should have a time horizon that makes sense in terms of the shareholders' interests. If shareholders desire long-term capital growth, the remuneration package should encourage decisions whose objective is to maximise long-term growth. Short-termism in such circumstances should be discouraged.

Management remuneration packages for RZP Co

Remuneration packages are often based on a performance measure linked to the income statement, such as growth in turnover or profit before tax. However, such performance measures could lead to maximisation of short term profit at the expense of long term investment in growth. They could also lead to manipulation of accounting figures and hence reported profit.

RZP Co has delivered earnings growth of more than 20% in both 20X3 and 20X4. If annual earnings growth were to be part of a remuneration package for RZP Co, earnings growth should be compared to the sector, and any bonus made conditional upon long term performance.

Alternatively, remuneration packages may be based on a performance measure linked to inventory market performance, such as share price growth compared to average share price growth for the sector, or compared to growth in a inventory market index. This would be consistent with shareholder wealth maximisation, and is likely to work well if the managers were to received shares or share options as part of the remuneration package. However, factors such as general economic changes or market conditions can have an effect on share prices, and so managers may fail to be rewarded when circumstances are beyond their control.

4 Tagna

Marking scheme

			Marks
(a)	Up to 2 marks for each detailed consequence		10
(b)	Value for money	3	
	Maximisation of shareholder wealth	3	
			6
(a)	Meaning of monopoly	1	
	Discussion of economic problems of monopoly	5	
	Discussion of role of government	3	
			9
			25

(a) (i)   If interest rates increase significantly, it is likely to have an adverse impact on Tagna's sales. As it sells luxury goods, it could be expected that these would be the first to be sacrificed by consumers if they are feeling 'the pinch' in other areas (such as mortgage payments) and their disposable income is reduced. The cost of consumer credit might also be pushed up to dampen spending, further denting consumer confidence and the willingness to spend money on luxury items.

(ii) Interest rates may also push up input costs such as materials and labour, although this would probably not be seen as immediately as an effect of higher interest rates upon sales, as the effect of the rise would have to make itself felt throughout the economy. Wages could go up as a result of inflation, but this will be countered by the effect of the interest rate increase on consumer demand.

(iii) Profit after tax will fall as a result of the interest rate increase, both for the reasons outlined above but also because the cost of servicing Tagna's overdraft will increase. With a fall in sales, increased operating costs and increased interest charges, there is likely to be a significant fall in earnings. As Tagna's profits have been low, this could represent a real threat to future profitability and dividend payments.

(b) Public sector organisations are generally set up with a prime objective which is not related to making profits. These organisations exist to pursue non-financial aims, such as providing a service to the community. However, there will be financial constraints which limit what any such organisation can do. A not-for-profit organisation **needs finance** to pay for its operations, and the major financial constraint is the amount of funds that it can obtain. Having obtained funds, a not-for-profit organisation should seek to get **value for money** from use of the funds:

(i) **Economy**: not spending $2 when the same thing can be bought for $1
(ii) **Efficiency**: getting the best use out of what money is spent on
(iii) **Effectiveness**: spending funds so as to achieve the organisation's objectives

Since managing government (for example) is different from managing a company, a different framework is needed for **planning and control**. This is achieved by:

- setting **objectives** for each
- **careful planning** of public expenditure proposals
- emphasis on getting **value for money**

A private sector organisation has as its primary objective the making of sufficient profits to provide a satisfactory return for its owners and to keep the business operating.

So, it is job of senior management to **maximise the market value** of the company. Specifically, the main financial objective of a company should be to maximise the wealth of its ordinary shareholders. Within this context, the financial manager seeks to ensure that investments earn a **return**, for the benefit of shareholders. Part of this job will involve attracting funds from the market, such as new investors, but as with public sector organisations it is also important that the operations of the company are run economically and efficiently.

(c) Regulation can be defined as any form of state interference with the operation of the free market. This could involve regulating demand, supply, price, profit, quantity, quality, entry, exit, information, technology, or any other aspect of production and consumption in the market.

An important role for the government is the regulation of markets when these fail to bring about an efficient use of resources. In response to the existence of market failure, and as an alternative to taxation and public provision of production, the state often resorts to regulating economic activity. Where one company's large share or complete domination of the market is leading to inefficiency or excessive profits, the state may intervene, for example through controls on prices or profits, in order to try to reduce the effects of this power. Abuse of a dominant position will cause economic problems and economic inefficiency, because there will be no incentive for the company to improve its processes or cut its costs, as it can pass on all inefficiencies to customers in the form of higher prices.

In a pure **monopoly**, there is only one firm, the sole producer of a good, which has no closely competing substitutes. In practice government policy is concerned not just with situations where one firm has a 100% market share, but other situations where an organisation has a significant market share. In the UK, a monopoly is said to occur if an organisation controls 25% or more of the market. The Office of Fair Trading and the Competition Commission monitor the market.

The Competition Commission can be asked to investigate what could be called 'oligopoly situations' involving explicit or implicit collusion between firms. The Commission must decide whether or not any monopoly is acting 'against the public interest. In its report, the Commission will say if a monopoly situation has been found to exist and, if so, will make recommendations to deal with it. These may involve various measures.

- Price cuts
- Price and profit controls
- Removal of entry barriers

5 Investment

Text references. Financial intermediation is covered in Chapter 2.

Top tips. Your answer to this question must be presented in the form of a report to a private client. Presentation will be improved by the use of appropriate sub-headings for the different parts of the question, and you should also make the explanation clear enough for non-accountants to understand.

Your answer should be wider than just the factors affecting equity investment; you should also mention other securities such as gilts, corporate bonds and derivatives. Other important points included time scale, income versus capital gains and the risk-return problem. In (c), note who are classified as financial intermediaries; they are not the same as independent financial advisers. You should *not* get a full economics question in the exam, but you may get a question like (d) for 5-6 marks, asking about the effect of an important economic development on a business.

(a) To: Private client
     From: Accountant
     Date: 14 December 20X8
     Subject: Purchase of traded investments

Introduction

There is a wide variety of traded investments, ie investment assets that can be bought and sold on the financial markets, now available to the private investor. These range from the traditional equity shares traded on the stock exchange to newer forms of derivative products, such as financial futures. When constructing a portfolio of such investments, the first step must always be to specify very clearly the requirements and individual situation of the investor, before looking for investments to deliver these requirements.

Key criteria

(i)   **Risk and security**

The investor should always seek to minimise risk by spreading his investments over a reasonable range of assets. However, it is important to specify at the outset the overall amount of risk that the investor is prepared to accept, and to seek to construct a portfolio that reflects this. The amount of risk that an investor will tolerate is closely linked to the second criterion (below).

(ii) **Purpose for which the investment is being made**

Investments may be made with a variety of motives, for example to provide a regular income, or to accumulate sufficient capital to meet a long-term financial commitment. This will affect the choice of investments. For example, high yielding loan notes may be selected if a regular income is required.

(iii) **Liquidity**

This refers to the nature of the funds that are being invested. If the funds could be required at short notice for an alternative purpose, then the investment must be capable of being liquidated quickly.

(iv) **Tax situation**

Investments should be chosen that help to minimise the tax liability of the investor. For example, a higher rate taxpayer may choose to opt for investments that offer high growth and low income.

A broad classification of investment types

The following list offers a broad indication of the relative levels of risk associated with different types of investment. Those at the start of the list offer the lowest level of risk/return, while those at the end of the list offer the highest level.

- Bank and building society deposits (although not classed as 'traded', this forms some basis for comparison)

- Government securities – gilts

- Corporate bonds and loan notes

- Unit trusts and investment trusts

- Preference shares

- Equity in 'blue chip' companies quoted on the stock exchange

- Equity in smaller companies that may be quoted on the main market or on the AIM (Alternative Investment Market)

- Derivative products such as financial futures

(b) **The risk/return trade-off**

There is a **trade-off** between **risk and return**. Investors in riskier assets expect to be compensated for the risk. In the case of ordinary shares, investors hope to achieve their return in the form of an increase in the share price (a capital gain) as well as from dividends.

An investor has the choice between different forms of investment. The investor may earn interest by depositing funds with a financial intermediary who will lend on to, say, a company, or it may invest in loan notes of a company. Alternatively, the investor may invest directly in a company by purchasing shares in it.

The current market price of a security is found by discounting the future expected earnings stream at a rate suitably adjusted for risk. This means that investments carrying a **higher degree of risk** will demand a **higher rate of return**. This rate of return or yield has two components:

- **Annual income** (dividend or interest)
- **Expected capital gain**

In general, the **higher the risk** of the security, the **more important is the capital gain** component of the expected yield.

(c) **The role of financial intermediaries**

A financial intermediary is an institution that links lenders with borrowers, by obtaining deposits from lenders and then re-lending them to borrowers. In the UK, the intermediaries include:

- Commercial banks
- Finance houses
- Building societies
- National Savings Bank
- Insurance companies
- Pension funds
- Unit trust companies
- Investment trust companies

Benefits of financial intermediation

(i) **Reduction of risk through pooling**

Since financial intermediaries lend to a large number of individuals and organisations, any losses suffered through default by borrowers or through capital losses are effectively pooled and borne as costs by the intermediary. Provided that the intermediary is itself financially sound, the lender should not run the risk of losing his investment. Bad debts are borne by the financial intermediary in its re-lending operation.

(ii)   **Maturity transformation**

An example of this is the building society, which allows depositors to have immediate access to their savings while lending to mortgage holders for 25 years. The intermediary takes advantage of the continual turnover of cash between borrowers and investors to achieve this.

(iii)   **Convenience**

They provide a simple way for the lender to invest, without him having personally to find a suitable borrower directly. All the investor has to decide is for how long the money is to be deposited and what sort of return is required; all he then has to do is to choose an appropriate intermediary and form of deposit.

(iv)   **Regulation**

There is a comprehensive system of regulation in place in the financial markets that is aimed at protecting the investor against negligence or malpractice.

(v)   **Information**

Intermediaries can offer a wide range of specialist expert advice on the various investment opportunities that is not directly available to the private investor.

Benefits of financial intermediaries

Financial intermediaries therefore have many benefits to offer the private investor, both in terms of general information and the investments available.

(d)   **A public sector budget deficit**

A **public sector budget deficit** arises when government spending exceeds the amount of money raised through taxes. The government will be forced to raise money to finance the deficit, either through borrowing or issuing securities. The effects of a higher level of government spending and the need of the government to raise money to finance the deficit will affect private sector businesses in a number of ways.

(i)   A proportion of the higher spending is likely to be with private sector businesses. Thus a high level of public spending can **boost demand** in the economy and have a positive impact on business either directly or through the multiplier effect.

(ii)   If the deficit is financed by government borrowings this will put upward **pressure on interest rates** and thus increase the financing costs of private sector business, as well as putting pressure on their cash flow and restricting the funds available for new investment.

(iii)   A further effect of high interest rates may be to **depress share prices,** thereby reducing the ability of businesses to raise new capital for investment.

(iv)   The additional level of demand in the economy may boost inflationary pressures. Expectations of higher inflation will generally cause a **fall in the level of optimism** about the economy and place pressure on private sector investment.

(v)   High domestic interest rates are likely to **strengthen the exchange rate** making it harder for businesses to export. At the same time imports will become cheaper thus increasing competitive pressures in the home market.

6 East Meets West Co

> **Text references.** Working capital is covered in Chapter 4 and inflation is discussed in Chapter 2.
>
> **Top tips.** Part (a) requires you to calculate each part of the cash operating cycle, with three types of inventory. In part (b) make sure you apply your suggestions to this particular organisation. In (c)(i) it is helpful to explain the components of working capital and their inter-relationships linking working capital with cash. In (c)(ii) you should consider not only the direct costs and dangers of reliance on trade credit, but also some of the potential dangers that it entails in terms of threat to supplies of goods and the potential to obtain credit from new suppliers in the future.
>
> Part (d) requires you to use your knowledge of economics from Part B of the syllabus. It is important to remember that exam questions may cover a number of different areas of the syllabus.

(a) Cost of sales $= 5{,}600{,}000 \times (100 - 25)\%$
$$= \$4{,}200{,}000$$

Purchases $= 4{,}200{,}000 \times 50\%$
$$= \$2{,}100{,}000$$

		Days
Raw material inventory period	$\dfrac{\text{Raw materials}}{\text{Purchases}} \times 365$	
	$\dfrac{220{,}000}{2{,}100{,}000} \times 365$	38.2
Credit taken from suppliers	$\dfrac{\text{Payables}}{\text{Purchases}} \times 365$	
	$\dfrac{210{,}000}{2{,}100{,}000} \times 365$	(36.5)
Work in progress	$\dfrac{\text{Work in progress}}{\text{Cost of sales} \times \text{Degree of completion}} \times 365$	
	$\dfrac{550{,}000}{4{,}200{,}000 \times 80\%} \times 365$	59.7
Finished goods	$\dfrac{\text{Finished goods}}{\text{Cost of sales}} \times 365$	
	$\dfrac{350{,}000}{4{,}200{,}000} \times 365$	30.4
Credit allowed to receivables	$\dfrac{\text{Receivables}}{\text{Sales}} \times 365$	
	$\dfrac{506{,}000}{5{,}600{,}000} \times 365$	33.0
		124.8

(b) The cash operating cycle can be reduced in the following ways

   (i) **Reduce raw material inventory**

   Arrangements can be made with suppliers so raw materials are only ordered when they are needed for production.

   (ii) **Credit taken from suppliers**

   East Meets West could negotiate a **longer credit period** from suppliers.

   (iii) **Reduce work-in-progress**

Work-in-progress might be reduced by using **more advanced technology** or improving **production processes.**

(iv) **Reduce finished goods inventory**

Finished goods inventory could be reduced by not holding as much **safety inventory** to guard against unexpected demands.

(v) **Reduce receivables**

Credit control procedures could be **tightened**, or incentives such as discounts be offered for early payment.

(c) (i) **Working capital**

The net working capital of a business can be defined as its current assets less its current liabilities. The management of working capital is concerned with ensuring that **sufficient liquid resources** are maintained within the business. For the majority of businesses, particularly manufacturing businesses, trade payables will form the major part of the current liabilities figure, and will be a significant element in the make-up of the working capital balance.

Trade credit period

It follows that the trade credit period taken will be a major determinant of the working capital requirement of the company. This is calculated (in days) as the total value of trade payables divided by the level of credit purchases times 365. The actual length of the period will depend partly on the credit terms offered by suppliers and partly on the decisions made by the company. For example, the company may choose to negotiate longer terms with its suppliers although this may be at the expense of any available settlement discounts.

Cash conversion cycle

A link can be made between working capital and liquidity by means of the **cash conversion cycle**. This measures the length of time that elapses between a firm paying for its various purchases and receiving payment for its sales. It can be calculated as the receivable days plus the inventory holding period less the trade credit period, and it measures the length of time for which net current assets must be financed.

This emphasises the important role of the trade credit period in the overall liquidity of the company.

(ii) **Importance of trade payables**

For many firms, trade payables provide a very important source of short-term credit. Since very few companies currently impose interest charges on overdue accounts, taking extended credit can appear to be a very cheap form of short-term finance. However, such a policy entails some risks and costs that are not immediately apparent, as follows.

(1) If discounts are being forgone, the **effective cost** of this should be evaluated – it may be more beneficial to shorten the credit period and take the discounts.

(2) If the company gains a reputation for slow payment this will **damage its credit references** and it may find it difficult to obtain credit from new suppliers in the future.

(3) Suppliers who are having to wait for their money may seek recompense in other ways, for example by raising prices or by placing a lower priority on new orders. Such actions could do **damage** to both the **efficiency and profitability** of the company.

(4) Suppliers may place the company **'on stop'** until the account is paid. This can jeopardise supplies of essential raw materials which in turn could cause production to stop: this will obviously provide the company with a high level of unwanted costs.

(d) **Problems with inflation**

(i) **Increase in raw material prices**

The **raw material prices** that a business faces may increase, but the business may not be able to pass these increases on to its customers in the form of higher prices for its finished goods.

(ii) **Uncertainty**

Inflation may lead to **economic uncertainty**, which decreases the demand for consumer goods. Increased uncertainty will also mean that **business decision-making** becomes more difficult. Businesses also have to **expend resources** keeping track of price changes.

(iii) **Higher interest rates**

Governments or the central bank may counter inflation by raising interest rates, and this will make the cost of borrowing for businesses more expensive and **limit their** opportunities to invest.

(iv) **Decreased overseas demand**

If a business in Pernisia has to raise its prices because it **faces increased costs**, it may come under increasing pressure from overseas competitors who do not face the same price increases.

(v) **Change in the value of debt**

Payables will be disadvantaged by inflation, as it will mean a **fall in the real value of debt**, although receivables will be advantaged for the same reason.

7 JIT and EOQ

Text references. Inventory management is covered in Chapter 5.

Top tips. It is easy to go off on the wrong track when answering (a). Make quite sure you know what you are going to do before you start! Don't forget you are asking for the effect on *profit*, not cash flow. The effect of the investment in equipment is shown as the sum of interest cost and depreciation.

Remember also that the reduced receivable payment period will be on an increased sales value.

In (b), it is the company's perspective you are concerned with, not its customers'.

In (c) we use the annuity factor to discount the cash flow. Don't forget the tax. You may not have covered this part of the syllabus yet so just read through the answers for now.

(a) **Improvement in first year profit before tax attributable to the JIT agreement**

		$'000	$'000
Equipment: interest cost	13% × $0.5m		(65.00)
depreciation cost	$0.5m/5		(100.00)
Main customer:			
Original value of annual sales	20% × $20m	4,000.00	
Increased value of annual sales	1.05 × $4m	4,200.00	
Increase in sales			200.00
Original receivables	90/365 × $4m	986.30	
Revised receivables	60/365 × $4.2m	690.41	
Reduction in receivables		295.89	
Annual interest saving from			
reduction in receivables	13% × 295.89		38.47
Penalty payment for default	10% × $4.2m	420	
Expected value of penalty	5% × $420,000		(21.00)
Net benefit to year 1 profits			52.47

The **JIT arrangement** appears to be worthwhile in expected value terms.

Other considerations

However, the expected value figure conceals the risk of adverse results if the company fails to meet delivery guarantees: the 'worst case' scenario in one year is that a penalty of $420,000 is payable (more than 5% of operating profit). The directors should make sure that the company is insured against all the normal risks outside its direct control (eg fire, theft, flood) and also invest in a total quality programme to underpin the JIT arrangement by eliminating any defective output.

(b) **Other benefits from the JIT agreement**

Closer relationship between organisations

The Just in Time arrangement with its major customer will promote a closer relationship between the two organisations. This will lower PS's **medium term operating risk** and enable it to plan its own materials requirements, although in the short term the company must be prepared to be very flexible in its delivery procedures. It may also result in PS entering into JIT arrangements with its own suppliers. The strengthened link between the companies may result in further co-operation in other fields (eg design of new products).

Just in time and total quality

A **Just in Time arrangement** with a customer works best when the company uses a **Total Quality** approach to eliminate defective products from its output. The growing reputation for 'zero defectives' is an advantage of implementing the system effectively. This growing reputation will boost PS's sales and enable it to negotiate JIT arrangements with other customers.

(c) (i) The **Economic Order Quantity (EOQ)** can be found as follows.

$$EOQ = \sqrt{\frac{2 \times \text{demand (units)} \times \text{ordering cost}}{\text{holding cost}}}$$

Before reorganisation

Demand	=	40,000 units per annum
Ordering cost	=	$100 per order
Holding cost	=	20% × $2.50

$$EOQ = \sqrt{\frac{2 \times 40,000 \times 100}{0.2 \times 2.50}}$$

$$EOQ = \sqrt{16,000,000} = 4,000 \text{ units}$$

After reorganisation

Demand	=	40,000 units per annum
Ordering cost	=	$25 per order
Holding cost	=	20% × $2.50

$$EOQ = \sqrt{\frac{2 \times 40,000 \times 25}{0.2 \times 2.50}}$$

$$EOQ = \sqrt{4,000,000} = 2,000 \text{ units}$$

(ii) Implementation of the new system will affect both the total ordering costs per annum and the inventory holding cost. **Under the existing system** these costs are as follows.

Ordering cost

	$
EOQ is 4,000 units; demand is 40,000 units.	
Number of orders per year is therefore 10.	
Cost per order is $100.	
Total ordering cost per annum ($100 × 10) =	1,000

Carrying cost

	$
EOQ is 4,000 units.	
Average inventory is therefore 2,000 units.	
Cost is 2,000 × $2.50 × 20% =	1,000
Total annual cost	2,000

Under the proposed system the costs would become as follows.

Ordering cost

	$
EOQ is 2,000 units; demand is 40,000 units.	
Number of orders per year is therefore 20. Cost per order is $25.	
Total ordering cost per annum ($25 × 20) =	500

Carrying cost

	$
EOQ is 2,000 units. Average inventory is therefore 1,000 units.	
Cost is 1,000 × $2.50 × 20%	500
Total annual cost	1,000

The **annual cost saving** is therefore $1,000 ($2,000 – $1,000). This will give rise to an **after tax cash flow** of $700 ($1,000 × (1 – 0.3)). The cash flows can now be **discounted** at the cost of finance of 12%. It is **assumed** that tax is payable in the year in which it arises, and that the reorganisation costs are fully tax allowable.

		$
Year 0	$4,000 × (1 – 0.3) × 1.000 =	(2,800.00)
Years 1-8	$700 × 4.968 =	3,477.60
NPV of reorganisation		677.60

8 TNG Co

Text references. Inventory management is covered in Chapter 5.

Top tips. This question is made up of five smaller parts. Part (e) is written and could be answered separately to the other parts. You could do this part first as long as you leave space in your answer book.

Easy marks. Using the EOQ model to calculate the requirements of part (b).

Examiner's comments. This was one of the most popular questions in Section B and many candidates who attempted it gained high marks. Part (a) asked for a calculation of the cost of the current ordering policy of a company. Three costs were needed: the cost of ordering inventory, the annual cost of the buffer inventory held, and the annual cost of additional inventory equal to half of the order size. A common problem was an inability to calculate the cost of holding inventory, the most common error being including buffer inventory but omitting half of the order size, or vice versa. Most answers calculated the annual ordering cost correctly.

Candidates were asked in part (b) to calculate the economic order quantity (the formula for this was provided in the formulae sheet), and the annual saving if an EOQ-based optimal ordering policy were used rather than the current policy. Answers were often of an acceptable standard, although tending to show similar errors to those found in part (a). Most answers were able to calculate correctly the economic order quantity, allowing for errors carried forward from part (a).

Part (c) asked for an evaluation of whether a discount offered by a supplier was financially acceptable. Answers showed that there were many ways to prove that the offered discount was financially acceptable and many answers gained full credit.

The requirement in part (d) was to discuss the limitations of the economic order quantity model as a way of managing inventory. Many answers gained good marks by focusing on the limitations imposed by the assumptions underlying the model, such as constant demand, zero lead time, and constant ordering cost and holding cost.

A discussion of the advantages and disadvantages of using just-in-time inventory management methods was required in part (e) and many answers gained high marks, although there was a tendency to list brief points rather than offer the discussion that was asked for.

Marking scheme

			Marks
(a)	Annual ordering cost	1	
	Annual holding cost	2	
	Annual cost of current policy	1	
			4
(b)	Calculation of economic order quantity	1	
	Annual ordering cost	1	
	Annual holding cost	1	
	Annual cost of EOQ policy	1	
	Saving from using EOQ policy or discussion	1	
			5
(c)	Analysis	2–3	
	Discussion	1–2	
		Maximum	4
(d)	Discussion of limitations of EOQ model		4
(e)	Advantages of JIT inventory management methods	4–5	
	Disadvantages of JIT inventory management methods	4–5	
		Maximum	8
			25

(a)   Current order size = 50,000 units
Average number of orders per year = demand/order size = 255,380/50,000 = 5.11 orders
Annual ordering cost = 5.11 × $25 = $127.75
Buffer inventory held = 255,380 × 28/365 = 19,591 units
Average inventory held = 19,591 + (50,000/2) = 44,591 units
Annual holding cost = 44,591 × 0.1 = $4,459.10
Annual cost of current ordering policy = 4,459.10 + 127.75 = $4,587

(b)   Economic order quantity:
EOQ = ((2 × 255,380 × 25)/0.1)0.5 = 11,300 units
Average number of orders per year = 255,380/11,300 = 22.6 orders
Annual ordering cost = 22.6 × $25 = $565.00
Average inventory held = 19,591 + (11,300/2) = 25,241 units
Annual holding cost = 25,241 × 0.1 = $2,524.10
Annual cost of EOQ ordering policy = 2,524.10 + 565.00 = $3,089
Saving compared to current policy = $4,587 – $3,089 = $1,498

(c)   Annual credit purchases = 255,380 × $11 = $2,809,180
Current payables = $2,809,180 × 60/365 = $461,783
Payables if discount is taken = $2,809,180 × 20/365 × 99% = $152,388
Reduction in payables = $461,783 – $152,388 = $309,395
Finance cost increase = $309,395 × 8% = $24,752
Discount gained = $2,809,180 × 1% = $28,091
Net benefit of taking discount = $28,091 – $24,752 = $3,339
The discount is therefore financially worthwhile.

(d)   Some businesses attempt to control inventories on a 'scientific' basis by balancing the costs of inventory shortages against those of inventory holding. The economic order quantity (EOQ) model can be used to decide the optimum order size for inventories which will minimise the costs of ordering inventories plus inventoryholding costs.

The calculation of EOQ is based upon a set formula which has two main inputs – holding cost and ordering cost, which must be known with certainty and which are assumed not to change. It is also assumed that demand is constant, the lead time is constant or zero and purchase costs per unit are constant (ie there are no bulk discounts). In practice, all of these assumptions are likely to be unrealistic – costs are going to vary and demand will never be constant.

(e)   Some manufacturing companies have sought to reduce their inventories of raw materials and components to as low a level as possible. Just-in-time procurement and stockless production are terms which describe a policy of obtaining goods from suppliers at the latest possible time (ie when they are needed) and so avoiding the need to carry any materials or components inventory.

Introducing just-in-time (JIT) inventory management methods have been said to deliver the following potential benefits.

- Reduction in inventory holding costs
- Reduced manufacturing lead times
- Improved labour productivity
- Reduced scrap/rework/warranty costs – improved quality
- Price reductions on purchased materials
- Reduction in the number of accounting transactions
- Stronger relationship between buyer and supplier

Reduced inventory levels mean that a lower level of investment in working capital will be required.

JIT will not be appropriate in some cases. For example, a restaurant might find it preferable to use the traditional economic order quantity approach for staple non-perishable food inventories, but adopt JIT for perishable and 'exotic' items. In a hospital, a stock-out could quite literally be fatal and so JIT would be quite unsuitable. There is little room for error in such a system, so if there are likely to be supplier delays or variable delivery times that could have disastrous consequences, then JIT is not suitable. The system also makes the buyer heavily dependent on the supplier for both delivery and quality of supply.

9 Thorne Co

Top tips. There are lots of opportunities for gaining at least a couple of marks in each of the three shorter parts.

Easy marks. The question is split into three smaller calculation elements as noted above. Parts (b) and (c) allow you to write what you know as well as apply this knowledge to the company's specific circumstances.

Marking scheme

			Marks
(a)	Credit sales	2	
	Cash sales	1	
	Proceeds from asset disposal	1	
	Salaries	1	
	Bonus	1	
	Expenses	1	
	Fixed overheads	1	
	Taxation and interest	1	
	Closing balances	1	
			10
(b)	Discussion of factors		5
(c)	Discussion of advantages and disadvantages		5
(d)	Discussion of Baumol model	2-3	
	Discussion of applicability in this case	2-3	
			5
			25

Answer plan

This question has four parts, which cover several aspects of cash flow.

It might be useful to jot down thoughts for your answers to parts (b) to (d) before you embark on this question so that you know you have enough material to answer these.

Step 1   For part (a)

- Set out a proforma for the cash budget. Calculate the monthly cash balances as stated in the question.

Step 2   Part (b)

- Write down the factors and discuss these. Are there any cash surpluses – refer to numbers calculated.

Step 3   Part (c)

- Write out advantages and disadvantages. Refer to any cash shortages calculated in part (a).

Step 4   Part (d)

- Outline Baumol cash model. Refer to specific circumstances of company.

(a) **Cash budget**

	Jan $'000	Feb $'000	March $'000	April $'000
Receipts				
Fee on sale (W1)	54	63	99	144
Receipt on sale of vehicles				20
	54	63	99	164
Payments				
Salaries	26.25	26.25	26.25	26.25
Bonus (W2)			6.3	12.6
Variable expenses (W3)	9	13.5	22.5	27
Fixed overheads	4.3	4.3	4.3	4.3
Interest on loan			3.0	
Tax liability				95.80
	39.55	44.05	62.35	165.95
Net cash flow	14.45	18.95	36.65	(1.95)
Balance b/fwd	(40.00)	(25.55)	(6.6)	30.05
Balance c/fwd	(25.55)	(6.6)	30.05	28.10

Working 1

	Jan	Feb	March	April
Receipts				
Unit sales	10	15	25	30
	$'000	$'000	$'000	$'000
Fee at 3% × $180,000 × numbers sold	54	81	135	162
Received				
– 1% in month of sale	18	27	45	54
– 2% in following month				
(January receipt relates to December sale)	36	36	54	90
	54	63	99	144

Working 2

	Jan	Feb	March	April
Receipts				
Unit sales	10	15	25	30
	$'000	$'000	$'000	$'000
Bonus based on numbers sold over 20	0	0		
– $140 × 9 × numbers sold over 20	0	0	6.3	12.6

BPP))))
LEARNING MEDIA

Working 3

	Jan	Feb	March	April
Receipts				
Unit sales	10	15	25	30
	$'000	$'000	$'000	$'000
Variable overheads at 0.5% × $180,000 × numbers sold	9	13.5	22.5	27

(b) **Factors to consider when investing any cash surplus**

The cash budget for Thorne Co shows an increase in sales over the period, which suggests higher sales as the spring approaches. However, the payment of tax in April meant that a trend of increasing net cash flows was temporarily reversed.

Thorne needs to consider the following when investing any surpluses:

(i) Short-term investments with no capital risk as these may be called upon at any time. Short-term investments include bank deposit accounts, certificates of deposit, term bills and gilts, which are short-dated.

   In choosing between these, Thorne Co will consider the size of the surplus, the length of time it is available, the yield offered and the risk associated with each instrument.

(ii) On an annual basis, look at any surpluses and invest these in longer-term higher yield assets. The company will most probably call on these at some stage to fund expansion but needs to pick the investments carefully.

The investment of cash balances is part of the treasury function of a company. It is unlikely that Thorne Co is of a size to sustain a full time treasury activity but nonetheless there is a definite benefit in closely managing any surpluses.

(c) **Advantages and disadvantages of using overdraft finance to fund cash shortages**

Thorne Co has budgeted deficits in two of the months in the forecast. These are short term in nature so it is unlikely that a long-term loan will be required to fund these.

Typically, temporary deficits are funded by an **overdraft** granted by the company's bank where interest is charged on the overdrawn amount at a rate over base.

Advantages of overdraft finance include its flexibility and that interest is only due on the actual overdrawn amount. The rate of interest is flexible as it is variable and linked to a base rate and so can go down as well as up.

Disadvantages of overdraft finance include the risk of an interest rate increase as the rate is not fixed. Also, the overdraft is repayable on demand. Banks usually ask for some collateral when lending such as a fixed or floating charge on the company's assets.

(d) **The Baumol model and cash management**

A number of different cash management models indicate the **optimum amount of cash** that a company should hold. One such model is based on the idea that deciding on optimum cash balances is like deciding on optimum inventory levels, and suggests the optimum amount to be transferred regularly from investments to current account.

We can distinguish two types of cost which are involved in obtaining cash:

(i) The **fixed cost** represented, for example, by the issue cost of equity finance or the cost of negotiating an overdraft

(ii) The **variable cost** (opportunity cost) of keeping the money in the form of cash

The inventory approach or Baumol model uses an equation of the same form as the EOQ formula for inventory management. The average total cost incurred for period in holding a certain average level of cash (C) is:

$$\frac{Qi}{2} + \frac{FS}{Q}$$

Where S   = the amount of cash to be used in each time period
F   = the fixed cost of obtaining new funds
i   = the interest cost of holding cash or near cash equivalents
Q   = the total amount to be transferred to provide for S

Similarly to the EOQ, C is minimised when:

$$Q = \sqrt{\frac{2FS}{i}}$$

The inventory approach illustrated above has the following drawbacks for companies such as Thorne Co.

(i)   In reality, it is unlikely to be **possible** to **predict amounts required** over future periods with much certainty.

(ii)   No **buffer inventory** of cash is allowed for. There may be costs associated with running out of cash.

(iii)   There may be other **normal costs** of holding cash, which increase with the average amount held.

(iv)   It assumes **constant transaction costs** and **interest rates**.

10 Plankers Co

Text references. Working capital management is covered in Chapter 5 and financial objectives in Chapter 1.

Top tips. In (a) (i) you need to realise that the company's demands can partly be met from cash earnings that it has retained. You need to revise ratios thoroughly if you used the wrong figures in the calculations in (a) (ii).

In (a) (iii) there is information in the question that you can use and you can also suggest other remedies that will be appropriate for most companies. You only needed to suggest five remedies, but we have given more to show you a range of potential solutions. Note however the point in (a) (iv) about which methods provide the major finance required.

In (b) you need to concentrate on what stakeholders require and expect, and costs of objectives and conflicts between them.

Examiner's comment. Most candidates wrongly assumed in (a) that all investment funds needed would have to be borrowed, failing to take account of the cash that was already available.

Answers to (b) were generally good, with candidates showing good appreciation of the requirements of stakeholders, although answers on multiple objectives were often unfocused.

(a)   (i)   Cash available for investment = 8.48m – 1m (minimum balance) = $7.48m

                Therefore extra loan balance required = 12m – 7.48m = $4.52m

	20X5
	$m
PBIT exc extra depreciation(20X4 + 5%)	1.985
Depreciation ($6m × 0.15)	(0.900)
PBIT	1.085
Interest charges (9% × ($7 + 4.52m))	(1.037)
Profit before tax	0.048
Tax (30%)	(0.014)
Profit after tax	0.034

(ii)   Interest cover $= \dfrac{\text{PBIT}}{\text{Interest}}$

$= \dfrac{1.085}{1.037}$

$= 1.046$

Earnings per share $= \dfrac{\text{Profit after tax}}{\text{No of shares}}$

$= \dfrac{0.034}{4,000}$

$= 0.85\text{c per share}$

Cash balance $=$ Balance at start of year + Profit after tax + Extra depn

$= 1.000 + 0.034 + 0.900$

$= \$1.934 \text{ million}$

Only the cash balance condition would be met

(iii)   **Methods of improving cash balances**

Postpone building programme

The company could clearly **avoid a cash shortage** by **postponing the building programme** until it had sufficient funds from retaining cash earnings.

Postponing other capital expenditure

Capital expenditure on **other non-current assets** could be **postponed** until the company had more cash. Some non-current assets, such as cars, tend to be replaced on a regular basis, and the **replacement cycle** on these could be **lengthened**.

Selling assets

The company could sell assets that were **not essential for operations**, for example investments. Alternatively the company could enter a **sale and leaseback** arrangement for certain assets, gaining the cash for selling them to third parties.

Taking longer credit

Plankers could take **longer periods of credit** from its **suppliers**.

Accelerating cash receipts

The company could **press receivables** for **earlier payment**, or could offer **discounts** as an incentive for prompt payment.

Loan terms

Plankers might be able to **negotiate** more **favourable terms** from the bank, perhaps lower interest, an easing of the loan conditions, or additional amounts lent.

Equity issue

The company could obtain money by means of a **rights issue** to existing shareholders.

Dividends

As well as not paying out dividends in 20X5, the company could **reduce or stop dividend payments** in other years.

(iv)   **Scale of investment**

Because of the large amount of the **equity investment**, only an equity issue or **increased loan finance** would provide the level of finance Plankers needs. The other methods by themselves would not provide enough finance, and some of them would only provide one-off or shorter term benefits which would not fulfil the need for longer term finance of the building programme.

Effect on interest cover

The problem with taking out an **increased loan** is that interest cover is likely to deteriorate as a result.

(b)   **Constraints faced by Plankers**

(i)   **Responding to stakeholder groups**

Organisations have a large number of **stakeholders** including **internal** stakeholders (employees, managers), **connected** stakeholders (shareholders, customers, suppliers, finance providers) and **external** stakeholders (government, community at large).

Conflict between stakeholders

Perhaps the main conflict that businesses can face is between shareholders, who wish to see long-term company value and hence their own income maximised, and other stakeholders. Employees and managers will wish to **maximise their own rewards** and lead to greater costs. Other stakeholders such as suppliers or finance providers will wish to **guarantee** their own revenues, which may limit the cash available for investment. External stakeholders such as the government or community will wish the business to be a good **corporate citizen**, which may involve additional costs in return for no financial benefits.

Results of conflict

In drawing up long-term plans the directors must take into account the consequences of conflict. If the company is not doing well, shareholders will wish to **sell their shares** and the value of the company **will fall**. However if other stakeholders' demands are not satisfied, they can employ sanctions of their own such as **not providing sufficient resources** (employees, finance providers), **not buying goods and services** (customers) and **forcing the business to incur legal burdens or costs** (government, community).

Other demands on managers

Even if it is possible to keep all stakeholders happy, management time will be needed to ascertain whether all stakeholders are **content** and to **identify** any **additional stakeholders** whose concerns will need to be addressed.

(ii)   **Conflicting demands of objectives**

Long-term and short-term profits

One possible conflict is between the basic objective to **maximise the company's value long-term** whilst making enough profits each year to satisfy shareholders' expectations of income. Shareholders' expectations that dividends remain constant or increase steadily may result in insufficient internal funds being available to finance the investment required to maximise long-term profitability.

Different financial objectives

As well as maximising profits, the company may set other objectives such as **limiting risk** by **limiting the level of debt the company takes on** or achieving other financial targets such as **increasing turnover**. There may be conflicts between these objectives, for example long-term investment planning being limited by an unwillingness to take on new funds, or turnover targets being achieved at the expense of keeping levels of working capital low.

Financial objectives and non-financial objectives

As indicated above, the company will need to consider non-financial objectives to satisfy certain external stakeholders. The **costs** of these may be quantifiable (such as the costs of employing extra staff to operate controls or the costs of taking anti-pollution measures) but it may be less easy to **quantify the long-term benefits**. This will make long-term planning more difficult, as the company may have to decide whether to **do the minimum** it needs to do, or whether there will be advantages from **going beyond the minimum** and showing itself to be an **'ethical' company**.

Resolving conflicts

Some conflicts may have to be resolved by **compromise**, in which case managers will need to decide how far the company can afford to fall short on each objective. Compromises will not always be possible, and managers may need to **rank the importance of objectives** in order to decide which have to be fulfilled.

Management time

Managers will need to **spend time and incur costs** monitoring the fulfilment of different objectives.

11 Question with analysis: Velm Co

Text references. Working capital management is covered in Chapters 4, 5 and 6.

Top tips. There isn't much to calculate here so just make sure you know your receivable days formula and think about the relationship between receivables and cash flow.

Most of the marks on this question are for a discussion of working capital in one form or another. So think about sources of finance and policies for managing working capital. The final part of the question does need you to think a bit more widely about cashflow and business policy.

Easy marks. Any of the discussion parts.

Examiner's comments. This was the most popular question in Section B. Part (a) was answered moderately well. Most candidates were able to identify the savings in bad debts and salary, and the cost of the discount, but the calculations of the reduced financing cost arising from the discount were often confused. In general, the approach taken by most candidates would have been improved if they had focused on the incremental costs and benefits. Good answers to part (b) on the relative merits of short and long-term finance for the financing of working capital discussed factors such as relative cost, availability, security and risk. Part (c) asked candidates to discuss the different policies that could be adopted towards the financing of working capital – a discussion of aggressive, conservative and matching policies was expected. Part (d) on working capital management was generally answered pretty well. There was a general tendency to mix up the answers to parts (b), (c) and (d).

		Marks
(a)	Reduction in receivables	1
	Cost of discount	1
	Reduction in financing cost	1
	Reduction in bad debts and salary saving	1
	Calculation of net benefit and conclusion	1
		5
(b)	Risks of short-term finance	2
	Cost of short-term finance	1
	Risks of long-term finance	1
	Cost of long-term finance	1
	Discussion and conclusion	1
		6
(c)	Permanent and fluctuating current assets	2
	Explanation of financing policies	4
	Discussion and link to Velm Co	1
		7
(d)	Advantages of working capital management	2
	Credit management	2
	Inventory management	2
	Discussion and link to Velm Co	1
		7
		25

(a) Receivables are currently taking on average ($550,000/$4,000,000) × 365 = 50 days to pay. This is in excess of Velm's stated terms. The discount, to be taken up by 2/3 of customers, will cost the company $4,000,000 × 1% × 2/3 = $26,667. It is stated that this will bring the receivables' payment period down to 26 days, which is represented by a new receivables level of ($4,000,000 – $26,667) × 26/365 = $283,000. This is a reduction in receivables of $267,000. At current overdraft costs of 9%, this would be a saving of $267,000 × 0.09 = $24,030.

Bad debts would decrease from 3% to 2.4% of turnover, which saves a total of $4,000,000 × 0.006 = $24,000. There would also be a salary saving from early retirement of $12,000.

So the net effect on Velm's profitability is as follows:

	$	
Saving on overdraft costs	24,030	
Decreased bad debts	24,000	
Salary saving	12,000	
Less: cost of discount	(26,667)	
	33,363	net saving

(b) Short-term sources of finance include overdrafts and short-term loans. Long-term sources of finance include loan notes and long-term loans. The choice is between cheaper but riskier short-term finance and more expensive but less risky long-term debt. A customer might ask the bank for a short term overdraft facility when the bank would wish to suggest a loan instead; alternatively, a customer might ask for a loan when an overdraft would be more appropriate.

In most cases, when a customer wants finance to help with **'day to day' trading** and cash flow needs, an overdraft would be the appropriate method of financing. The customer should not be short of cash all the time, and should expect to be in credit in some days, but in need of an overdraft on others.

When a customer wants to borrow from a bank for only a short period of time, even for the purchase of a major non-current asset such as an item of plant or machinery, an overdraft facility might be **more suitable** than a loan, because the customer will stop paying interest as soon as his account goes into credit.

However, when a customer wants to borrow from a bank, but cannot see his way to repaying the bank except over the course of a few years, the required financing is best catered for by the provision of a loan rather than an overdraft facility.

Short-term financing

Advantages of an overdraft over a loan

(i)   The customer **only pays interest when he is overdrawn**.

(ii) The bank has the flexibility to **review** the customer's overdraft facility periodically, and perhaps agree to additional facilities, or insist on a reduction in the facility.

(iii) An overdraft can do the same job as a **loan**: a facility can simply be renewed every time it comes up for review.

(iv) Being short-term debt, an overdraft will not affect the calculation of a company's **gearing**.

Bear in mind, however, that overdrafts are technically **repayable on demand**, so even though they are cheaper than longer term sources of debt finance, they are more risky.

Long-term financing

Advantages of a long term loan

(i)   Both the customer and the bank know exactly what the repayments of the loan will be and how much interest is payable, and when. This makes planning (budgeting) simpler.

(ii) The customer does not have to worry about the bank deciding to reduce or withdraw an overdraft facility before he is in a position to repay what is owed. There is an element of 'security' or 'peace of mind' in being able to arrange a loan for an agreed term. However, long term finance is generally more expensive than short term finance.

(iii) Loans normally carry a facility letter setting out the precise terms of the agreement.

Working capital policies can be characterised as **conservative**, **moderate** and **aggressive**. A conservative policy would finance working capital needs primarily from long term sources of finance, so all long term assets and some fluctuating current assets. However, Velm Co is following an aggressive financing policy as long term debt only makes up 2.75% (40/1,450) of non-cash current assets and most finance is provided by short term debt ($1,530k).

(c)   As a general rule, assets which yield profits over a long period of time should be financed by long-term funds. This is an application of the **matching principle.** ——————— | Policy of matching asset life to debt |

In this way, the returns made by the asset will be sufficient to pay either the interest cost of the loans raised to buy it, or dividends on its equity funding.

If, however a long-term asset is financed by short-term funds, the company cannot be certain that when the loan becomes repayable, it will have enough cash (from profits) to repay it.

Types of policy

Under a moderate or matching approach, a company would normally finance short-term assets partly with short-term funding and partly with long-term funding. However, Velm appears to be conducting an aggressive financing policy, as short term finance is being used for most of its current assets. This is a higher risk source of finance.

(d)   Every business needs adequate **liquid resources** to maintain day-to-day cash flow. It needs enough to pay wages and salaries as they fall due and enough to pay payables if it is to keep its workforce and ensure its supplies.

Note the key terms in bold

Maintaining adequate working capital is not just important in the **short term**. Sufficient liquidity must be maintained in order to ensure the **survival of the business** in the long term as well. Even a profitable company may fail if it does not have adequate cash flow to meet its liabilities as they fall due.

On the other hand, an excessively conservative approach to working capital management resulting in **high levels of cash holdings** will harm profits because the opportunity to make a return on the assets tied up as cash will have been missed.

If the turnover periods for inventories and receivables lengthen, or the payment period to payables shortens, then the **operating cycle** will lengthen and the investment in working capital will have to increase. This will increase costs (and decrease shareholder wealth) so it is important that receivables are properly managed and chased up, inventory is maintained at optimum levels (perhaps using the economic order quantity model), and full advantage is taken of suppliers' credit terms.

Since a company must have adequate cash inflows to survive, management should plan and control cash flows as well as profitability. **Cash budgeting** is an important element in short-term cash flow planning. If a budget reveals that a short-term cash shortage can be expected, steps will be taken to meet the problem (perhaps by arranging a bigger bank overdraft facility).

In summary, **working capital management** seeks to improve cash flows by reducing inventories and receivables, taking more credit, or even negotiating a higher bank overdraft facility.

12 PCB Co

Text references. Working capital management is covered in Chapters 4, 5 and 6.

Top tips. This question requires an understanding of working capital and the causes and consequences of overtrading. There is plenty of information available in the example that you will find helpful to analyse and incorporate in your answer, in order to provide a good illustration of the points that you make.

The symptoms in (a) are common signs which you will often see in questions on overtrading. The basic point is that increased activity requires more cash to pay for increased assets (fixed and current), and greater levels of expenditure. Ideally the cash should come from long-term sources (shareholders and long-term lenders), but short-term sources (bank overdraft) will have to be used if long-term sources are not available. The result is the lack of matching described in (c).

(b) is all about using the other information given in the question to come up with reasons for the change in the profit figures.

Note in (c) that the company is in a precarious position, needing more finance (preferably long-term), but will find it difficult to obtain more finance because it is in a precarious position. Even if the interest burden can be sustained, it may be at the expense of shareholders' income.

In (d) you need to consider both sides of the problem, whether and how the growth in non-cash assets and expenditure can be controlled, and possible internal and external sources of finance obtained. PCB is the sort of company in which venture capitalists often invest, but venture capitalists must be convinced that PCB is a worthwhile investment.

(a)   Manufacturing companies generally have a relatively **long operating cycle** and a correspondingly large working capital requirement. When the level of sales increases, there is an increased investment in:

   (i)   **Inventory**, as additional raw materials are purchased to produce the additional goods.

   (ii)   **Staff costs**, both direct in production, and indirect in sales and credit control overhead.

   (iii)   **Receivables** since most manufacturing companies sell on credit, and additional sales will therefore translate into a higher level of receivables.

Need for working capital investment

The company may also need to purchase equipment to increase its capacity. All of these areas require an immediate investment of cash, in advance of the cash flow benefits of the additional sales and operating profits being felt. Although the company may also benefit from an increased level of payables, this will not be enough to offset the other factors, and therefore additional cash will be required to finance this process.

Problems of PCB

This problem can be illustrated using PCB as an example.

(i)   During the last year, **sales** have **increased** by $1.3m from $1.7m to $3m, an increase of 76%.

(ii)   There has been **additional investment** of $44,000 in **non-current assets** during the same period.

(iii)   The **level of inventory** has **more than doubled** from $95,000 to $220,000.

(iv)   **Receivables** have **increased** by $102,000 from $108,000 to $210,000, an increase of 94%.

(v)   **Six additional sales** staff have been **recruited**.

(vi)   This has resulted in a **massive increase** in the **bank overdraft** of $116,750 from $41,250 to $158,000, and in the level of trade payables, which has increased by nearly 150% from $82,500 to $205,000.

The cash resources at the start of the year were only $1,750, and the increased level of trading has been financed entirely from short-term bank borrowings and trade payables.

(b)   The change in the trading position has been as follows.

	Y/e 30.11.X8		Y/e 30.11.X7		Change
Sales	3,000,000		1,700,000		+76%
Gross profit	450,000	15%	330,000	19%	+36%
Net profit before tax	60,000	2%	82,000	5%	–27%

Both gross and net margins have fallen. Contributory factors are likely to include the following.

(i)   **Selling prices may have been reduced** to achieve the increase in sales. This will result in depressed gross margins.

(ii)   The additional investment in non-current assets will have led to an **increase in the depreciation charge**.

(iii)   **Interest costs will have increased** due to the higher level of bank borrowings.

(iv)   **Staff costs will have increased** because of the larger number of sales staff now employed.

(c)   **Increase in debt levels**

It has been seen that there has been a large increase in the level of short-term borrowings in the form of bank loans and trade payables. The ratio of equity: bank debt has fallen from 8.4 times ($345,000 ÷ $41,250) to 2.4 times ($375,000 ÷ $158,000), and the real level of reliance on debt is even higher if the increase in the level of trade payables is taken into account. In effect, PCB has financed its expansion wholly by using short-term debt.

Dangers of PCB's position

(i)   **Lack of matching**

The company should **match long-term assets** with **long-term funds**. At present, both the increase in working capital and the increase in non-current assets are being financed out of short-term debt.

(ii) Exceeding terms of trade

Although the use of trade payables as a source of finance is attractive because there is rarely any interest charge, it is likely that PCB is **exceeding its terms** of **trade**, since the increase in the level of payables is so much greater than the increase in the level of sales. It is therefore running the risk of losing the goodwill of its suppliers.

(iii) Inability to obtain credit

The current state of the funding means that, on the basis of the balance sheet figures, PCB may find it **hard to obtain additional credit** from existing or new suppliers. This is because of the high level of financial risk now being carried by the trade payables who have no security for their credit.

(iv) Problems with bank

There is no information on the **nature of any agreements** that PCB has with the bank over funding, or any indication as to the size of the overdraft limit. However, as the level of short-term funding increases, the bank will want to review the current and forecast trading situation with the company before increasing its stake in the company any further. It would be in the interest of both parties if the existing overdraft were replaced with some form of secured medium-term bank debt.

(v) Increase in risk levels

The current situation represents an **increase** in the **level of risk** carried by the equity shareholders. As the gearing increases, so the level of the **interest charge** will **increase**, and thus there will be greater volatility in the level of returns to equity, particularly if the business is cyclical in nature. The current cash shortage also means that even if the company continues to be profitable, it will be difficult to sustain the level of dividend payments. This situation is already arising, since dividends have been cut drastically from $35,000 in 20X7 to $12,000 in 20X8.

(d) The main needs of PCB are to reduce its reliance on short-term debt and to ease its current cash shortage. This could be achieved in the following ways.

(i) Conversion of loan

The short-term bank loan could be **converted** to a **longer-term loan** or debenture as discussed in (c) above.

(ii) Increase equity

The company could seek to **increase the level** of **equity investment**, which would reduce the level of gearing to a safer level. The exact means by which this should be achieved is difficult to specify, since it is not clear from the question whether PCB is a quoted or unquoted company.

(iii) Venture capital

It is possible that additional funding in the form of **venture capital** could be appropriate, given the fact that the company is growing. However, PCB would need to satisfy potential investors that it will be able to improve its earnings performance as well as its sales performance.

(iv) Improved inventory and receivable control

As has already been shown, certain elements of working capital have increased at a faster rate than the sales growth would appear to warrant. In particular, there appears to be scope for improving the **control of inventory and receivables**. If both these elements were restricted to a 76% increase in line with the growth in sales, this would release over $72,000 of working capital. This would reduce the need for additional external funding.

13 Special gift suppliers

(a)   Funding requirement = Average inventory holding period
                        + Average receivables' collection period
                        − Average payables' payment period
                        = 3.5 + 2.5 − 2.0
                        = 4.0 months

(b)   **Current arrangements**

	$
Bad debts (3% × 90% × $2.5m)	67,500
Salary of sales ledger administrator	12,500
Cost of financing debts (90% × (2.5/12) × 12% × $2.5m)	56,250
	136,250

Factor

	$
Cost of advancing funds (90% × 80% × (1/12) × 15% × $2.5m)	22,500
Cost of financing remaining debts (90% × 20% × (1/12) × 12% × $2.5m)	4,500
Charge for factoring services (4% × 90% × $2.5m)	90,000
One-off payment to factor (25,000 × 12%)	3,000
	120,000

Hence it is worthwhile to factor the debts.

(c)   To: Financial Controller, Special Gift Department

From: Adviser
Subject: Working capital
Date: 27 September 20X2

This memo covers a number of aspects of managing working capital.

(i)   **Functioning of a credit control department**

The credit control department should be involved with customers at all stages of the credit control cycle.

(1)   When customers **first request credit**, the credit control department should **obtain references** and **credit ratings, analyse their accounts** and obtain other information such as **press comment** as appropriate. Staff may also **visit the customer**. A **credit limit** should be

recommended based on the information obtained; initially the limit should be **low**, and only raised over time if the **customer's payment record** is good.

(2) When the customer makes an order, the credit control department should check whether the **new order** will cause the customer to **exceed** their limits.

(3) Staff should also **review regularly** the **appropriateness of credit limits**, and **check the aged receivable listing** to see if debts are overdue and **report problems** to **designated senior managers**.

(4) The credit control department will be responsible for issuing documentation such as **monthly statements** and **demands for payment**. Staff should **maintain contacts** with other departments, trying to ensure that orders are not accepted from customers who are in difficulties. The department will **pursue slow payers**, ultimately **employing debt collectors** and **initiating legal action**.

(5) The **department's procedures** should be set out in a **credit control manual**.

(ii) **Benefits of factoring**

(1) The business can **pay** its **suppliers promptly**, and so be able to take advantage of any early payment discounts that are available.

(2) **Optimum inventory levels** can be **maintained**, because the business will have enough cash to pay for the inventories it needs.

(3) **Growth** can be **financed** through **sales** rather than by injecting fresh external capital.

(4) The business gets **finance linked** to its **volume of sales**. In contrast, overdraft limits tend to be determined by historical balance sheets.

(5) The **managers** of the business **do not** have to **spend** their **time** on the problems of **slow paying receivables**.

(6) The business does **not incur** the **costs** of **running** its own **sales ledger department**, and can use the **expertise** of receivable management that the factor has.

(7) Because they are managing a number of sales ledgers, factors can **manage receivables more efficiently** than individual businesses through economies of scale.

(iii) **Financing of working capital**

Types of current assets

(1) The **permanent current assets** businesses hold will include a minimum level of receivables owing money, and minimum balances of inventory and cash held for safety reasons. These minimum levels represent permanent working capital.

(2) **Fluctuating current assets** are assets held over and above the minimum amounts.

Aggressive management

If working capital is managed **aggressively**, all **fluctuating assets** plus a **certain proportion of permanent current assets** will be **financed by short-term capital** such as **bank overdrafts** and **trade payables**. Aggressive management will mean that there is an **increased risk** of **cash flow** and **liquidity problems**. Businesses may also suffer **higher interest costs** on short-term sources of finance.

Use of long-term capital

If short-term methods cannot be used, **long-term funding** such as **long-term loans** or **share capital** not tied up in funding non-current assets will be used to support **working capital**. This will mean that working capital is managed **conservatively**, with **all non-current assets** and **permanent current assets**, as well as part of **fluctuating current assets**, being **financed by long-term capital**. When fluctuating current assets are low, there will be surplus cash which the company will be able to invest in marketable securities.

14 Chromex Co

> **Text references.** Payback is covered in Chapter 7, government intervention in Chapter 2 and ratio analysis in Chapter 1.
>
> **Top tips.** Section (a) is the type of part-question that may well occur on your paper; a discussion of one or other methods of investment appraisal. In (b) the calculations must be based on *cash flows* and not profits.
>
> In (d) you should consider the specifics of the Chromex bid in order to assess the probability of a referral to the Competition Commission. You do not need to have a detailed understanding of the Commission's work, but you should be able to show that you understand the type of issues that it addresses and the actions that it may take in this type of case. Do not forget that EU legislation may also be relevant in this situation.
>
> You are not required to *calculate* any ratios in (e) and you should not waste time in trying to do so. However it is important to explain why you have arrived at your choice – you may find it helpful to structure your answer around the four categories into which financial ratios are commonly divided. (e) represents a good test not only of your knowledge of ratios, but what determines the usefulness of ratio analysis.

(a) **Payback**

The payback method of project appraisal involves calculating the period of time that it is likely to take to recoup the initial outlay on a project, and then comparing this with what the company defines as an acceptable period. If the payment period is less than that defined as acceptable, and provided that there are no other constraints for example capital rationing, the project will be accepted.

Limitations of payback

(i) It **ignores** the **timing of cash flows** within the payback period, the cash flows at the payback period and therefore the total project return.

(ii) It **ignores** the time **value of money.**

(iii) It is **unable** to **distinguish between projects** with the same payback period.

(iv) It **tends** to **favour short term** (often smaller) projects over longer term projects.

(v) It takes account of the **risk** of the timing of cash flows but **not** the **variability** of those cash flows.

Popularity of payback

(i) It is **simple to calculate** and **simple to understand**, and this may be important when management resources are limited. It is similarly helpful in communicating information about minimum requirements to managers responsible for submitting projects.

(ii) It **can be used** as a **screening device** as a first stage in eliminating obviously inappropriate projects prior to more detailed evaluation.

(iii) The fact that it tends **to bias in favour of short term projects** means that it tends to minimise both financial and business risk.

(iv) It can be used when there is a **capital rationing situation** to identify those projects which generate additional cash for investment quickly.

(b) The **payback period** is calculated on the basis of the **incremental cash flows** arising to Chromex following the acquisition.

The annual cash flows will be:

	$'000
Operating profit	10,000
Add back non-cash items:	
Depreciation	500
Annual labour savings	700
Annual incremental cash flow	11,200

The net cost of the acquisition is the bid value of $150m *less* the actual income of $10m ($15m-$5m) received from the sale of the land and buildings, ie $140m.

The payback period is therefore 140m ÷ 11.2m = **12.5 years**

(c) **Additional information required**

(i) Details of the **timescale** over which the investment is to be assessed

(ii) **Annual cashflow forecasts** for the appraisal period, adjusted for inflation as necessary

(iii) An appropriate estimate of the **cost of capital** to be used in the calculations

(iv) An estimate of the **terminal value**, ie the amount that could be realised from the investment at the end of the period

(v) An indication of the proposed **financing mix** in order to account for the effect of the tax shield on debt interest

(vi) Information on the effective rate of **tax** on profit and the possibility of claiming **tax allowable depreciation**

(d) **Competition authorities**

Chromex already supplies nearly one quarter of the UK bicycle market, and the Bexell acquisition would push the market share up to 34%. In view of this it is possible that the government might decide that there is a potential monopoly situation and refer the bid to the **Competition Commission**. The role of the Commission would be to assess the likely effect of the bid on the **public interest**. If it decides that the bid could have an adverse effect on the public, for example due to the restriction of choice, it may request the companies involved to change the terms of the deal. One of the main effects of this would obviously be to delay the progress of the bid. In reaching its decision, the government must also take into account whether the proposals contravene any of the EU regulations on fair competition.

(e) **Choice of ratios**

There are a large number of ratios that could be chosen in this context. However, a range of ratios should be chosen to ensure that an analysis is made of the four main areas of company performance as follows.

	Performance area	Ratios that could be selected
1.	**Profitability and return:**	Return on sales Return on investment Asset turnover
2.	**Debt and gearing:**	Gearing ratio Debt ratio Interest cover
3.	**Liquidity:**	Current ratio Quick ratio Receivable payment period Payable payment period Inventory turnover
4.	**Shareholders' investment ratios:**	Dividend yield Earnings per share Price/earnings ratio Dividend cover Earnings yield

Some of the reasons why comparison should be based on companies in the same sector are as follows.

(i) **Working capital requirements**

Different industries have very **different working capital requirements**. For example, a supermarket will have a much lower level of receivables than an aerospace manufacturer due to the differing levels of credit sales. Similarly, manufacturing businesses generally require a much greater investment in inventories than do service businesses. This makes a meaningful comparison of the liquidity ratios impossible.

(ii) **Fixed costs**

Different industries have **different levels of fixed costs**. For example, the fixed costs of a small management consultancy will be much lower than those of a capital equipment manufacturer. Different cost structures make it difficult to compare relative levels of profitability and gearing.

(iii) **Business risk**

There will be **different levels of business risk and earnings volatility** in different industrial sectors. Again, this makes it impossible to compare the investment and gearing ratios of different companies.

15 Charm Co

> **Text references.** Investment appraisal methods are covered in Chapters 7, 8 and 9.
>
> **Top tips.** Be careful with the fixed costs in part (a). They are relevant but incremental does not mean variable. Make sure you focus on NPV in part (c).
>
> **Easy marks.** The calculations in parts (a) and (b) should be straightforward and gain easy marks.
>
> **Examiner's comments.** This was the most popular question on this paper and many answers gained high marks in parts (a) and (b). Many answers showed a shallow understanding of the issues in part (c).

Marking scheme

		Marks	
(a)	Sales revenue	1	
	Material costs	1	
	Variable production costs	1	
	Advertising	1	
	Incremental fixed costs	2	
	Taxation	1	
	Capital allowance tax benefits	1	
	Discount factors	1	
	Net present value	1	
	Comment	1	
			11
(b)	Net present value	1	
	IRR	3	
	Comment	1	
			5
(c)	Up to 2 marks for each detailed point made		9
			25

ANSWERS

(a) **Calculation of net present value of proposed investment**

Year	1	2	3	4
	$'000	$'000	$'000	$'000
Sales	3,750	1,680	1,380	1,320
Direct materials	(810)	(378)	(324)	(324)
Variable production cost	(900)	(420)	(360)	(360)
Advertising	(650)	(100)		
Fixed costs (W1)	(600)	(600)	(600)	(600)
Operating cash flow	790	182	96	36
Tax at 30%	(237)	(55)	(29)	(11)
Tax saved by capital allowance (W2)	60	60	60	60
Net cash flow	613	187	127	85
10% discount factors	0.909	0.826	0.751	0.683
Present value	557.2	154.5	95.4	58.1

Workings

(1) Fixed costs in year 1 = 150,000 × $4.

This is a one-off increase in fixed costs and will not then vary with production.

(2) Tax saved by capital allowance = $800,000/4 × 30% = $60,000 per annum

Total present value = $865,200

Net present value = $(865,200 − 800,000) = $65,200

This net present value is **positive** and the investment is therefore worthwhile on financial grounds. However this does depend on very high sales in the first year which may not be achievable.

(b) **Calculation of NPV using a discount rate of 20%**

Year	1	2	3	4
	$'000	$'000	$'000	$'000
Net cash flow	613	187	127	85
20% discount factors	0.833	0.694	0.579	0.482
Present value	510.6	129.8	73.5	41.0

Net present value = $(754,900 − 800,000) = − $45,100

Using the formula

$$ IRR \approx a + \left(\left(\frac{NPV_a}{NPV_a - NPV_b} \right) (b - a) \right) \% $$

$$ IRR \approx 10 + \left[\frac{65,200}{65,200 + 45,100} \times (20 - 10) \right] \% = 15.91\%, \text{ say } 16\% $$

An IRR of 16% is higher than the discount rate of 10% used to appraise new investments. The investment is therefore financially acceptable.

(c) The net present value method of investment appraisal has a number of **advantages** over other methods.

(i) It is based on **cash flows** not accounting profit unlike ROCE. Accounting profits are subject to a number of different accounting treatments and cash flows can add to the wealth of the shareholders via increased dividends.

(ii) NPV looks at cash flows throughout the **whole** of an investment period unlike payback, which ignores cash flows after the end of the payback period. This avoids the incorrect rejection of projects with later high returns, although it is unlikely in practice that payback would be used in isolation.

BPP
LEARNING MEDIA

(iii)   NPV incorporates the **time value of money** by using discounted cash flows whereas ROCE and payback do not. This means that it takes account of the fact that $1 today is worth more than $1 in one year's time. Discounted payback can be used but this will still ignore cash flows after the payback period.

(iv)   NPV is viewed as being **technically superior** to IRR and **simpler to calculate**. It reflects the amount of the initial value rather than a relative measure of return and represents the change in total market value that will occur if the investment project is accepted. Other investment appraisal methods do not directly show the potential increase in shareholder wealth, which is a primary financial management objective.

(v)   The NPV method is superior for ranking **mutually exclusive projects** in order of attractiveness. IRR will give an incorrect indication where discount rates are less than the IRR of incremental cash flows.

(vi)   Where cash flow patterns are **non-conventional,** for example where the sign of the net cash flow changes in successive periods, there may be several IRRs which decision makers must be aware of to avoid making the wrong decision. NPV however can accommodate these non-conventional cash flows.

(vii)   When discount rates are expected to **differ** over the life of the project, such variations can be incorporated easily into NPV calculations, but not into IRR calculations.

(viii)   An assumption underlying the NPV method is that any net cash inflows generated during the life of the project will be **reinvested at the cost of capital** (that is, the discount rate). The IRR method, on the other hand, assumes these cash flows can be reinvested to earn a return equal to the IRR of the original project, which is not necessarily reasonable.

16 Zedland Postal Services

Text references. Investment appraisal is covered in Chapters 7, 8 and 9.

Top tips. As you are given the opportunity cost of capital for the postal service, you should use that in the investment appraisal and not the cost of debt. You can assume, as you are not told otherwise, that the 14% is a nominal rate, and as the cash flows increase at different rates, they have to be stated at nominal rates. Don't forget when carrying out the return on investment calculation that average investment does not equal initial investment;

average investment = initial investment + end value of investment (here 0)/2.

The calculations indicate important points of difference between return on investment and net present value calculations – the treatment of non-cash expenses and timing differences on tax. The line on taxable profits indicates that the new investment makes no difference to the tax rate Zedland suffers.

Make sure you write a full answer in part (c) even if you have not completed the calculations in the earlier parts of the question.

Easy marks. Easy marks will be available for the early stages of the calculations in parts (a) and (b).

(a) **Return on average investment**

Year	1	2	3	4	5
	$'000	$'000	$'000	$'000	$'000
Revenue					
Letters	2,048	2,867	3,010	3,160	3,318
Parcels	682	1,075	1,129	1,185	1,244
	2,730	3,942	4,139	4,345	4,562
Expenses					
Staff	2,340	2,457	2,580	2,709	2,844
Premises	150	158	165	174	182
Vehicle maintenance					
Vans	200	250	313	391	488
Trucks	20	25	31	39	49
Advertising	1,300	263			
Depreciation	232	232	232	232	232
	4,242	3,385	3,321	3,545	3,795
Revenue less expenses	(1,512)	557	818	800	767
Taxation (40%)	605	(223)	(327)	(320)	(307)
Profit after tax	(907)	334	491	480	460

Total profit after tax = $858,000

Average profit after tax = $858,000/5 = $171,600

Average investment = $1,160,000/2 = $580,000

Average annual after tax return on investment = $\dfrac{\$171{,}600}{\$580{,}000} \times 100\% = 30\%$

(b) **Net present value**

Year	0	1	2	3	4	5	6
	$'000	$'000	$'000	$'000	$'000	$'000	$'000
Revenue less expenses		(1,512)	557	818	800	767	
Add depreciation		232	232	232	232	232	
Taxation			605	(223)	(327)	(320)	(307)
Initial investment	(1,160)						
Cash flow	(1,160)	(1,280)	1,394	827	705	679	(307)
Discount factor (14%)	1	0.877	0.769	0.675	0.592	0.519	0.456
Present value	(1,160)	(1,123)	1,072	558	417	352	(140)

Net present value = ($24,000).

Assumptions made

(i) The **inflation rate**, for both revenue per unit and costs (excluding depreciation) will be 5%.

(ii) The cost of **preliminary research** is to be ignored, as it has already been incurred.

(iii) If the five managers were not needed for this new service, they would **remain** in their **present posts** rather than being made redundant.

(iv) **Return on average investment** is to be computed ignoring financing costs.

(d) The two targets which need to be met are a return on investment of at least 5% and a non-negative net present value.

The proposed new service has an annual **average return on average investment of 30%**, but it has a **negative net present value** ($24,000). Because projects must meet both targets to be acceptable, it is recommended that the service is not provided. However, this is subject to the further factors considered below.

Further factors

The proposed service might well be of **great value** to the public. It should perhaps be provided on that ground.

If the postal service's other projects have large positive net present values, it might be possible to net them off against the negative net present value here, to give an acceptable overall result. This is, of course, tantamount to **cross-subsidisation**.

It may be that charges could be increased and/or costs reduced, so that the net present value could become positive. In particular, planned staffing levels may be excessive.

Before any final decision is taken, the **reliability** of all forecasts should be reviewed, and a **sensitivity analysis** should be carried out.

17 Preparation question: Sensitivity analysis

(a)   *Original forecast*

	$'000
Sales revenue 20,000 × $20	400
Less variable costs 20,000 × $15	300
Contribution	100
Less cash fixed costs	25
Annual cash inflow	75

Characteristic

	A	B	C	D	E	F
(i) Investment ($'000)	385	350	350	350	350	350
(ii) Annual cash flow ($'000)	75	75	65(W1)	35(W2)	45(W3)	72.5(W4)
(i) ÷ (ii) = DCF index	5.133	4.667	5.385	10.000	7.778	4.828
From cumulative tables,						
IRR = approx	14.5%	15.5%	13.5%	0.0%	5.0%	16.0%

These returns are found for A and C to F by looking along the ten year line of cumulative PV factors for the value nearest to the calculated DCF index. For B, the factor is found by looking along the nine year line.

Workings

1   10% reduction in sales volume = 10% × $100,000 contribution
       = $10,000 reduction in cash flow

2   10% reduction in selling price = 10% × $400,000 sales
       = $40,000 reduction in cash flow

3   10% increase in variable cost = 10% × $300,000 cost
       = $30,000 reduction in cash flow

4   10% increase in fixed cost = 10% × $25,000 cost
       = $2,500 reduction in cash flow

(b)   The first step is to list the recalculated IRR's in ascending order.

Characteristic altered by 10%		*Resulting IRR*
		%
D:	selling price	0.0
E:	variable cost	5.0
C:	sales volume	13.5
A:	initial investment	14.5
B:	expected life	15.5
F:	fixed cost	16.0

This ranking shows that the selling price is the most vulnerable area likely to prevent the project meeting the company's hurdle rate. A 10% reduction in selling price would cause a dramatic drop in IRR.

(c) **Improving sensitivity analysis**

Further work which might be undertaken to improve the value of the sensitivity analysis is as follows.

(i)   We could **assess** the **probabilities** of **changes** in each of the characteristics, and use these probabilities to calculate an expected value for the project.

(ii)   We could use a **computer simulation** model to assess the likelihood of not meeting the company's hurdle rate.

(iii)   We could assess the effect of **other magnitudes** of **changes**, not only 10%.

(iv)   We could assess the effect of **combinations** of **simultaneous changes** in characteristics.

(v)   We could assess the effect of **favourable changes** in **characteristics**.

(d)   Revised contribution per unit = $(20 – 18) = $2

	$
Total contribution: $2 × 20,000	40,000
Less fixed cost	10,000
Cash inflow	30,000
Investment	$25,000

The investment would be repaid in the first year, therefore this is almost certain to be a successful project.

From a purely financial viewpoint, the company should accept the offer. However, consideration should be given to **non-financial factors** such as the quality and reliability of supply.

18 Question with analysis: Umunat Co

Text references. Dealing with risk is covered in Chapter 10.

Top tips. This question has four parts which include both written and numerical elements. Therefore a fair chance to show both skills. In part (a) you must define and distinguish risk and uncertainty. In parts (b) and (d) you need to know the techniques required.

Easy marks. In part (a), a general discussion of risk and uncertainty can get you up to 5 marks.

Examiner's comments. In part (a), many candidates did not draw an adequate distinction between risk (which can be quantified) and uncertainty (which cannot). Many obtained full marks in part (b), but candidates need to note that incremental fixed costs are relevant for any appraisal decision. The answers offered for part (c) were of variable quality, with only a small number of answers correctly evaluating the sensitivity of the project's NPV to changes in the specified variables. In part (d), the majority of candidates calculated the expected sales volume but did not comment on the ENPV. Few noted that the NPV of the worst case was negative, and that there was a 30% chance of this occurring. Some managers might regard a 30% chance of negative returns as an unacceptable risk. As in part (b), many candidates calculated and discounted itemised annual cash flows for each year of the project life, when an annuity factor approach would have saved a considerable amount of time.

Marking scheme

		Marks	
(a)	Discussion of risk	2	
	Discussion of uncertainty	1	
	Value of considering risk and uncertainty	2	
			5
(b)	Calculation of payback period	2	
	Discussion of payback period	2	
			4
(c)	Calculation of net present value	2	
	Sensitivity of NPV to sales volume	2	
	Sensitivity of NPV to sales price	2	
	Sensitivity of NPV to variable cost	1	
	Discussion of sensitivity analysis	3	
			10
(d)	Calculation of expected value of sales	1	
	Calculation of expected net present value	1	
	Discussion of expected net present value	4	
			6
			25

(a) The terms risk and uncertainty are often used interchangeably but a distinction should be made between them. With risk, there are several possible outcomes, which upon the basis of past relevant experience, can be quantified. In areas of uncertainty, again there are several possible outcomes, but with little past experience, it will be difficult to quantify its likely effects.

[Definitions of risk and uncertainty]

A risky situation is one where we can say that there is a 70% probability that returns from a project will be in excess of $100,000 but a 30% probability that returns will be less than $100,000. If, however, no information can be provided on the returns from the project, we are faced with an uncertain situation. Managers need to exercise caution when assessing future cash flows to ensure that they make appropriate decisions. If a project is too risky, it might need to be rejected, depending upon the prevailing attitude to risk.

In general, risky projects are those whose future cash flows, and hence the project returns, are likely to be variable. The greater the variability is, the greater the risk. The problem of risk is more acute with capital investment decisions than other decisions because estimates of cash flows might be for several years ahead, such as for major construction projects. Actual costs and revenues may vary well above or below budget as the work progresses.

(b) Assuming that cash flows occur evenly throughout the year:

Contribution per unit = $3.00 − $1.65 = $1.35

Total contribution = 20,000 units × $1.35 = $27,000 per year

Annual cash flow = $27,000 − $10,000 = $17,000

Payback = $50,000/$17,000 = 2.9 years

[Calculation]

[Comment on your findings]

This exceeds the company's hurdle payback period of two years. Payback is often used as a first screening method. By this, we mean that the first question to ask is: 'How long will it take to pay back its cost?' Umunat has a target payback, and so it might be tempted to reject this project. However, a project should not be evaluated on the basis of payback alone. If a project gets through the payback test, it ought then to be evaluated with a more sophisticated investment appraisal technique, such as NPV. Payback ignores the timing of cash flows within the payback period, the cash flows after the end of payback period and therefore the total project return. It also ignores the time value of money (a concept incorporated into more sophisticated appraisal methods).

(c)

> Need to calculate NPV first

Year	Investment $	Contribution $	Fixed costs $	Net $	Discount factor 12%	Total $
0	(50,000)			(50,000)	1	(50,000)
1-5		27,000	(10,000)	17,000	3.605	61,285
						11,285

NPV of sales revenue = 20,000 × $3.00 × 3.605 = $216,300
NPV of variable costs = 20,000 × $1.65 × 3.605 = $118,965
NPV of contribution = $97,335.

(i) **Sensitivity to sales volume**

For an NPV of zero, contribution has to decrease by $11,285. This represents a reduction in sales of 11,285/97,335 = 11.6%

(ii) **Sensitivity to sales price**

As before, for an NPV of zero, contribution has to decrease by $11,285. This represents a reduction in selling price of 11,285/216,300 = 5.2%

(iii) **Sensitivity to variable cost**

As before, for an NPV of zero, contribution has to decrease by $11,285. This represents an increase in variable costs of 11,285/118,965 = 9.5%

The basic approach of sensitivity analysis is to calculate the project's NPV under alternative assumptions to determine how sensitive it is to changing conditions. An indication is thus provided of those variables to which the NPV is most sensitive (critical variables) and the extent to which those variables may change before the investment results in a negative NPV.

Sensitivity analysis therefore provides an indication of why a project might fail. Management should review critical variables to assess whether or not there is a strong possibility of events occurring which will lead to a negative NPV. Management should also pay particular attention to controlling those variables to which the NPV is particularly sensitive, once the decision has been taken to accept the investment.

(d) Expected sales = (17,500 × 0.3) + (20,000 × 0.6) + (22,500 × 0.1) = 19,500 units

Expected contribution = 19,500 units × $1.35 = $26,325

> Calculation of ENPV

Year	Investment $	Contribution $	Fixed costs $	Net $	Discount factor 12%	Total $
0	(50,000)			(50,000)	1	(50,000)
1-5		26,325	(10,000)	16,325	3.605	58,852
						8,852

The expected net present value is positive, but it represents a value that would never actually be achieved, as it is an amalgamation of various probabilities. Examining each possibility:

> Looking at individual scenarios

Worst case (sales of 17,500 units, 30% probability):

Year	Investment	Contribution	Fixed costs	Net	Discount factor	Total
	$	$	$	$	12%	$
0	(50,000)			(50,000)	1	(50,000)
1-5		23,625	(10,000)	13,625	3.605	49,118
						(882)

We already know the NPV of sales of 20,000 units to be $11,285

Best case (sales of 22,500, 10% probability):

Year	Investment	Contribution	Fixed cost:	Net	Discount factor	Total
	$	$	$	$	12%	$
0	(50,000)			(50,000)	1	(50,000)
1-5		30,375	(10,000)	20,375	3.605	73,452
						23,452

The managers of Umunat will need to satisfy themselves as to the accuracy of this latest information, but the fact that there is a 30% chance that the project will produce a negative NPV could be considered too high a risk. ⎯⎯⎯ From sales of 17,500 units

It can be argued that assigning probabilities to expected economic states or sales volumes gives the managers information to make better investment decisions. The difficulty with this approach is that probability estimates of project variables can carry a high degree of uncertainty and subjectivity.

19 AGD Co

Text references. Leasing is covered in Chapter 11.

Top tips. This question is in three parts. Nearly 50% of the marks are available for a purchase or lease investment appraisal and a further eight marks for a discussion of operating and finance leases.

The reminder of the marks, five in total, can be earned for a tail end two-part question requiring you to calculate APRs and repayments of loans.

All three parts could be answered separately.

Easy marks. The question is split into two smaller calculation elements in part (c)that will gain you easy marks if you know how to calculate APRs and repayments. The written part allows you to list what you know of both types of lease but you need to note the differences as required in the question. Look at using pro forma workings for the investment appraisal in part (a).

Examiner's comments. While many candidates made errors in this popular question, answers were usually of a satisfactory overall standard. Common errors included timing the investment when borrowing to buy as occurring at the end of the first year, omitting the tax savings on the maintenance costs incurred by buying the asset, and omitting the tax savings on the lease rental payments.

The overall standard of answers to part (b) was not strong and many candidates used a 'double-list' approach that supports contrast rather than discussion. A degree of confusion between finance leasing and lease-purchase was in evidence, but this was dealt with sympathetically.

Many candidates either did not answer part (c) or gave answers that were incorrect. The overall standard of answers was very poor.

Marking scheme

			Marks
(a)	Purchase price	1	
	Sale proceeds	1	
	Capital allowances	1	
	Balancing allowance	1	
	Capital allowance tax benefits	1	
	Maintenance costs	1	
	Maintenance cost tax benefits	1	
	NPV of borrowing to buy	1	
	Lease rentals	1	
	Lease rental tax benefits	1	
	NPV of leasing	1	
	Selection of cheapest option	1	
			12
(b)	Explanation and discussion		
	Finance lease	4-5	
	Operating lease	4-5	
	Maximum		8
(c)	Annual percentage rate	2	
	Amount of equal instalments	3	
			5
			25

Answer plan

This question has three parts, which cover several aspects of financing and investment appraisal.

It might be useful to sketch out an answer plan for part (b), before you embark on this part of the question so that you pick up the requirements of the question and don't just do a mind dump of all you know on leases.

Step 1 For part (a)

Calculate the NPVs for each of the two alternatives. Remember tax benefits of leasing and capital allowances available for the purchase option. Conclude which option is preferable.

Step 2 Part (b)

- Define a finance lease
- Define an operating lease and compare with a finance lease

Step 3 Part (c)

- Calculate the APR required
- Calculate the repayments due at the end of each six-month period

(a) **(i)** **Net present value of purchasing machine**

	Year 0 $'000	Year 1 $'000	Year 2 $'000	Year 3 $'000	Year 4 $'000
Cash outflows					
Capital costs	(320)				
Annual maintenance costs		(25)	(25)	(25)	
	(320)	(25)	(25)	(25)	0
Cash inflows					
Disposal proceeds				50	
Taxation (at 30% in following year)			8	8	8
Writing down allowances (W1)			24	18	39
			32	76	47
	–	–			
Net cash flows	(320)	(25)	7	51	47
Discount at 7%	× 1.000	× 0.935	× 0.873	× 0.816	× 0.763
PV of cash flow	(320)	(23)	6	42	36
NPV of cash flow	$259,000				

Working 1. Writing down allowances

	$'000	Capital allowance $'000	Tax benefit $'000	Year of cash flow
Initial investment	320			
Allowances at 25% pa on a reducing balance basis over 3 years				
Year 1	(80)	(80)	24	Y2
	240			
Year 2	(60)	(60)	18	Y3
	180			
Year 3				
Proceeds on sale	(50)			
Balancing allowance	130		39	Y4

(ii) **Net present value of leasing machine**

	Year 0 $'000	Year 1 $'000	Year 2 $'000	Year 3 $'000	Year 4 $'000
Cash outflows					
Annual lease rentals	(120)	(120)	(120)		
	(120)	(120)	(120)		
Cash inflows					
Taxation (at 30% in following year) – tax deduction for lease rentals			36	36	36
Net cash flows	(120)	(120)	(84)	36	36
Discount at 7%	× 1.000	× 0.935	× 0.873	× 0.816	× 0.763
PV of cash flow	(120)	(112)	(73)	29	27
NPV of cash flow	$249,000				

(b)   **Key differences between operating and finance leases**

Finance lease

A finance lease is an agreement between the user of the leased asset and a provider of finance that covers the majority of the asset's useful life.

Key features of a finance lease

(i)   The provider of finance is usually a **third party finance house** and not the original provider of the equipment.

(ii)   The **lessee is responsible for the upkeep**, servicing and maintenance of the asset.

(iii)   The lease has a **primary period**, which covers all or most of the useful economic life of the asset. At the end of the primary period the lessor would not be able to lease the equipment to someone else because it would be worn out.

(iv)   It is common at the end of the primary period to allow the lessee to continue to lease the asset for an indefinite **secondary period**, in return for a very low nominal rent, sometimes known as a 'peppercorn' rent.

(v)   The lessee bears most of the risks and rewards and so the asset is shown on the lessee's balance sheet.

Operating leases are rental agreements between a lessor and a lessee

Key features of an operating lease

(i)   The lessor supplies the equipment to the lessee.

(ii)   The **lessor is responsible for the upkeep**, servicing and maintenance of the asset.

(iii)   The lease period is fairly short, less than the expected economic life of the asset. At the end of one lease agreement the lessor can either lease the same equipment to someone else and obtain a rent for it or sell it second-hand.

(iv)   The asset is not shown on the lessee's balance sheet.

(c)   (i)   **Annual percentage rate (APR)** on a 10% loan by the bank with two six-monthly interest payments.

As interest is due every six months, this is equivalent to 5% every six months.

As this would be compounded, therefore the APR would be $(1.05 \times 1.05 - 1) = 0.1025$ or 10.25%

(ii) The term of the loan is $320,000 at 10% pa over 5 years with six-monthly payments of interest.

In (i) above, we established that the rate was 5% every six months. There are 10 equal payments due. Treating this as an annuity at 5% over 10 periods gives a discount rate of 7.722.

Therefore dividing $320,000/7.722 gives $41,440 as each equal payment due.

20 Leaminger Co

Text references. Leasing and capital rationing are covered in Chapter 11.

Top tips. Make sure you take into account all the detail given in the question; it's easy to miss or misinterpret the timing of flows or the maintenance costs. Note that annuity factors can be used to save time in (a) (ii) and (iii), whereas in (a) (i) a more complicated calculation is required. Most points in the NPV calculation were worth 1 mark, although 3 marks were available for the capital allowances.

The key point in (b) is that capital rationing affects the purchase and operating lease options, but does not affect the finance lease option since the first payments do not take place until capital rationing has ended.

Examiner's comment. There were a number of errors in (a) that many candidates made including: omitting maintenance costs and their tax benefits from the purchase and finance lease calculations; including the writing down allowance rather than the tax benefit of the writing down allowance in the purchase calculation; including the tax benefits of writing down allowances in the lease calculations (they were only available on ownership); only considering one year of the operating lease.

In (b) few candidates recognised the opportunity cost element in the purchase and operating lease options. Candidates gained marks for using a profitability index approach. Many answers in (c) just consisted of a discussion of hard and soft capital rationing. Few candidates considered the short-term cash flows, the cost of capital, the possibility of failure to renew the operating lease, other alternatives to immediate purchasing and other sources of finance.

(a) (i) **Purchase**

	20X2 $	20X3 $	20X4 $	20X5 $	20X6 $	20X7 $
Purchase price	(360,000)					
Rental		(15,000)	(15,000)	(15,000)	(15,000)	
Tax on rental			4,500	4,500	4,500	4,500
Tax allowable depreciation (W)		27,000	20,250	15,188	11,391	28,172
Disposal proceeds					20,000	
Net cash flow	(360,000)	12,000	9,750	4,688	20,891	32,672
Discount factor	1.000	0.909	0.826	0.751	0.683	0.621
Present value	(360,000)	10,908	8,054	3,521	14,269	20,289

Net present value = $(302,959)

Working

Tax allowable depreciation

Year of claim	Depreciation $	Tax saved $	Year of tax payment/saving
20X2	90,000	27,000	20X3
20X3	67,500	20,250	20X4
20X4	50,625	15,188	20X5
20X5	37,969	11,391	20X6
20X6	93,906	28,172	20X7

Depreciation

20X2 $360,000 \times 25\% = 90,000$

20X3-5   75% of previous year

20X6   Balancing allowance = Purchase price – Depreciation – Sale proceeds

= 360,000 – 90,000 – 67,500 – 50,625 – 37,969 – 20,000

= 93,906

(ii) **Finance lease**

Year		Cash flow	Discount factor	Present value
		$	10%	$
20X3-6	Rental and maintenance (135,000 + 15,000)	(150,000)	3.170	(475,500)
20X4-7	Tax on payments	45,000	2.882*	129,690
	Present value			(345,810)

20X4-7 factor = Year 1-5 Factor – Year 1 Factor
= 3.791 – 0.909
= 2.882

(iii) **Operating lease**

Year		Cash flow $	Discount factor 10%	Present value $
20X2-5	Rental	(140,000)	3.487	(488,180)
20X3-6	Tax on rental	42,000	3.170	133,140
	Present value			(355,040)

Based on these calculations, purchase would appear to be the best option.

(b) Every $ of year 0 expenditure will involve a loss of profit of 100,000/500,000 = 20p

Purchase

	$
Present value	(302,959)
Profits foregone (360,000 × 0.20)	(72,000)
Revised present value	(374,959)

Finance lease

$345,810 as before.

Operating lease

	$
Present value	(355,040)
Profits foregone (140,000 × 0.20)	(28,000)
Revised present value	(383,040)

If capital rationing applies, the finance lease is the best option.

(c)
REPORT

To: Directors
From: Business Adviser
Date: 14 November 20X2
Subject: Acquisition of turbine

This report covers the issues influencing the decision to acquire the turbine.

Effect of capital rationing

Without capital rationing, the most economic decision would be to purchase the turbine; with capital rationing taking out a finance lease would appear to be the best decision.

Continued capital rationing

However this analysis assumes capital rationing only lasts for a single period. Existence of capital rationing in future periods will mean a greater loss of profits if we have used lease finance (because rentals have to be paid), than if the machine is purchased outright (where the only costs after initial purchase are maintenance costs).

Postponement of purchase decision

The implications of taking out an operating lease until the period of capital rationing has ended and then purchasing a new turbine need to be investigated. Maybe a turbine purchased in a couple of years' time will incorporate technological advances and thus be able to be used beyond 20X6.

Cash flow patterns

Cash flow patterns may be a significant factor in the financing decision. The purchase option requires a significant upfront cash payment. The rental cash flows are evenly spread over the next few years.

Cost of capital

Connected to the last point, the current cost of capital may not be appropriate for assessing the decision, if new sources of finance are needed, particularly to provide short-term funds if acquisition results in a cash shortage. The financial risk of the company may change as a result.

Renewal of operating lease

We need to assess the possibility that the operating lease will not be renewed by the lessor or the rentals raised significantly. However using an operating lease does give us the flexibility to cancel the arrangement if business conditions change.

Problems with the turbine

If the turbine breaks down, the lessor will have to deal with the problems if Leaminger has taken out an operating lease, but the company will have to solve the problems and incur costs if it uses a finance lease or purchases the machine outright. If the warranty has expired when the problems arise, Leaminger could incur significant extra costs.

21 Bread Products Co

Text references. Asset replacement decisions are covered in Chapter 11.

Top tips. In part (a), the lowest common multiple is to be preferred over the equivalent annual cost method of evaluation because it allows the effects of the different rates of inflation that affect the various costs and revenues to be included. The large number of marks available in (b) indicated that the points you raised needed to be discussed in a degree of depth; one-line answers would not have been enough.

(a) In order to compare the replacement policies, we must calculate the costs of each approach over a number of complete cycles. The timescale to be used will be the lowest common multiple of the lifecycles, ie $2 \times 3 = 6$ years.

All costs and revenues will be inflated into nominal terms, and then discounted at the nominal rate of 15%.

The first stage is to calculate the nominal costs and revenues over the six year period, and then to apply 15% discount factors to find the NPV cost of each policy.

Replace every two years (Revenues shown as credits)

	Year 0	Year 1	Year 2	Year 3	Year 4	Year 5	Year 6
Oven purchase (+ 5% pa)	24,500		27,011		29,780		
Maintenance (+ 10% pa)		550	968	666	1,171	805	1,417
Resale proceeds (+ 5% pa)			(17,199)		(18,962)		(20,905)
Total cash flow	24,500	550	10,780	666	11,989	805	(19,488)
15% discount factors	1.000	0.870	0.756	0.658	0.572	0.497	0.432
PV cash flow	24,500	479	8,150	438	6,858	400	(8,419)
Total PV cost over 6 years	32,406						

Replace every three years (Revenues shown as credits)

	Year 0	Year 1	Year 2	Year 3	Year 4	Year 5	Year 6
Oven purchase (+ 5% pa)	24,500			28,362			
Maintenance (+ 10% pa)		550	968	1,997	732	1,288	2,657
Resale proceeds (+ 5% pa)				(12,965)			(15,009)
Total cash flow	24,500	550	968	17,394	732	1,288	(12,352)
15% discount factors	1.000	0.870	0.756	0.658	0.572	0.497	0.432
PV cash flow	24,500	479	732	11,445	419	640	(5,336)
Total PV cost over 6 years	32,879						

A two year replacement cycle is to be preferred since this costs the least in present value terms.

(b) **Limitations of net present value techniques**

(i) **Shareholder wealth maximisation**

NPV is based on the **assumption that the primary aim of the organisation is to maximise the wealth of the ordinary shareholders**. This is valid for many companies, but in some investment decisions there may be other overriding factors that make the NPV approach less relevant. This is particularly true when the investment under consideration is fundamental to the strategic direction of the business.

(ii) **Public sector problems**

The technique is **difficult to apply in the public sector**, partly due to methods of accounting, and partly because other organisational aims will be more important than the maximisation of profit. Public sector operations are commonly judged in terms of economy, efficiency and effectiveness, and the NPV approach can only provide a partial answer to these issues.

(iii) **Discount rate**

A major problem in the use of NPV in practice is the **choice of the discount rate**. It is generally accepted that the rate to be used should be the cost of capital, but this in itself may be difficult to determine. The problem is particularly tricky when the size of the investment means that the company will need to acquire a significant amount of additional capital, and there is uncertainty about the cost of new funds.

(iv) **Risk**

A related problem to the choice of the discount rate is the **incorporation of risk**. The simplest approach is to apply a risk premium to the cost of capital, but the amount of this is subjective. Other approaches include the use of sensitivity analysis and probability analysis, but these too have limitations, and involve the use of subjective judgements.

(v) **Subjectivity**

It follows from (iv) that NPV techniques may appear to be very scientific and rational whereas in fact there is a large component of subjectivity in the assumptions and forecasts used. However, this **subjectivity is masked** by the precise format in which results are communicated.

(vi) **Cash flow timing**

The technique **assumes that all cash flows arise at the end of the time period** (which is usually one year). This is obviously untrue, and large fluctuations in this pattern may distort the results. Breaking the analysis down into small periods leads to complication, and may be unsatisfactory due to the problems of forecasting in such a precise way.

(vii) **Long-term measure**

Although the NPV approach may lead to the correct financial decision in the long-term, this **timescale may be too long** to be appropriate for the business to use in practice. For example, it

BPP
LEARNING MEDIA

could lead to an unacceptable reduction in short-term accounting profits which will impact upon the share price and on confidence in the company. Similarly, it may conflict with incentive arrangements for managers, which are usually geared to short-term profitability.

(viii) **Non quantifiable costs and benefits**

Some costs and benefits that arise are not quantifiable. There may be important non-financial factors that are relevant to the decision, but which are difficult to quantify. For example, undertaking a new investment may enhance the standing of the company, making it more attractive to customers, investors and potential employees. This could have an important impact on the performance of the company, but cannot be quantified in an NPV analysis.

22 Filtrex Co

Text references. Capital rationing is covered in Chapter 11.

Top tips. (a) is a good summary of why long-term profits don't always lead to positive cash flows. (b) demonstrates why capital rationing may be a matter of choice; certain sources of funds may not be felt desirable and projects have to be properly controlled.

(c)(i) of the question can be approached by means of the Profitability Index (PI); the optimal mix of project can then be found by trial and error. In addition you need to be clear about mutual exclusivity and indivisibility. Mutual exclusivity means that if you choose one project, you cannot choose other projects with which the chosen project is mutually exclusive. Indivisibility means that you cannot carry out part of a project; it is all or nothing.

In (d) it is helpful to consider the situation from the point of view of developing the projects themselves and in terms of alternative sources of funds.

(a) **Cash shortages**

A period of capital rationing is often associated with more general problems of cash shortage. Possible reasons for this include the following.

(i)   The business has become **loss making** and is unable to cover the depreciation charge. Since one purpose of the depreciation charge is to allow for the cost of the assets used in the profit and loss account, the implication is that there will be insufficient cash with which to replace these assets when necessary.

(ii)   High inflation may mean that even though the business is profitable in historical cost terms, it is still failing to **generate sufficient funds** to replace assets.

(iii)   If the business is growing it may face a **shortage of working capital** with which to finance expansion, and this may result in a period of capital rationing.

(iv)   If the business is **seasonal or cyclical** it may **face times of cash shortage** despite being fundamentally sound. In this situation, there may be a periodic need for capital rationing.

(v)   A **large one-off item** of **expenditure** such as a property purchase may mean that the company faces a temporary shortage of cash for further investment.

Investment opportunities

A further reason for capital rationing arises in the situation where the company has **more investment opportunities** available than the **funds allocated** to the capital budget permit. This means that projects must be ranked for investment, taking into account both financial and strategic factors.

(b) **Hard capital rationing**

Hard capital rationing describes the situation when a firm is prevented from undertaking attractive investments for reasons external to the firm.

Soft capital rationing

Soft capital rationing describes the position when management places a limit on the amount of capital investment that may be undertaken: it is due to factors internal to the firm.

Reasons for the deliberate restriction of capital expenditure include the following.

(i)   Management may decide to **limit the funds available** to those which can be generated from retained earnings, for the following reasons.

   (1)   They **do not wish** to **issue further equity** to prevent outsiders from gaining control of the business.

   (2)   They **do not wish** to **raise further equity** to avoid earnings dilution.

   (3)   They **do not wish to commit the company** to meeting large fixed interest payments on additional debt capital.

(ii)   A **capital budgeting procedure** may be used to ensure that only the best projects are undertaken.

(iii)   The **number of projects** undertaken may be **restricted** in order to ensure that there are adequate management resources available for them to realise their full potential.

(c)   (i)   **Profitability index**

When resources are limited, the aim must be to maximise the productivity of the scarce resource, in this case capital. It is therefore helpful to calculate the **Profitability Index (PI)** for each project to determine which delivers the most NPV per dollar of investment.

Project	Outlay	NPV	PI(NPV/Outlay)
	$	$	
A	150,000	65,000	0.43
B	120,000	50,000	0.42
C	200,000	80,000	0.40
D	80,000	30,000	0.38
E	400,000	120,000	0.30

On this basis, project A is the most attractive since it shows the highest PI, and project E is the least attractive. Since the projects are not divisible and projects A and C are mutually exclusive it is not possible simply to work down the rankings to determine the optimum combination. Instead this must be done algebraically or by trial and error. Various combinations of projects can be evaluated using the latter approach.

	Outlay	NPV
	$	$
A, B, D	350,000	145,000
B, C, D	400,000	160,000
E	400,000	120,000

It appears that the **optimum combination** of projects is B, C and D. As well as delivering the highest NPV it also has the **benefit that all the funds available** for investment are used and Filtrex does not face the choice between investments showing a poorer return or returning excess funds to its shareholders.

Opportunity costs

However, Filtrex may also wish to consider the **opportunity cost** of failing to undertake attractive projects. One way of approaching this is by the application of **linear programming techniques** and the calculation of dual values. The dual value shows the amount by which total NPV would rise if the organisation were able to obtain one more unit of the scarce resource at the market cost of funds. It therefore indicates how much it is worth paying over and above the market rate of funds used in the NPV calculation for additional funds. This might help Filtrex to decide whether it should change its financing policies and look at the possibility of raising additional external funds.

(ii) **Useful further information**

(1) The **possibility** of **raising additional finance** and at what cost.

(2) If **rationing** is to continue, then the **effect on the NPV** of **postponing projects becomes relevant**. If all the projects are equally postponable than Filtrex should select those which provide the fastest flow of funds in order to finance those which have been postponed as quickly as possible.

(3) It has been assumed that all the projects carry a **similar degree of risk**. If this is not the case then Filtrex should allow for this, for example by the use of sensitivity analysis in its evaluations.

(4) It may be that some of the projects carry a **greater strategic significance** than others. Information on this area should also be taken into account in the investment decision.

(d) **Further opportunity**

Filtrex might consider some of the **following options** as a means of exploiting more of these opportunities.

(i) **Sale of patent rights**

It could accept that it will be **unable to manage** all the **later stages** of development itself and could decide to sell some of the patent rights once they have been obtained.

(ii) **Joint ventures**

It could seek **joint venture partners** to share in the development.

(iii) **Licensing or franchising**

Some of the areas may be appropriate **for licensing or franchising** with a royalty being payable to Filtrex. This in turn could help to finance the development of those projects which are retained for in-house promotion.

(iv) **Additional finance**

It could seek additional finance in the following forms.

(1) **Further equity** by way of a rights issue or, by agreement with existing shareholders, via a public issue.

(2) **Debt finance secured** on the **assets**. This should be possible since the company is currently ungeared.

(3) **Debt finance secured** against the **working capital** ie factoring or invoice discounting.

(4) It may be possible to arrange a **sale and leaseback** of some of the company's property or equipment.

(5) Depending on its location and business there may be the possibility of applying for **grant aid**, for example from one of the EU regional development funds.

23 Basril Co

Text references. Capital rationing is covered in Chapter 11.

Top tips. In part (a) calculate the NPVs for each project first and then look at the best combination of divisible or indivisible projects. Part (b) just needs a short answer. Part (c) needs a longer explanation of capital rationing and the use of key terms as highlighted in the answer. Part (d) asks you to explain and how you apply relevant cashflow calculations in investment appraisal.

Easy marks. Setting out formats for calculating NPVs in part (a). In part (c) providing definitions of hard and soft capital rationing.

Examiner's comments. This question asked for optimal selection under capital rationing, an explanation of how NPV is applied under capital rationing, a discussion of the causes of capital rationing, and an explanation of the term 'relevant cost' in the context of investment appraisal.

Part (a), required three projects with a variety of cash flow profiles to be evaluated. Good answers calculated the NPV and profitability index, and gave the optimum investment schedule and total NPV for the cases of divisible and non-divisible projects. Errors included: failing to calculate profitability indexes, not calculating the total NPV (even though required by the question), failing to account correctly for inflation in the case of the project where real cash flows were provided (inflating real cash flows to money terms or deflating the nominal rate were both acceptable), and using annuity factors rather than discount factors in calculations.

Marking scheme

			Marks
(a)	(i)	NPV of project 1	1
		NPV of project 2	1
		NPV of project 3	2
		Calculation of profitability indices	2
		Optimum investment schedule	2
	(ii)	Selection of optimum combination	2
			10
(b)		NPV decision rule	1
		Link to perfect capital markets	1
		Explanation to ranking problem and solution	1
			3
(c)		Hard capital rationing	3
		Soft capital rationing	4
			7
(d)		Explanation of relevant cash flows	2
		Examples of relevant cash flows	3
			5
			25

(a) (i)

Project 1

	$	12% discount factor	$
Initial investment	(300,000)	1	(300,000)
Year 1	85,000	0.893	75,905
Year 2	90,000	0.797	71,730
Year 3	95,000	0.712	67,640
Year 4	100,000	0.636	63,600
Year 5	95,000	0.567	53,865
			32,740
Profitability	332,740/300,000		1.11

Project 2

	$	12% discount factor	$
Initial investment	(450,000)	1	(450,000)
Year 1	140,800	0.893	125,734
Year 2	140,800	0.797	112,218
Year 3	140,800	0.712	100,250
Year 4	140,800	0.636	89,549
Year 5	140,800	0.567	79,834
			57,585
Profitability	507,585/450,000		1.13

Project 3

	$	12% discount factor	$
Initial investment	(400,000)	1	(400,000)
Year 1	124,320	0.893	111,018
Year 2	128,796	0.797	102,650
Year 3	133,432	0.712	95,004
Year 4	138,236	0.636	87,918
Year 5	143,212	0.567	81,201
			77,791
Profitability	477,791/400,000		1.19

The most profitable projects are Projects 3 and 2, so if they are **divisible** it is suggested that Basril invests $400k in Project 3 for an NPV of $77,791, and the remaining $400k in Project 2 for an NPV of 400/450 × $57,584 = $51,186.

(ii)   If the projects are **indivisible**, then Basril can either invest in Project 1 + Project 2 at a cost of $750,000, or Project 1 + Project 3 at a cost of $700,000 (Project 2 + Project 3 would cost too much). The NPV of 1 + 2 = $32,740 + $57,584 = $90,324. The NPV of 1 + 3 = $32,740 + $77,791 = $110,531. Therefore the best combination is Projects 1 and 3.

> **Examiner's comments.** Part (b) required a discussion of how the NPV approach is applied via the profitability index in the case where capital is rationed and projects are divisible, and via the NPV of possible combinations in the case where projects are indivisible. Other valid answers discussed single-period and multiple period capital rationing, and linear programming as a solution in multiple-period capital rationing.

(b)   When capital is rationed, a company cannot invest in every opportunity that comes its way with a positive NPV. The basic approach in such circumstances is to rank all investment opportunities so that the NPVs can be maximised from the use of the available funds.

Ranking in terms of absolute NPVs will normally give incorrect results, because it leads to the selection of large projects, each of which has a high individual NPV but which may have, in total, a lower NPV than a large number of smaller projects with lower individual NPVs.

Ranking should therefore be carried out in terms of what is called the profitability index. This ratio measures the present value of future cash flows per $1 of investment, and so indicates which investments make the best use of the limited resources available. Projects may or may not be divisible when performing this analysis. Different combinations of projects will need to be assessed.

> **Examiner's comments.** Part (c) asked candidates to explain the causes of capital rationing, and many answers discussed hard and soft capital rationing, as well as offering examples of each. Credit was given to answers that explained in more general terms why a company might find its investment funds to be restricted, as long as the reasons had credibility.

(c)   **Capital rationing** is a situation in which a company has a limited amount of capital to invest in potential projects, such that the different possible investments need to be compared with one another in order to allocate the capital available most effectively. If an organisation is in a capital rationing situation it will not be able to enter into all projects with positive NPVs because there is not enough capital for all of the investments.

Soft capital rationing is brought about by internal factors; **hard capital rationing** is brought about by external factors.

Soft capital rationing may arise for one of the following reasons.

(i)   Management may be reluctant to issue additional share capital because of concern that this may lead to outsiders gaining control of the business.

(ii)   Management may be unwilling to issue additional share capital if it will lead to a dilution of earnings per share.

(iii)   Management may not want to raise additional debt capital because they do not wish to be committed to large fixed interest payments.

(iv)   Management may wish to limit investment to a level that can be financed solely from retained earnings. They may not want to grow the company too quickly.

Hard capital rationing may arise for one of the following reasons.

(i)   Raising money through the inventory market may not be possible if share prices are depressed.

(ii)   There may be restrictions on bank lending due to government control.

(iii)   Lending institutions may consider an organisation to be too risky (eg, too highly geared, poor prospects) to be granted further loan facilities.

(iv)   The costs associated with making small issues of capital may be too great.

Examiner's comments. Part (d) asked for an explanation, with examples, of 'relevant cost' in the context of investment appraisal. Weaker answers showed a lack of understanding of cost classification.

(d)   When appraising an investment project, it is essential that only those cash flows relevant to the project be taken into account, otherwise an incorrect investment decision could be made. A 'relevant cash flow' is an incremental cash flow that arises or changes as a direct result of the investment being made.

Some costs will be sunk before an investment decision is made. An example would be research and development or market research costs into the viability of a new product. Once incurred, such costs become irrelevant to the decision as to whether or not to proceed, and so should be excluded from the analysis.

Cash flows that would be relevant include an increase in production overheads or labour costs, new purchases that are necessary, and any incremental tax effects.

It is important to note that any interest payments on the finance for a new project are relevant to the project decision, but are not taken into account in any NPV calculation. The interest payments will already be 'built in' to the calculation in the discount factor that is being applied.

24 Burnsall Co

Text references. Sources of finance are covered in Chapter 12.

Top tips. In (a) the approach is to calculate the amount of additional working and fixed capital required, and then to compare this with the level of internally generated funds in order to establish the external financing requirement. You will need to make an assumption about the operating margin for 20X5/X6.

In (b) take into account the size and status of the company (ie listed) as well as the funds required when deciding on the appropriate financing alternatives.

In (c) you should make sure you refer to Armada's circumstances.

(a)   The first step is to calculate Burnsall's total **additional financing requirement**.

	$m
Existing working capital:	
Current assets	45.0
Payables	(18.0)
	27.0
Additional working capital (+20%)	5.4
Additional fixed capital	20.0
Total	25.4

This can be met in part from internal sources as follows. It is assumed that the margin before depreciation will remain unchanged. The profit in 20X4/X5 before depreciation was $100m × 16% + $5m = $21m.

	$m
20X5/X6 profit before depreciation ($21m × 120%)	25.2
Less outflows:	
Interest ($20m × 12%)	(2.4)
Tax (20X4/X5)	(5.0)
Dividends ($5m × 110%)	(5.5)
Net additional internal funds generated	12.3

Internally generated funds are therefore inadequate to finance the costs of expansion, there being a shortfall of $13.1m ($25.4m – $12.3m) which will have to be raised externally.

(b)   The factors to be taken into account include the following.

(i)   **Matching**

The asset structure of a company generally approximates to the following diagram.

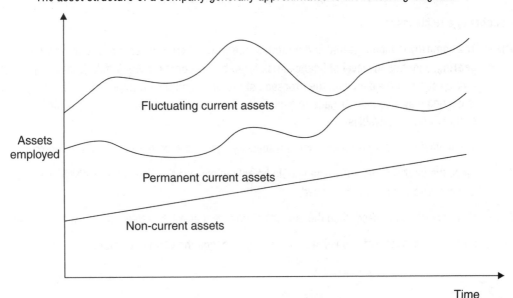

The traditional view is that **non-current assets** should be **financed** by **long-term sources** of **finance** and **current assets** by a **mixture of long-term and short-term sources**. If a company finances illiquid assets from short-term debt it faces the risk of insolvency in the event of its being unable to renegotiate the loans when they fall due. Thus a company with a greater proportion of non-current assets and permanent current assets is also likely to have a higher proportion of long-term debt in its capital structure.

(ii) **Cost**

The company will seek to **minimise its cost of capital**. The cost of debt capital will be made up of the interest cost of the debt and the transaction costs incurred in arranging the finance. **Transaction costs vary** according to the type of finance being raised, for example it will be cheaper to arrange a medium-term bank loan than a public issue of dated loan notes. Short-term debt will need to be renegotiated more frequently and this will give rise to recurring transaction costs.

The **relative interest rates** carried by long-term and short-term debt will **vary over time** according to supply and demand and to market expectations of interest rate changes. Rates are generally higher on long-term loans than on short-term since the level of risk faced by the lender that interest rates may rise before repayment is due is higher.

(iii) **Security**

The company may find it easier to **raise short-term finance** with **low security** than long-term finance. However the cost of such loans is likely to be higher.

(iv) **Risk**

In opting for short-term debt, the company faces the risk that it may **not** be able to **renegotiate the loan** on such good terms, or even at all, when the repayment date is reached. Long-term loans are thus less risky. The fact that a firm is seeking a large amount of short-term debt, and is frequently going back to the market, may lead to a loss of confidence in the firm on the part of investors.

(v) **Flexibility**

Long-term debt may carry **early repayment penalties** if it is found that the loan is no longer needed or a more attractive form of finance becomes available. Short-term debt is **more flexible** since it allows the firm to react to interest rate changes and to avoid being locked into an expensive long-term fixed rate commitment at a time when rates are falling. Many firms use overdraft finance – a form of short-term credit whose amount varies from day to day according to the needs of the company. This avoids the company having to pay interest on funds which it does not actually need.

(c) **Benefits of a rights issue**

(i) The company is highly geared and a rights issue would therefore serve to **reduce the level of gearing**, and thus the level of financial risk faced by the company would fall. It may be possible to replace some of the debt with the proceeds of the issue and thus further reduce the ratio. A reduction in gearing may also help Armada to avoid breaching any loan covenants and to achieve greater security from its payables.

(ii) The market has been rising and rights issues are easier to accomplish on a **rising market**.

(iii) Since the market is high, Armada should be able to achieve the issue at a relatively **low cost** since fewer shares will need to be issued.

(iv) If **underwriters** are used, then the amount of finance that will be raised is known and guaranteed.

(v) If the issue is successful, it will not significantly change the **voting structure**.

Drawbacks of rights issue

(i)   The issue will need to be priced at a discount to the current share price in order to make it attractive to investors. This will result in a **dilution in earnings per share** and a **drop in the share price**.

(ii)   Since the economic outlook is poor, it is unlikely that the market will **rise much further** and thus Armada may be too late to take advantage of the benefits of issuing on a rising market.

(iii)   If the issue is not successful, a significant number of shares will be taken up by underwriters. This may **alter the voting structure and control** of the company.

(iv)   **Administration and underwriting costs** are high.

(v)   It could be difficult to **convince the markets** of the need for the issue – it may be assumed that Armada is facing a cash crisis. If the issue fails then this problem will be compounded and it will be harder for Armada to achieve a successful issue in the future.

(vi)   Shareholders may be unable or **unwilling to increase their investment** in Armada.

25 Question with answer plan: Tirwen Co

Text references. Sources of finance are covered in Chapter 12.

Top tips. This question needs to be answered in sequence. Take each part in turn and remember some earlier analysis may be useful in later parts of the question, for instance in parts (c) to (e).

Easy marks. In part (a), the calculation of the theoretical ex-rights price per share. Make sure you are confident in calculating this.

In part (c) calculation of current EPS and earnings.

Examiner's comments. In part (a), almost all candidates calculated correctly the theoretical ex-rights price per share, but some calculated the value of rights per new share rather than per existing share. Some candidates disregarded the instruction to ignore issue costs. Answers to part (b) indicated that many candidates are unclear about the effect of a rights issue on shareholder wealth. Candidates could have calculated the current EPS in part (c) by dividing the share price by the PE ratio, but a significant number divided reserves by the number of shares. In part (d), the share price following redemption of some of the loan notes was found by multiplying the revised earnings per share by the constant price/earnings ratio. Most answers to part (e) did not include an evaluation of the effect of the rights issue on the debt/equity ratio and interest cover, even though this was required by the question. A comparison with sector averages was also required in order to gain full marks.

			Marks
(a)	Theoretical ex rights price per share	2	
	Values of rights per existing share	1	
			3
(b)	Effect on wealth of exercising rights	2	
	Effect on wealth of sale of rights	2	
	Discussion of rights issues and shareholder wealth	2	
			6
(c)	Current earnings per share	1	
	Current earnings	1	
	Funds raised via rights issue	1	
	Interest saved by redeeming loan notes	1	
	Revised earnings	1	
	Revised earnings per share	1	
			6
(d)	Expected share price after redeeming loan notes	1	
	Comparison with theoretical ex rights price	1	
	Discussion and conclusion	1	
			3
(e)	Effect of rights issue on debt/equity ratio	2	
	Effect of rights issue on interest cover	2	
	Discussion and link to Tirwen Co	3	
			7
			25

Answer Plan

Step 1   Part (a). Calculate the theoretical ex rights price (TERP).

Use this to value the rights PER EXISTING SHARE (ie 5 shares).

Step 2   Part (b). There are 3 possible actions for an investor: buy, sell or let the rights lapse.

In the first 2 cases, the shareholder should not lose out from the rights.

If the rights lapse, the shareholder will lose out by the difference between the cum rights price and the TERP by the number of shares held.

Step 3   Revise the balance sheet for the repayment of debt. As no income statement is given, manipulate the P/E ratio given to calculate EPS and then earnings.

Then calculate revised Profit after Tax and EPS.

Step 4   Using the answer in part (c) work out the share price after the redemption of debt and compare this to the current market price.

Step 5   Finally, a discussion is required which should talk in ratio analysis (refer to the sector averages) pre and post the issue of shares and/or redemption of loan notes.

(a) (i) Issue price of new shares = 85% × $4.00 = $3.40. The theoretical ex-rights price = ((5 × $4.00) + $3.40)/6 = $3.90.

(ii) The value of rights per existing share = ($3.90 – $3.40)/5 = 10c

(b) Choices open to the investor are to either refuse the offer, take up the offered rights or sell the rights (or a combination).

If the investor does not subscribe to the offer, a loss of $100 will occur, being the difference between the value of 1,000 shares before the rights issue ($4,000) and the value of 1,000 shares after the rights issue ($3,900).

If the investor takes up the offered rights, he will purchase an additional 200 shares at $3.40 = $680. This will give the investor 1,200 shares at $3.90 each = $4,680. This is equal to the sum of the value of 1,000 shares before the rights issue ($4,000) plus the cash subscribed. As a result there is no overall change in wealth. Some cash has merely been transferred into shares.

If the rights are sold (1,000 rights at 10c each) then again there is no overall change in wealth. The $100 proceeds plus the value of the shares after the rights issue (1,000 shares at $3.90 each = $3,900) is the same as the value of the holding before the rights issue. Part of the wealth has been converted from shares into cash.

(c) Current EPS = share price / PE ratio = $4.00/ 15.24 = 26.25c

Number of shares = $2,000,000/ 50c = 4 million

Earnings = number of shares × EPS = 4m × 0.2625 = $1,050,000

Funds raised from rights issue = 4m/ 5 = 800,000 × $3.40 = $2,720,000

Net of issue costs = $2,500,000.

If this is entirely used to redeem loan notes, this will save $2,500,000 @ 12% = $300,000

	$	
Earnings before tax	1,500,000	$1.05 m grossed up for 30% tax rate
Debenture interest	540,000	$4.5m @ 12%
Overdraft interest	87,500	$1.25m @ 7%
Current PBIT	2,127,500	
Revised interest cost	(327,500)	$540k + $87.5k – $300k
	1,800,000	
Tax at 30%	(540,000)	
Revised profit after tax	1,260,000	
Total new shares	4,800,000	
Revised EPS	26.25	

(d) As it is stated that the PE ratio will remain constant, and EPS has not changed, this means that the share price will remain unchanged at EPS × PE = 26.25c × 15.24 = $4.00. As the theoretical ex rights price is $3.90 for each share, this results in a gain of 10c per share.

(e) **Debt equity ratio** (using debenture debt only)

Current: 4,500/ 3,500   129%

This is above the sector average. If $2.5m of debenture debt is redeemed:

2,000/ 6,000   33%

If the debt is not reduced:

4,500/ 6,000   75%

These are both less than the sector average, and will indicate reduced financial risk.

Interest cover

Current: 2,127,500/ 627,500   3.4

If $2.5m of debenture debt is redeemed:

2,127,500/ 327,500   6.5

Thus interest cover improves to above the sector average.

A rights issue is therefore an attractive source of finance for Tirwen, although it must be noted that equity finance is relatively more expensive than debt finance and will affect the company's cost of capital when assessing projects in the future.

A rights issue will decrease gearing and improve interest cover if the funds are used to redeem some of the debenture debt. The reduction in debt on the balance sheet will make it more likely that Tirwen can raise additional finance in the future, perhaps at a cheaper rate.

26 RG

Text reference. Dividend policy is covered in Chapter 13.

Top tips. (a) provides the opportunity to display your knowledge of recent developments in the discussion of dividend policy. Examples of the more extreme policies can be given, together with examples of pronouncements made by some of the institutions.

(b) starts by explaining an important point – that cash does not have to be given back to shareholders but can be retained in the business for investment. (b) brings out the importance of signalling, suggesting that markets are not always strongly efficient. Hence they may not be able to recognise a large payment as being one-off, they may instead view the payment as a sign that the directors have run out of ideas for investments. Because markets are not strongly efficient, a steady stream approach may be best, supported on occasions by short-term borrowing as brought out in (c). Note in (d) that an increase in financial risk caused by higher gearing is likely to be outweighed by the benefits of obtaining cheaper finance provided gearing levels are not too great.

Easy marks. The parts look fairly even in terms of difficulty, so marks are maximised by ensuring you make some reasonable comments for each part, and don't miss any out.

(a)   **Dividend policy**

The policy being put forward is consistent with the basic accounting concept that dividends should only be paid if there are **sufficient distributable profits** available to cover the payout. However, profits vary from one accounting period to the next, and companies face the conflicting demands of maintaining a **constant payout ratio** and level of dividend cover against maintaining a **consistent level of actual dividend payments**. In recent recessions some firms adopted a conservative policy and severely cut the dividend, while others maintained the level of payments in line with their view of longer term future prospects rather than short-term current performance.

(i)   **Financial institutions**

Financial institutions tend to prefer **dividend income** to **capital growth** because cash flows are required to meet their liabilities and, if these cash flows are in the form of dividend payments, they can **avoid the transaction costs** involved in realising capital gains. It is therefore likely that institutional shareholders would prefer the increased payout ratio in the period of reduced growth. Institutions often put pressure on companies to ensure that dividend levels are maintained during periods of reduced profit performance.

(ii)   **Small private investors**

The **position of small private investors** will vary. Where they **fall below the income tax threshold** then they too are likely to express a preference for an **increased payout ratio**. However these tax advantages are not available to other investors, who will **prefer capital gains** if they can take advantage of any exemption from tax on capital gains below a certain limit. They will also be able to time their realisation of capital gains in order to minimise their tax liability.

(b)/(c)/(d)   REPORT

To: The Directors of DV
From: IFA Financial Advisers
Date: 15 May 20X7
Subject: Dividend policy and share buybacks

We set out below our comments on the matters we talked about at our recent meeting.

(b)   **Implications of share repurchase**

Before deciding on a **share repurchase**, you must clarify the company's overall cash requirements for the foreseeable future. Our assumption in this discussion is that the company will have a substantial temporary surplus of funds this year but that, if this is distributed to shareholders, additional funds will be needed for the subsequent two years.

Cash retention

Your first decision is whether to retain the cash until it is needed next year, or to distribute it to shareholders, or to retain a proportion, distributing the balance. **Retained cash** could be placed on deposit or invested in a suitable **financial portfolio**. Secondly, if you decide to distribute the cash to shareholders, this can be done either as a dividend or by buying back some shares.

Deciding level of cash retention

The argument against retaining too much cash is that it can give the impression that the directors have 'run out of ideas' for expanding the company's operations. This may cause the **share price to drop** and attract unwanted takeover bids. On the other hand, the retention is logical if the company can **invest the cash short term** at a higher interest rate than individual shareholders. Any such retention of cash must be accompanied by careful explanations to the market of the company's investment plans over the following two years.

Implications of dividend payment

If the surplus cash is distributed to shareholders as a **dividend**, this will cause a big percentage increase in dividend this year. Shareholders will be happy with the cash received but, in the absence of further explanations, will become confused by what the company is trying to **'signal'** by this dividend increase. Some may assume that further large increases in dividend can be expected in future years, and may develop over-optimistic expectations of the company's prospects.

Buyback as use for surplus cash

Most finance directors take the view that it is best to increase dividends at a steady rate which **signals the company's long-run growth prospects**. If you agree with this view and you wish to make an **above-average distribution** to shareholders, you may consider using the balance of surplus cash to buy back some of the company's shares. For example, GEC, which for many years was criticised for holding too much cash, has more recently adopted a policy of share buy-backs.

Mechanism of buyback

The share buy-back requires provision in the company's constitution and approval in general meeting. It can be arranged as a series of purchases on the open market or as a **private purchase** from a number of large shareholders. Assuming that the buy-back is at **market price**, the **share price** should be **unaffected**, whereas if a dividend payout is made, the share price will fall (from cum div to ex div). With a buy-back, the remaining shares will effectively be worth more, reflecting the higher future earnings per share.

Strategic share buybacks

Share buy-backs are sometimes made for **strategic reasons** separate from the dividend policy considerations outlined above. These include:

(i)   The wish to **re-privatise a business**; in this case all the shares were bought back from investors
(ii)   To make **shares available for employee share option schemes**
(iii)   As a **defence** against a **hostile takeover bid**
(iv)   To **increase** the **company's gearing**

(c)   **Advisability of borrowing money to pay dividends in years 2 and 3**

Borrowing money to pay dividends is legal provided that the dividends are **covered by the accumulated balance of distributable profits**. The question is whether it is financially advisable.

Maintaining dividend growth

In theory, if cash is invested and dividends are reduced, this should not worry shareholders provided that they can see the prospect of **increased future dividends.** In practice, for 'signalling' reasons mentioned above, it is believed that shareholders are happiest when they receive a steady stream of dividends increasing from year to year. This is an argument in favour of borrowing in order to maintain the dividend growth. Shareholders receive more cash in years 2 and 3 but less in future years because of the need to repay the loans with interest.

Recommendation

Given that the company is not highly geared we recommend that the company borrows as much as is needed to **maintain dividend growth** in line with long-term earnings growth.

(d)   **Effect on the company's cost of equity**

If shares are repurchased, the **total value of equity goes down** by the amount of cash paid out while debt remains unchanged. This **increase in gearing** will cause the **cost of equity to rise** because of the increased financial risk (volatility of equity earnings) experienced by the shareholders. In the same way, if the company increases its borrowings in order to pay dividends, the gearing will increase and the **cost of equity capital** will rise.

Effect on cost of debt

However, DV is operating at a **low level of gearing**. The increase in the **cost of equity** is likely to be **outweighed** by the **cheap after-tax cost of debt** compared with equity. The tax savings resulting from debt interest will mean that, even though the cost of equity goes up, the weighted average cost of capital will be reduced.

I hope these notes address the points you have raised with us. If you require any further clarification please contact us at any time.

Signed: IFA Financial Advisers

27 PG

Text references. Sources of finance are covered in Chapter 12.

Top tips. Be warned if you got (a) (i) wrong that manipulation of the earnings and price formulae may come up in this paper. (a)(ii) brings out the limitations of the theoretical ex rights price calculation. Actual price movements depend on the state of the market, the degree of market efficiency and, very importantly, the risk profile.

In (b) (ii) you are only asked about the advantages of issuing convertible loan stock; the principal feature is short-term benefits from being able to raise funds at limited cost, with possible adverse consequences (dilution of earnings, change in control) only happening long-term.

The dividend valuation model is at the heart of the answer to (b) (iii). You may not have covered this yet so read through the answer provided.

(a) (i) The **current market price** can be found by multiplying the earnings per share (EPS) by the price/earnings (P/E) ratio.

EPS is $3.6/6m = 60c per share

P/E ratio is 15

Market price of shares is $15 \times 60c$ = **$9.00 per share**

(ii) In order to raise $10,500,000 at a price of 800 cents, the company will need to issue an additional 1,312,500 ($10,500,000/$8.00) shares.

Following the investment, the total number of shares in issue will be 7,312,500 (6,000,000 + 1,312,500).

At this point, the total value of the company will be:

$(6m \times \$9) + \$10,500,000 = \$64,500,000$

The **theoretical ex-rights price** will therefore be $64.5m/7.3125m = **$8.82**.

Problems with calculations

(1) The **costs of arranging the issue** have not been included in the calculations.

(2) The **market view** of the **quality of the new investment** will affect the actual price of the company's shares.

(3) If the **issue** is **not fully subscribed** and a significant number of shares remain with the underwriters, this will **depress the share price**.

(4) The effect of the new investment on the **risk profile** of the company and the expected **future dividend stream** could also cause the share price to differ from that predicted.

(5) The price of the shares depends not only on the financial performance of the company, but also on the **overall level of demand** in the inventory market. If the market moves significantly following the announcement of the issue, this will affect the actual price at which the shares are traded.

(iii) **Features of deep discounted rights issue**

In a **deep-discounted** rights issue, the new shares are priced at a **large discount** to the current market price of the shares. The purpose of this is to ensure that the issue is well subscribed and that shares are not left with the underwriters, and thus this form of issue pricing is attractive when the inventory market is particularly volatile. However, the shares cannot be issued at a price which is below their nominal value.

Disadvantage of deep discounted rights issue

The main drawback to this approach is that a **larger number of shares** will need to be **issued** in order to raise the required amount of finance, and this will lead to a larger dilution of earnings per share and dividends per share.

(b) (i) **Conversion premium**

The **conversion premium** is the **difference** between the **issue value** of the **inventory** and the **conversion value** as at the date of issue. In other words it is the measure of the additional expense involved in buying shares via the convertible loan notes as compared with buying the shares on the open market immediately.

In this case, $100 loan notes can be converted into 11 ordinary shares. The **effective price** of these shares is therefore $9.09 per share.

The **current market price** of the shares is $9.00. The **conversion premium** is therefore $9.00 – $9.00 = **9 cents**. This can also be expressed in percentage terms as **1%** (0.09/9).

(ii) **Advantages of issuing convertible loan notes**

(1) **Convertibles** should be **cheaper than equity** because they offer greater security to the investor. This may make them particularly attractive in fast growing but high-risk companies.

(2) **Issue costs** are **lower** for loan notes than for equity.

(3) **Interest** on the **loan notes** is **tax deductible**, unlike dividends on ordinary shares.

(4) There is **no immediate change** in the **existing structure** of control, although this will change over time as conversion rights are exercised.

(5) There is no **immediate dilution** in **earnings** and **dividends per share**.

(iii) **Dividend policy**

Dividend policy is one of the major factors which determines the share price. Under the **dividend valuation model**, the share price is held to be directly related both to the current dividend and to the expected future growth in dividends:

$$P_0 = \frac{D_0(1+g)}{(r-g)}$$

where: P_0 = market price of shares
D_0 = current level of dividend
r = required rate of return
g = expected annual growth in dividend

Impact of dividend growth

Thus it can be seen that dividend growth is important in determining the likely market value of the shares. As has already been discussed above, the market value of the shares is very important in determining the price of convertibles, and therefore the dividend policy of the company will have an important effect on the value of convertible loan notes.

28 Newsam Co

Text references. Gearing and capital structure is discussed in Chapter 14.

Top tips. This question offered a substantial amount of accounting information to enable you to illustrate the answers numerically but, more importantly, to allow an opportunity to show your expertise in interpreting accounting statements. (a) does not specify the ways in which the gearing has been calculated. You should therefore define clearly your basis of calculation of gearing and explain the reasons for your choice.

Note carefully how the market price of the shares is arrived at in (a) if you failed to get that part of the question correct.

The availability in (c) of 6 marks should have suggested that the answer was not clear-cut. Despite the bank reservations, Newsam does not do too badly on the important measures of interest cover and asset backing.

In (d) do not limit your discussion to the options suggested in the question, but consider what else might be available to Newsam. Note that some of the measures proposed (revaluation of non-current assets and brands) do not bring any additional funds, they just make the balance sheet 'look better'. As a quoted company, Eurodollar funding is available for Newsam.

(a) **Capital gearing**

Capital gearing is concerned with a company's **long-term capital structure**. The covenants attaching to the debenture do not define clearly what they mean by capital gearing in this context, in particular whether the bank overdraft should be included as long-term debt capital. However, since it appears that the overdraft has been used principally to finance non-current assets in the form of machinery rather than as a source of working capital, it is probably reasonable to argue that it should be included as part of the prior charge capital. The gearing ratio can thus be defined as:

$$\frac{\text{Prior charge capital}}{\text{Shareholders' funds}} = \frac{\text{Debentures} + \text{overdraft}}{\text{Ordinary shares} + \text{reserves}}$$

The gearing ratios can now be calculated.

(i) **Book values**: $\dfrac{\$5.0m + \$3.0m}{\$5.0 + \$10.0m} = 53.3\%$

(ii) **Market values**

Market value of loan notes:

$\$5.0m \times 115\%$	$= \$5.75m$
Market price of shares	$= \text{P/E ratio} \times \text{Earnings per share}$
	$= \text{P/E} \times \dfrac{\text{Profit after tax}}{\text{Number of shares}}$
	$= 14 \times \$1.34m/20m = 93.8c$
Market value of equity	$= \text{Market price} \times \text{number of shares}$
	$= 93.8c \times 20m = \$18.76m$
Gearing ratio	$= \dfrac{\$5.75m + \$3.0m}{\$18.76m} = 46.6\%$

(b) **Terms of covenant**

It appears from the calculations above that if calculated on the basis of **book values**, Newsam has already breached the covenant relating to the gearing level. If the gearing is calculated using **market values**, then

Newsam has not yet breached this covenant, but with a gearing of 46.6% is very close to doing so. If short-term payables were included, the gearing measures would be increased.

The required liquidity range for the current ratio is 1.08 (1.35 × 80%) to 1.62 (1.35 × 120%). Newsam's current ratio (current assets: current liabilities) is 1.0 ($7.0m:$7.0m). The company is therefore in breach of the covenant with respect to liquidity.

(c) **Dangers of high gearing**

A **high gearing level** only constitutes a danger when the level and volatility of earnings is such that the company is at risk of being unable to meet the interest payments as they fall due. If this situation arises the company could be forced to **liquidate assets** to meet the demands of its payables, and this in turn could jeopardise its operating viability. It follows that the absolute level of gearing cannot be used to assess the financial risk faced by the company. It is more helpful to assess the level of interest cover in the light of the degree of volatility in earnings.

Interest coverage

Interest coverage can be calculated as the rate of operating profit: interest payable. In Newsam's case, the cover is currently 3.0 times ($3.0m:$1.0m). There is little evidence available on which to assess earnings stability, but the fact that sales growth has been steady rather than spectacular may be taken to imply that earnings are not especially volatile. If this is the case then the existing level of gearing does not appear to be dangerous.

Quality of asset backing

A further factor to take into account is the **quality of the asset backing** since this will influence the attitude of its lenders if Newsam faces problems in repaying its debt. Land and buildings currently appear in the accounts at $9.0m, and it is of crucial importance to know how this relates to **current market valuations**. If this figure is conservative then the payables' security could be fairly good. Land and buildings at $9m represent 75% of the value of total payables (including trade payables). It is unlikely that anything close to the book valuation of plant and machinery and inventory could be realised in the event of a forced sale; however, it is to be hoped that the major part of the receivables figures is collectable. Thus, in summary, the company appears to have adequate asset backing in the event of a forced restructuring or liquidation.

Conclusion

The factors discussed above, when taken together, suggest that the **level of gearing** is not particularly dangerous. However, if the company is actually in breach of its debenture covenants, the courses of action available to the debenture holders and their attitude towards the situation will be of key importance in determining the true dangers of the company's position.

(d) (i) **Operating leases**

If the company is to **lower its capital gearing** it needs either to **increase** the value of its **issued share capital** and reserves or to **decrease the size of its borrowings**. Since growth is low and cash resources relatively small it seems unlikely the company will be able to repay much of the debt in the short-term future from operational funds. However, one option might be to **convert** some of the owned plant and vehicles onto **operating leases** and thus reduce the size of the bank overdraft.

Sale and leaseback

Similarly the company might be able to raise funds through a **sale and leaseback** of property which could be used to reduce the level of debt. There may also be some scope to reduce the level of working capital through improving inventory and receivable turnovers and increasing the amount of credit taken from suppliers. However, the opportunities are likely to be limited: for example, the average debt collection period could probably not be reduced much below the current level of 52 days.

Increasing shareholders' funds

Policies that could be used to increase the size of shareholders' funds include the following.

(1) **Non-current asset revaluation**

It is implied that land and buildings have not been revalued since their acquisition twelve years ago. Despite a slump in the property market it is possible that land and buildings may be undervalued, and a revaluation could result in a **strengthening of reserves** and hence an improvement in the capital gearing.

(2) **Rights issue**

The reaction of the market to a rights issue will depend on the **rating** of the company and the **purpose** for which the issue is being made. In this case, growth has been slow, the P/E ratio is low in relation to the sector average implying a low rating, and the purpose of the issue is not to finance new growth opportunities but to reduce the level of debt. Given a relatively flat market, investors are unlikely to view such an issue positively. As a result the issue would need to be **priced** at a **relatively large discount** to make it attractive; this in turn would increase the earnings dilution and impact badly upon the share price.

(3) **Placing**

The company may find it easier to make a placing with the institutions. However, it might need to gain the agreement of the shareholders to forgo their pre-emptive rights in this situation.

(4) **Brand capitalisation**

The appearance of the balance sheet could be improved by this method, but investors and payables may not place much weight on such a valuation.

(ii) **Reduction in interest charges**

In order to improve the level of interest coverage, Newsam will need to **reduce the level of its interest charges**. Options available include the following.

(1) **Redeem the loan notes and replace with additional overdraft**

This would reduce the interest cost as follows.

$5m × (15% − 9%) = $0.3m

The interest coverage would then become:

$3m ÷ ($1.0m − $0.3m) = 4.3 times

(2) **Redeem the loan notes and replace with Eurodollar bond**

This would reduce the interest cost:

$5m × (15% − 5%) = $0.5m

The interest coverage would become:

$3m ÷ ($1.0m − $0.5m) = 6 times

The improvement in interest coverage makes this appear an attractive option. However if the dollar continues to strengthen in the manner suggested by the forward rates, at 4% per annum, this would effectively wipe out the benefit by the end of the first year.

(3) **Redeem the loan notes and replace medium to long-term debt**

A medium term bank loan would be a possibility.

Although probably more expensive than the overdraft or eurodollar bond, this would be free from the risk of foreign currency movements and would offer more security than the use of short-term finance which is repayable on demand.

Conclusion

It is therefore suggested that, unless Newsam has significant dollar incomes, it should investigate the possibility of a medium-term sterling loan.

(e) **Convertibles**

Companies normally issue convertibles in the expectation that the **holders will exercise their options**. Convertibles can therefore be seen as a form of **delayed equity**. They are attractive to the firm when the price of the ordinary shares is **abnormally low** at the date of issue, and at times when to issue a further tranche of equity would result in a significant drop in earnings per share. However they also carry the risk that the **share price will not rise** in line with expectations at the time of issue and that holders will not therefore convert. If the loan notes are dated, then the company must have funds in place to **allow redemption** on the due date. Convertibles also have a short term benefit in that interest payments are allowable against tax.

Consequences of issuing convertibles

Convertibles therefore may form part of the strategy of a company whose objective is to raise new equity, but which for various reasons does not wish to go directly to the market in the short term. They are often preferable to straight loan notes since they **do not commit the company indefinitely** to the payment of large interest bills. They further allow the company to **widen the investment base** by attracting investors looking for a guaranteed short term income plus the possibility of a capital gain at a later date. They have also recently formed a part of the strategy of companies that wished to **manipulate their reported gearing** and earnings per share, since they could choose whether to show them as equity or debt. However, this loophole has now been closed.

29 Question with analysis: Arwin

Text references. Gearing and the capital structure decision is covered in Chapter 14.

Top tips. This question expected you to prepare a forecast income statement which would then be used in part (b) to calculate various ratios. Provided you know your ratios, parts (a) and (b) should be comfortably answered and a passmark attained already. Part (c) needs a formal discussion of the two types of risk. So define them and explain them in the context of the types of gearing already calculated.

Easy marks. The requirements of part (a) involved simple calculations.

Examiner's comments. This was a popular question, but many candidates experienced difficulty in producing forecast income statements for both of the financing proposals. Candidates must have a good understanding of sources of finance to be successful. The most common error was to omit fixed costs. Many markers commented that the standard of answers to part (b) was poor, with some candidates showing that they did not know how to calculate common ratios. Some even attempted to answer this part of the question without calculating any ratios at all. It is impossible to make reasoned comments in the absence of analysis. For example, the claim that earnings per share will decrease if more shares are issued will not be true if earnings have increased due to the investment of the funds raised. Most answers to part (c) were of an acceptable standard, although candidates often failed to frame their answers according to the wording of the question.

Marking scheme

		Marks
(a)	Sales and administration cost	1
	Cost of sales	1
	Interest	1
	Profit after tax	1
	Retained earnings	1
		5
(b)	Revised share capital and reserves	1
	Financial gearing	2
	Operational gearing	2
	Interest cover	2
	Earnings per share	2
	Calculation of current values	1
	Discussion	2
		12
(c)	Explanation of business risk	1
	Explanation of financial risk	1
	Up to 2 marks for each danger of high gearing	6
		8
		25

(a)

	Debt finance $'000	Equity finance $'000	
Sales	56,000	56,000	50,000 × 1.12 / 30,000 × 85% × 1.12
Variable cost of sales	(28,560)	(28,560)	
Fixed cost of sales	(4,500)	(4,500)	30,000 × 15%
Gross profit	22,940	22,940	
Administration costs	(14,700)	(14,700)	14,000 × 1.05
PBIT	8,240	8,240	
Interest	(800)	(300)	Debt finance cost 10% × $5m = $500k in addition to existing $300k
Profit before tax	7,440	7,940	
Tax at 30%	(2,232)	(2,382)	
Profit after tax	5,208	5,558	
Dividends at 60%	(3,125)	(3,335)	Remember distributions apply under either alternative
Retained earnings	2,083	2,223	

Note the workings here – these help the examiner

(b)

Financial gearing	Current	Debt finance	Equity finance
Debt/equity ratio:			
Debt	2,500	7,500	2,500
Share capital and reserves	22,560	24,643	29,783
Debt/equity ratio %	11.1%	30.4%	8.4%

Operational gearing	Current	Debt finance	Equity finance
Contribution/PBIT			
Contribution	24,500	27,440	27,440
PBIT	6,000	8,240	8,240
Operational gearing	4.1	3.3	3.3

Interest coverage	Current	Debt finance	Equity finance
PBIT	6,000	8,240	8,240
Debt interest	300	800	300
Interest coverage	20	10.3	27.5

Earnings per share	Current	Debt finance	Equity finance
Profit after tax	3,990	5,208	5,558
Number of shares	10,000	10,000	11,250
EPS	39.9	52.1	49.4

The debt finance proposal increases EPS by the largest amount, but will reduce interest coverage and increase financial gearing. Whether these changes are acceptable depends both upon sector averages and the response of investors and managers. A decision to use equity finance would decrease financial gearing but would increase interest coverage. EPS would increase too. A decrease in operational gearing would result from both proposals.

(c) (i)

definition

Business risk, the inherent risk of doing business for a company, refers to the risk of making only low profits, or even losses, due to the nature of the business that the company is involved in. One way of measuring business risk is by calculating a company's operating gearing or 'operational gearing'.

$$\text{Operating gearing} = \frac{\text{Contribution}}{\text{Profit before interest and tax (PBIT)}}$$

Operating gearing and business risk

The significance of operating gearing is as follows.

(1) **If contribution is high but PBIT is low**, fixed costs will be high, and only just covered by contribution. Business risk, as measured by operating gearing, will be high.

(2) **If contribution is not much bigger than PBIT**, fixed costs will be low, and fairly easily covered. Business risk, as measured by operating gearing, will be low.

(ii)

Financial gearing and financial risk

A high level of debt creates financial risk. This is the risk of a company not being able to meet other obligations as a result of the need to make interest payments. The proportion of debt finance carried by a company is therefore as significant as the level business risk. Financial risk can be seen from different points of view.

(1) **The company** as a whole. If a company builds up debts that it cannot pay when they fall due, it will be forced into liquidation.

(2) **Payables**. If a company cannot pay its debts, the company will go into liquidation owing payables money that they are unlikely to recover in full.

(3) **Ordinary shareholders**. A company will not make any distributable profits unless it is able to earn enough profit before interest and tax to pay all its interest charges, and then tax. The lower the profits or the higher the interest-bearing debts, the less there will be, if there is anything at all, for shareholders.

30 Food retailers

Text references. Sources of finance are covered in Chapter 12 and shareholder ratios in Chapter 1.

Top tips. In (a), as well as commenting on the P/E ratios given in the table, you could also calculate high and low P/E ratios for the year and use this information to illustrate the meaning of the ratio to investors.

In (b), it is possible to calculate the level of dividends using the share price information and the dividend yield, and then to calculate earnings using the share price information and the P/E ratio. These figures can then be used to calculate the dividend cover. However, it is quicker to take the inverse of the product of the two ratios, and this is the method illustrated in the suggested solution.

(c) is a good illustration of the importance of being able to predict market sentiment, as there are various different standpoints the market could take.

(a)   **Price-earnings ratio**

The **price earnings (P/E) ratio** is regarded by many as the most important yardstick for assessing the relative worth of a share. It is calculated as:

$$\frac{\text{Market price of share}}{\text{EPS}}$$

This can also be expressed as:

$$\frac{\text{Total market value of equity}}{\text{Total earnings}}$$

The P/E ratio is a measure of the **relationship** between the **market value** of a company's shares and the **earnings** from those shares. It is an important ratio because it relates **two key variables** for investors, the market price of a share and its earnings capacity.

Stock market appraisal

The value of the P/E ratio reflects the **market's appraisal** of the share's future prospects. In other words, if one company has a higher P/E ratio than another it is because investors either expect its earnings to increase faster than the other's, or they consider that it is a less risky company or in a more secure industry.

Influence of market efficiency

The level of the ratio will change directly in response to changes in the share price and may vary widely during the course of the year as **events alter investor perceptions**. The extent and timing of changes will depend on the **efficiency** of the market; the stronger the level of efficiency, the more the market will be able to anticipate events.

Comparisons

Earnings potential is strongly related to the sector in which the business operates, and therefore P/E **comparisons** are only valid in respect of **companies in the same market** sectors. They can be used in this case since all the companies are publicly quoted food retailers.

Price earnings ratios of companies being compared

Using the information given in the table, the P/E ratio for Axis is 13.0. This means that it would take thirteen years for the earnings from the share to equal the price paid for it. The ratio for Spin is 21.1, the higher ratio meaning that the time taken for the earnings to **equal** the price of the share is 21.1 years. The reason for the higher level is that investors expect **earnings** from Spin to rise at a **faster rate** than those from Axis. The P/E ratio gives no indication of itself as to *why* earnings are expected to increase at different rates, although possibilities include superior management quality or more aggressive investment plans.

Ply has a current share price of 63 cents and a P/E ratio of 14.2. Earnings for last year were therefore 4.437 cents per share (63/14.2). At its high point for the year when the share price was 112, the P/E ratio was 25.2, while at its low point, the P/E ratio was 12.2. The figures also demonstrate that Spin has the **lowest level of volatility**, Axis the **highest**. This appears to reinforce the point made above that investors are confident about Spin's prospects (hence the P/E ratio has not altered much over the year), but are rather less sure about Axis's future.

(b)   **Dividend cover**

The dividend cover is the number of times that the actual dividend could be paid out of current profits. It indicates the **proportion** of **distributable profits** for the year that is being **retained** by the company and the level of risk that the company will not be able to maintain the same dividend payments in future years, should earnings fall.

Calculation of dividend cover

In this case, the ratio must be approached by means of the dividend yield and the P/E ratio:

$$P/E = \frac{\text{Market share price}}{\text{Earnings}} \qquad \text{Div yield} = \frac{\text{Dividend paid}}{\text{Market share price}}$$

$$P/E \times \text{Div yield} = \frac{\text{Dividend paid}}{\text{Earnings}} \text{ (since the Market share price cancels out)}$$

This is the inverse of the dividend cover, and therefore:

Dividend cover = 1 ÷ (P/E × div yield)

	P/E	Div yield	P/E × div yield	Dividend cover
Spin	21.1	2.3%	0.4853	2.06 times
Axis	13.0	2.1%	0.2730	3.66 times

Comparisons

As with the P/E ratio, comparisons with other companies in the same sector are a lot more valuable than comparisons with companies in different sectors, as the 'typical rate' for different business sectors will vary widely.

Dividend covers of companies being compared

The lower level of dividend cover for Spin means that the company has paid out nearly **half** of its **earnings** in the form of dividends, while Axis has only paid out less than one third. This suggests that Axis has **retained a higher proportion of profits** for **reinvestment** within the business. If earnings are very volatile, the figures could suggest that Spin might have **problems** in continuing to **pay out dividends** at this level in the future. However as indicated above, the market appears confident about Spin's future, and rates Axis rather lower despite Axis retaining more funds for future expansion.

(c)   **Payment of dividends from reserves**

If a company pays dividends in excess of earnings, then this payment must be made out of **reserves**. The effect of this will be to **reduce the net asset value** of the business.

Reasons for payment from reserves

(i)   The company believes that it must continue to pay a **high level of dividends** in order to **support the share price**. If profits for the year are too low to support the previous level of dividends, the directors may decide that it should make a payment out of reserves rather than reduce the level of dividends.

(ii)   If a company has a **high level of reserves** for which it **cannot find** an attractive **investment opportunity**, it may decide that it is appropriate to repay part of those reserves to investors by means of a dividend payment.

Problems with payment from reserves

(i)   The fall in the net asset value of the business may make it **more vulnerable** to a **takeover** bid.

(ii)   The market may see the payment out of reserves as a **desperate measure** on the part of the directors, and this may trigger a **significant drop in the share price**.

(iii)   Payment of dividends that are in excess of earnings could lead to a **shortage of cash** for the business.

(d)   **Reasons for using loan notes**

(i)   **Loan notes** are a **cheaper form of finance** than preference shares because debenture interest is tax deductible, unlike preference dividends.

(ii)   **Loan stock** are **more attractive** to **investors** because they are secured against the company's assets.

(iii)   **Debenture holders rank before preference shareholders** in the event of a liquidation.

(iv)   **Issue costs** should be **lower for loan notes** than for preference shares.

31 CF Co

Text references. Cash budgets are explained in Chapter 6, sources of finance for SMEs are covered in Chapter 14 and venture capital in Chapter 12.

Top tips. Sources of finance discussion questions are very likely to be combined with cash flow or working capital calculations.

As with all cash budget questions, you should start your answer to (a) by setting up the proforma and slotting the easy figures such as non-current assets, rent and wages in, before going on to calculate sales and purchases. You should set out your workings for calculating the monthly sales clearly so as to avoid careless errors.

Make sure your answers in part (b) relate specifically to small businesses and are not a general description of sources of finance.

The common thread in (c) is that venture capital is often provided for a major business development in the medium to long-term, and would not normally be provided to sort out short-term day-to-day problems.

(a)   **Cash budget for the period January 20X2 to May 20X2**

	Workings	January $	February $	March $	April $	May $
Receipts						
Share capital		200,000				
Sales			9,360	28,440	40,320	66,240
Total receipts		200,000	9,360	28,440	40,320	66,240
Payments						
Non-current assets		250,000				
Material purchases		16,800	25,200	33,600	67,200	67,200
Wages		4,000	4,000	4,000	4,000	4,000
Overheads		3,000	6,000	6,000	6,000	6,000
Rent		6,000			6,000	
Total payments		279,800	35,200	43,600	83,200	77,200
Net cash flow		(79,800)	(25,840)	(15,160)	(42,880)	(10,960)
Opening cash balance		0	(79,800)	(105,640)	(120,800)	(163,680)
Closing cash balance		(79,800)	(105,640)	(120,800)	(163,680)	(174,640)

Workings

1

	January	February	March	April	May
Units sold	2,400	3,600	4,800	9,600	9,600
Turnover ($10/unit)	24,000	36,000	48,000	96,000	96,000
Rec'd after 1 mth (before discount)		9,600	14,400	19,200	38,400
Rec'd after 1 mth (net of discount)		9,360	14,040	18,720	37,440
Rec'd after 2 mths			14,400	21,600	28,800
Total sales receipts		9,360	28,440	40,320	66,240

2

	January	February	March	April	May
Units sold	2,400	3,600	4,800	9,600	9,600
Purchases $7/unit	16,800	25,200	33,600	67,200	67,200

(b) The cash budget for the first five months of trading by CF Co shows that the company will need additional financing throughout this period. The cash flow problem in this case has two components:

(1) There is a **large non-current asset investment** required in the first month of operation, the size of which exceeds the initial capital injection.

(2) Sales are **not forecast** to **reach a steady state** until April, and receipts from customers lag the sales.

Normal pattern

Once sales have stabilised, the typical **monthly cash flow** will be as follows:

	$	$
Sales: 9,600 units × $10 × 60%	57,600	
9,600 units × $10 × 40% × 97.5%	37,440	
Total receipts		95,040
Purchases: 9,600 units × $7	67,200	
Wages	4,000	
Overhead	6,000	
Rent (monthly charge)	2,000	
Total payments		79,200
Net monthly cash flow		15,840

The cash deficit at the end of May is forecast to be $174,640. It will therefore take **just over eleven months** for the **deficit to be eliminated, assuming that cash flows are in** line with forecasts.

CF will need to consider obtaining an **overdraft** from the bank and must also consider the need for **longer term funds** (loans or equity funds) to finance the permanent element of working capital and non-current assets.

(c) **Matching of funding**

A general principle of financing is that the funding term should match the asset life. Therefore, non-current assets should normally be financed using **long-term sources of funds**.

Possible finance sources

There is a wide variation in the size and type of non-current assets, from photocopiers to new buildings, and therefore the relative amount of funds required, and the most appropriate form of funding will vary. However, the following sources of finance could be considered by a small business.

(i) **Retained earnings**

Relatively small asset purchases, such as a new computer, can often be financed using cash arising from retentions, and thus no additional external funds will be required.

(ii)   **Leasing and hire purchase**

These can also be considered for **smaller assets**. They can be used to spread the cost of the asset over its **useful life**. The main types of agreement available are:

- **Operating leases**. These are generally for a period less than the economic life of the asset. The risks and rewards of ownership remain with the lessor. However, in areas where there is a fast rate of technological change, such as computers, they have the advantage of giving flexibility to the lessee.

- **Finance leases**. These generally cover the whole economic life of the asset, and the risks and rewards of ownership are transferred to the lessee.

- **Hire purchase**. This is a form of instalment credit, whereby the ownership of the goods passes to the customer on payment of the final credit instalment.

(iii)   **Secured loan**

Depending on the nature of the asset, it may be possible to obtain a **secured bank** loan (either medium or long-term) against the asset being purchased. The **Loan Guarantee Scheme** is an example of a government initiative to help small businesses. It is intended to help small businesses to get a loan from the bank, when a bank would otherwise be unwilling to lend because the business cannot offer the security that the bank would want.

Under the scheme, the bank can lend up to a certain limit without security over **personal** assets or a personal guarantee being required of the borrower. However, all available **business** assets must be used as security if required. The government will guarantee for example, 75% of the loan, while the borrower must pay an annual percentage premium on the guaranteed part of the loan.

(iv)   **Mortgage**

This may be appropriate if the assets being acquired are **land or buildings**.

(v)   **Grants**

A grant is a sum of money given to an individual or business for a specific project or purpose. A grant usually covers only part of the total costs involved.

Grants to help with **business development** are available from a variety of sources, such as the government, European Union, Regional Development Agencies, local authorities and some charitable organisations.

These grants may be linked to business activity or a specific industry sector. Some grants are linked to specific geographical areas, eg those in need of economic regeneration.

(vi)   **Venture capital**

This form of finance may be appropriate for larger investments related to expansion or new product development. Venture capital is essentially **risk capital**, and has the advantage that new equity funds are provided, generally for a restricted time period at the end of which the investor will seek an exit from the business. The benefit of this is that in the longer term the ownership structure of the business is unchanged.

(vii)   **Other sources of equity**

These include further investments from the existing shareholders, the use of a **'business angel'**, or possibly some form of Alternative Investment Market (AIM) flotation. The AIM route is only likely to be appropriate for significant long-term expansions.

If the company does not go down the AIM route, it may have difficulty in obtaining equity finance, because of its liquidity problems or because shareholders will find it difficult to sell their shares.

Enterprise capital funds (ECFs) were launched in the UK in 2005. ECFs are designed to be commercial funds, investing a combination of private and public money in small high-growth businesses. They are based on a variant of the Small Business Investment Company (SBIC) programme that has operated in the United States for the past 45 years. The SBIC programme has supported the early growth of companies such as FedEx, Apple, Intel and AOL.

For investment below £500,000 most SMEs can access an informal funding network of their friends, families and business angels. Once companies require funding above £2m they are usually quite established, generating revenues and therefore perceived as lower risk and are able to secure funding from institutional investors. The gap between these two finance situations is known as the 'equity gap'.

ECFs provide Government match funding for business angels and venture capitalists to help small and medium sized businesses bridge the equity gap. Each ECF will be able to make equity investments of up to £2 million into eligible SMEs that have genuine growth potential but whose funding needs currently are not met.

(d) **Expansion**

A private company might want to invest **more capital** in an **expansion** programme, but be unable to raise the funds internally or from a bank loan. It might therefore seek venture capital.

Management buy-out

A business might need capital for a **management buyout**. The management team buying out the business is unlikely to have enough capital of its own to buy the entire business.

Research and development

A business might want capital to invest in **research and development**, which would be regarded as a high-risk venture. Other sources of finance might therefore be unavailable.

Low share price

A public company might need **extra equity finance** but be unable to issue more shares because its share price is currently below par. (Companies are forbidden by law to issue shares at below their nominal value.)

Start-ups

Venture capital is sometimes available for **company start-ups**.

32 XYZ Co

Text references. Cost of capital is covered in Chapter 15 and sources of finance in Chapter 12.

Top tips. In (a), the actual values relating to the debt being raised have been used in the suggested solution. It would be equally appropriate to use values based on a $100 unit of debt. The exceptions to the rule about using WACC to appraise investments should be noted in (c). In (d) you should take into account operational as well as financial factors.

A table format for comparisons will not always be appropriate, but in (d) it provides a clear way of giving the detail needed on each option.

In (a) five marks were available for the two calculations necessary to find the IRR and three marks for the interpolation. In (b) you would have been given credit for using the cost of debt that you calculated in (a) and using market values of share capital and debt. In (c) most of the marks were available for explaining the importance of capital structure and financial risk. Answers to (d) needed to be quite broad to gain marks, covering cash flow, risk and security, but also mentioning financial reporting implications.

(a) The **after tax cost of debt equates** to the **discount rate** at which the cost of the debt over the ten year period is zero. This can be estimated by trying different discount rates and then interpolating.

In order to raise $72m, XYZ Co must issue $80m of debt, since the debt is to be issued at a **discount** of 10% on par value ($72m ÷ 0.9 = $80m).

The **annual interest cost** net of tax will be $8m × 6%(1 − 0.3) = $336,000.

The cash flows will be as follows:

Year		Cash flow $m	5% discount factors	PV $m	6% discount factors	PV $m
0	Issue proceeds	(72)	1.000	(72)	1.000	(72)
1-10	Interest	3.36	7.722	25.95	7.360	24.73
10	Capital repayment	80	0.614	49.12	0.558	44.64
				3.07		(2.63)

Calculate the cost of debt using an IRR calculation.

$$IRR = a\% + \left[\frac{NPV_a}{NPV_a - NPV_b} \times (b - a)\right]\%$$

$$= 5\% + \frac{3.07(6\% - 5\%)}{3.07 + 2.63} = 5.54\%$$

The **after tax cost of debt** is therefore 5.54%

(b) V_E = 200 million × $1.50

= 300 million

$$WACC = k_e\left(\frac{V_E}{V_E + V_D}\right) + k_d\left(\frac{V_D}{V_E + V_D}\right)$$

$$= 10\left(\frac{300}{300 + 72}\right) + 5.54\left(\frac{72}{300 + 72}\right)$$

= 9.14%

(c) **Cost of debt**

The cost of debt is an inappropriate rate to use, as if fails to recognise **any impact** on **existing providers** of finance.

Return in excess of cost of capital

Any new investment undertaken by a company should generate a return in **excess** of the **overall cost of capital** to the company. This is the **minimum return** that a company should make on its own investments, to earn the cash flows out of which investors can be paid their return.

Use of WACC

The current **weighted average cost of capital** should generally be used to **evaluate projects**. This is because the **marginal cost of new capital** should be **roughly equal** to the **weighted average cost of current capital**, provided that the **company's capital structure changes slowly** over time.

Exceptions to use of WACC

(i) Where the new investment has **different business risk characteristics** from the company's existing operations, and thus the **return required** by shareholders (**the cost of equity**) might **change** as a result of undertaking the investment.

(ii) Where the **finance** that is raised to fund the new investment **substantially changes** the **capital structure** and the perceived **financial risk** of investing in the company.

Implications for XYZ

XYZ Co is a large listed company, and therefore the **size** of this **investment**, although large, is unlikely to have a significant impact on the capital structure. The project itself is concerned with the **replacement** of **existing assets**, and is therefore unlikely to change the level of business risk faced by the company. There is therefore no reason why the weighted average cost of capital should not be used in this case, and the after tax cost of the new debt should not therefore be used to evaluate the investment.

(d)
To: Board of Directors, XYZ Co
From: Management Accountant
Date: 11 December 20X1
Subject: Choice of financing method

Introduction

This memorandum deals with the factors that should be considered when deciding which of the three methods of financing the grinding machines is the most appropriate.

Operational effects

These can be summarised as follows:

Option 1	Option 2	Option 3
Use of the machines **guaranteed** for the **full 10 year useful life.**	Use of the machines **guaranteed** for the **full 10 year useful life**.	Use of the machines would have to be **renegotiated annually**, with resulting insecurity.
XYZ **tied** into this **technology** for the full 10 year life of the machines. If the technology is superseded, change could be difficult and expensive.	XYZ **tied** into this **technology** for at least eight years of the ten year life of the machines.	The use of a series of annual contracts means that in the event of technological change, XYZ would be able to **adapt quickly** and would not need to write off obsolete plant.
XYZ **responsible** for **maintenance**.	XYZ **responsible** for **maintenance**.	**Lessor responsible** for **maintenance**. This could have quality implications.
Payables' **security** is a **fixed charge** over the machines and a **floating charge** over other assets.	Lessor's security is over the **machines alone.**	Lessor's security is over the **machines alone.**

Financial effects

Option 1	Option 2	Option 3
Interest payments on the debt interest would be **tax allowable**.	The **interest element** of the annual payments would be **allowable** against tax.	Although the lease rentals are higher than under option 2, they would be **fully tax allowable**.
XYZ would be able to **claim tax allowable depreciation** on the purchase of the machines.	**Tax allowable depreciation** is **not available**.	**Tax allowable depreciation** is **not available**.
Annual costs would be **low**, being only the interest payments on the debt.	Annual costs would be **higher** for the first eight years, but would be **insignificant** for the final two years.	**Annual costs** would be the **highest** for each of the ten years.
XYZ would have to **find $8m** to repay the debt at the end of the ten year period. Some of this might be recoverable from machine sale proceeds, but these are uncertain.	There would be **no terminal costs** at the end of the ten year period.	There would be **no terminal costs** at the end of the ten year period.
Key balance sheet ratios may be affected by including **assets** and **debt** on the balance sheet.	Key balance sheet ratios may be affected by including **assets** and **debt** on the balance sheet.	**Assets** and **finance** are **off balance sheet**.

Conclusions

The key factors to be considered are:

(i) **Operational**

Technological **flexibility** may be important, and **responsibility for maintenance** could prove expensive.

(ii) **Cash flow**

The different options have **different cash flow patterns**.

(iii) **Cost**

The total cost of the different options over the ten year life of the project should be evaluated using **discounted cash flow techniques**.

(iv) **Taxation**

The company should consider whether it could use all the **tax allowable depreciation** available under option 1, and whether it has sufficient annual income to benefit from the tax savings on expenses under options 2 and 3.

Signed: Management Accountant

33 D Co

Text references. Cost of capital is covered in Chapter 15.

Top tips. Unusually for gearing and WACC calculations the company has preference shares as well as equity shares and debt. As (a) does not specify which gearing ratio to use, you should begin your answer by stating how you are calculating gearing. Remember that you include reserves when you are calculating gearing using book values, and they should be excluded when you are calculating gearing using market values.

In (b) it is important to set out clearly which formula you're using; it demonstrates to the marker that you understand the principles. You wouldn't however need to define as we have done the symbols used in a formula that you are given on the exam paper. If you were unsure on how to calculate the cost of preference shares, you do so in exactly the same way as you calculate the cost of equity shares with g equalling 0. Note also that you do not adjust the cost of preference share capital for tax, but you must adjust the cost of loan stock for tax.

In (c) any answer on the CAPM must focus on the different types of risk.

In (d) you should consider the viewpoint of the investor as well as the viewpoint of the company.

(a)   The **gearing ratio** can be calculated using the following expression:

$$\text{Gearing} = \frac{\text{Prior charge capital}}{\text{Prior charge capital} + \text{equity}}$$

(i)   **Using book values**, prior charge capital includes:

	Book value $'000
9% loan notes	8,000
7% preference shares	1,000
	9,000

Equity:	
Ordinary share capital	2,000
Share premium account	1,100
Retained earnings	6,550
	9,650

$$\text{Gearing} = \frac{9,000}{9,000 + 9,650} = 48.3\%$$

(ii)   Using **market values**, prior charge capital includes:

	Market value $'000
9% loan notes @ 80c per $1	6,400
7% preference shares @ 77c per $1	770
	7,170

Equity:	
Ordinary shares @ $1.35 per 25c nominal value	10,800

$$\text{Gearing} = \frac{7,170}{7,170 + 10,800} = 39.9\%$$

BPP
LEARNING MEDIA

(b) The **weighted average cost of capital** (WACC) can be found using the following expression:

$$\text{WACC} = k_e\left[\frac{V_E}{V_E + V_P + V_D}\right] + k_{pref}\left[\frac{V_P}{V_E + V_P + V_D}\right] + k_{dnet}\left[\frac{V_D}{V_E + V_P + V_D}\right]$$

where:

k_e	=	cost of equity
k_{pref}	=	cost of preference shares
k_{dnet}	=	cost of debt (after tax)
V_E	=	market value of equity in the firm
V_P	=	market value of preference shares in the firm
V_D	=	market value of debt in the firm

The next step is to calculate the cost of the different sources of capital in D Co:

Cost of equity (k_e)

This can be found using the dividend growth model:

$$k_e = \frac{d_0(1+g)}{p_0} + g$$

where:

d_0	=	current level of dividends
g	=	dividend growth rate in perpetuity
p_0	=	current market price of equity
k_e	=	$\dfrac{10(1+0.09)}{135} + 0.09$
	=	17.1%

Cost of preference shares (k_{pref})

This can be found by dividing the preference dividend rate by the market price of the shares:

$$k_{pref} = \frac{7}{77}$$

$$= 9.1\%$$

Although preference shares are included with prior charge capital, the dividend is not allowable for tax, and therefore no adjustment needs to be made for this.

Cost of loan notes (k_{dnet})

The after tax cost of the loan notes can be found using the following expression:

$$k_{dnet} = \frac{i(1-T)}{p_0}$$

where:

i	=	rate of debenture interest
p_0	=	market price of loan stock
T	=	rate of tax
k_{dnet}	=	$\dfrac{9(1-0.3)}{80}$
	=	7.9%

The WACC can now be calculated:

$$\text{WACC} = \frac{(17.1 \times 10,800)}{17,970} + \frac{(9.1 \times 770)}{17,970} + \frac{(7.9 \times 6,400)}{17,970}$$

$$= 13.5\%$$

(c) **Role of CAPM**

The **capital asset pricing model** (CAPM) provides an alternative to the dividend valuation model in calculating the cost of equity. Unlike the dividend valuation model, the CAPM seeks to differentiate between the various types of risk faced by a firm and to allow for the fact that new projects undertaken may carry a different level of risk from the existing business.

Systematic risk

The model focuses on the level of **systematic risk** attaching to the firm, in other words, that element of risk which is common to all investments and which cannot be avoided by diversification. The model uses the **beta factor** as a measure of an individual share's volatility of expected returns as against the market average. A beta factor of less than 1.0 indicates that the expected volatility is less than that of the market as a whole, and vice versa.

Formulation of model

The model can be formulated as follows:

$$E(r_i) = R_f + \beta_i (E(r_m) - R_f)$$

where: $E(r_i)$ = cost of equity capital
β_i = beta factor for the firm's equity
$E(r_m)$ = market rate of return
R_f = risk free rate of return

Thus the additional information that would be required is as follows.

Beta factor

This can be calculated statistically from historical records of:

(i) The **returns earned** by the **share** in terms of capital gains/losses and dividends
(ii) The **overall returns** earned by the market

Market rate of return

The average annual rate of return on the securities market as a whole. This can be calculated from historical records.

Risk free rate of return

This is generally taken to be the rate of return on government bonds.

(d) **Reasons for using loan notes**

(i) **Loan notes** are a **cheaper form of finance** than preference shares because debenture interest is tax deductible, unlike preference dividends.

(ii) **Loan notes** are **more attractive** to **investors** because they are secured against the company's assets.

(iii) **Debenture holders rank before preference shareholders** in the event of a liquidation.

(iv) **Issue costs** should be **lower for loan notes** than for preference shares.

34 IML Co

Text references. CAPM is covered in Chapter 15 and the efficient market hypothesis in Chapter 18.

Top tips. Although this looks like a question on the CAPM, the final part of the question requires a discussion of the efficient markets hypothesis and you may not have come across this yet in your studies. It is covered in part G of the syllabus and again illustrates that questions may cover different parts of the syllabus.

Note the requirement for the discussion in (c) to be comprehensible to a non-financial manager. Discussion of the assumptions and limitations of CAPM carried most marks in (c), although to score heavily the efficient markets hypothesis and the chairman's assertions also needed to be discussed, and the calculations carried out in (a) and (b) used in support.

(a) The required rate of return on equity can be found using the capital asset pricing model:

$$E(r_i) = R_f + \beta_i (E(r_m) - R_f)$$

AZT Co

$$\begin{aligned} E(r_i) &= 5\% + 0.7(15\% - 5\%) \\ &= \textbf{12\%} \end{aligned}$$

BOR Co

$$\begin{aligned} E(r_i) &= 5\% + 1.4(15\% - 5\%) \\ &= \textbf{19\%} \end{aligned}$$

(b) The beta for IML can be found using the same expression:

$$17\% = 5\% + \beta(15\% - 5\%) \, E(r_i)$$

$$\beta = \frac{(17\% - 5\%)}{(15\% - 5\%)}$$

The beta factor = 1.2

The **beta factor** is a measure of the volatility of the return on a share relative to the stock market. If for example a share price moved at three times the market rate, its beta factor would be 3.0. The beta factor indicates the level of **systematic risk**, the risk of making an investment that cannot be diversified away. It is used in the capital asset pricing model to determine the level of return required by investors; the higher the level of systematic risk, the higher the required level of return.

(c) To: The Chairman
     From: Finance Director
     Date: 20 November 20X1
     Subject: The Capital Asset Pricing Model (CAPM) and stock market reactions

   (i) **Assumptions and limitations of CAPM**

   Diversification

   Under the CAPM, the return required from a security is **related** to its **systematic risk** rather than its total risk. Only the risks that **cannot** be **eliminated** by diversification are **relevant**. The assumption is that investors will hold a **fully diversified portfolio** and therefore deal with the unsystematic risk themselves. However, in practice, markets are **not totally efficient** and investors do not all hold fully diversified portfolios. This means that total risk is relevant to investment decisions, and that therefore the relevance of the CAPM may be limited.

Excess return

In practice, it is difficult to determine the excess return ($R_m - R_f$). **Expected rather than historical returns** should be used, although historical returns are used in practice.

Risk-free rate

It is similarly difficult to **determine the risk-free rate**. A risk-free investment might be a government security; however, interest rates vary with the term of the debt.

Risk aversion

Shareholders are risk averse, and therefore **demand higher returns** in compensation for increased levels of risk.

Beta factors

Beta factors based on historical data may be a **poor basis** for future **decision making**, since evidence suggests that beta values fluctuate over time.

Unusual circumstances

The CAPM is **unable** to **forecast accurately returns for companies** with **low price/earnings ratios**, and to take account of **seasonal 'month-of-the-year' effects** and **'day-of-the-week'** effects that appear to influence returns on shares.

Possible reasons for the apparent discrepancy in betas for AZT Co and BOR Co

The Chairman has expressed the view that AZT Co is a higher risk company than BOR because it operates in overseas markets. This factor gives rise to its **lower beta value**. Its returns are likely to have a **lower correlation** with those of the stock market as a whole, and therefore it has a **lower level of systematic risk**. It is also possible that the **level of total risk** faced by AZT Co is lower because it is **better diversified** than BOR.

Efficient markets hypothesis

The way in which the stock market responds to information released by a company can be understood with reference to the **efficient markets hypothesis** (EMH). It is generally accepted that most stock markets demonstrate a **semi-strong form** of **market efficiency**. This means that share prices **respond immediately** to all **publicly available information**, but not to information available only to insiders.

Implications of efficient markets hypothesis

- It is **not possible** consistently to **beat the market** (on a risk-adjusted basis) without the use of inside information

- **Past share prices** are **not** a **predictor** of future share prices

- The price of a share reflects **market expectations** of future performance

- Investors behave **rationally** and are not deceived by manipulation of accounting figures

(ii) **IML's position**

This can help to explain the situation of IML Co. The effect of an announcement of either profit or loss on the share price will not depend simply on the **magnitude** of the profit or loss, but in the relationship between the **announcement** and what the **market was expecting**. In this case, the company announced a loss and the share price rose. The market might have been expecting the **loss** to be **much larger** than it actually was, and the share price therefore adjusted in response to what was effectively good news. Alternatively, it could be that investors looked not simply at the loss, but at the **future prospects** of the company and decided that these were better than had been expected. The share price would then rise accordingly.

Signed: Finance Director

35 DEA Co

Text reference. Cost of capital is covered in Chapter 15.

Top tips. This question tests both your ability to calculate the cost of equity, debt and the WACC, and your understanding of the issues surrounding choice of a discount rate for investment appraisal. You also need to be able to discuss the relationships between dividends, retentions and financing policy. In (a) make sure you treat the cost of debt as redeemable. In part (b) focus your answer specifically on the comments made by the directors.

(a)   **Cost of debt**

Payments to be made over the next year prior to redemption

	$
Interest net of tax ($12.5m × 8% × (1 − 0.3))	700,000
Payment on redemption	12,500,000
	13,200,000

The current market value of the debt is $12.25m ($12.5m × 98%)

The cost of debt (k_d) can be found as follows:

$$\frac{\$13.2m}{(1+k_d)} = \$12.25m$$

$1 + k_d \quad = \$13.2m/\$12.25m$

$k_d \qquad = 7.755\%$

Cost of equity

This can be estimated using the dividend growth model.

$$\text{20X2 dividend} \times (1 + g)^4 = \text{20X6 dividend}$$

$$35.64 \times (1 + g)^4 = 45.00$$

$$(1 + g)^4 = 45.00 \div 35.64$$

$$\sqrt[4]{(1+g)} = 1.2626$$

$$1 + g = 1.06$$

$$g = 6\%$$

The dividend growth model can now be used:

where: $P_0 \quad = \$5.50 - \$0.45 = \$5.05$

             $d_0 \quad = \$0.45$

             $g \quad = 6\%$

$$k_e = \frac{d_0(1+g)}{P_0} + g$$

$$k_e = \frac{0.45(1+0.06)}{5.05} + 0.06$$

$$k_e = 15.45\%$$

Weighted average cost of capital (WACC)

Weightings will be based on market values.

$$\text{WACC} = k_e\left[\frac{V_E}{V_E + V_D}\right] + k_d\left[\frac{V_D}{V_E + V_D}\right]$$

where: $k_e = 15.45\%$
$k_d = 7.755\%$
$V_E = \$12m \times \$5.05 \quad = \$60.6m$
$V_D = \$12.5m \times 0.98 \quad = \$12.25m$

$$\text{WACC} = \frac{(15.45\% \times 60.6)}{(60.6 + 12.25)} + \frac{(7.775\% \times 12.25)}{(60.6 + 12.25)}$$

$$= 12.85\% + 1.31\%$$

$$= 14.16\%$$

(b) To: Directors of DEA Co
From: Treasury team member
Date: 17 November 20X1
Subject: Selection of a discount rate and dividend policy

This memorandum addresses the issues raised by the individual directors at the recent meeting.

(i) **The Marketing Director**

Assumptions of WACC

The weighted average cost of capital (WACC) does reflect the **average cost** of acquiring funds. Use of the WACC as the **discount rate** is the normal approach in appraising potential new investments. However, this is based on the assumption that the new investments are **small** in relation to the size of the company, and that they carry a **similar level of risk** to the existing business.

Japanese contract

The Japanese contract does not fulfil these conditions. First of all, it is **large** in relation to the size of the company, with revenues expected to amount to 25% of sales. Secondly, since this represents a **diversification** into a **new market**, it is possible that it will have **higher operating risk** than alternative investments. There is also **foreign currency risk** associated with the project, and, due to the size of the contract, the company will need to raise additional finance.

Risk analysis

It is therefore recommended that a **more detailed analysis of the risks and sensitivities** associated with the investment be made. If this suggests that the level of risk is significantly greater than for alternative UK projects, then the discount rate used should be adjusted to reflect this.

(ii) **The Production Director**

Cost of finance

The cost of finance used for a specific project should not be used as the discount rate. This approach ignores the effect of both undertaking the project, and the new source of finance, on the company as a whole. **Bank borrowings** are **cheaper** than **equity finance**, but an increase in borrowings will lead to an **increase** in the **level** of **financial gearing**, and therefore to an **increase in the financial risk** of the company. This will cause the **cost of equity** to **rise**, and this will be reflected in the weighted average cost of capital.

Investment and financing

If the project has a higher level of risk than the existing business of the company, then this will magnify the effect on the cost of capital. It is a good principle to **separate** the **investment decision** from the **financing decision** in project evaluation. The project should be evaluated from the point of view of its effect upon the cash flows of the company as a whole, while the financing decision will involve different considerations of the effect of the new funds upon the financial structure of the company.

(iii) **The Chairman**

Capital asset pricing model

The capital asset pricing model is not a means of calculating the weighted average cost of capital, but can be used as an alternative to the dividend growth model (used above) to calculate the **cost of equity**. Unlike the dividend growth model, the CAPM seeks to differentiate between the various types of risk faced by a firm and to allow for the fact that new projects undertaken may carry a different level of risk from the existing business.

Systematic risk

The model focuses on the level of **systematic risk** attaching to the firm, in other words that element of risk which is common to all investments and which cannot be avoided by diversification. The model uses the **beta factor** as a measure of an individual share's volatility of expected returns as against the market average. A beta factor of less than 1.0, for example, indicates that the expected volatility is less than that of the market as a whole.

Formulation of model

The model can be formulated as follows:

$$E(r_i) = R_f + \beta_i (E(r_m) - R_f)$$

Where: $E(r_i)$ = cost of equity capital
   β_i = beta factor for the firm's equity
   $E(r_m)$ = market rate of return
   R_f = risk free rate of return

Thus the additional information that would be required is as follows.

Beta factor

This can be calculated statistically from historical records of:

(1)   The **returns earned** by the **share** in terms of capital gains/losses and dividends
(2)   The **overall returns** earned by the market

Market rate of return

This is the average annual rate of return on the securities market as a whole. This can be calculated from historical records.

Risk free rate of return

This is generally taken to be the rate of return on government bonds.

(iv) **The Finance Director**

Retentions and dividends

It is true that if the company cannot earn a better return than could be made by individual investors, then funds should be returned to the shareholders. However it is incorrect to turn this statement round and to argue that retentions should be preferred to dividends. Investors require **dividends** to provide a **return** on their investment. They may lose confidence in the company if there are **wide fluctuations** in the level of dividends from year to year. Substituting small individual share sales for dividends has a **high transaction cost**, and may **increase** investors' **tax liabilities**.

Cost of retentions

The Finance Director also implies that there is no cost of finance associated with retentions. However, this is not the case – the **cost of retentions** is in fact the **same** as the **cost of equity**. It is not therefore cheaper to finance new investment using retentions rather than debt.

Need for both

In practice, the company needs cash both for **new investment** and to **pay dividends**. The best way in which to finance the cash requirements will depend on the financial structure and tax position of the company.

Investment and financing

The appropriate discount rate to use for evaluating the contract has been discussed above. However, the cost of raising new finance should be looked at **separately** from the **investment decision** itself, and the effect of the project upon the business risk profile of the company must also be taken into account.

Signed: Treasury team member

36 KJI

Text references. Shareholder ratios are covered in Chapter 1 and cost of capital in Chapters 15 and 16.

Top tips. The main difficulty in part (a) is answering all the parts in the time available; providing explanations, uses and limitations is a lot to do in the time you are given. You would maximise your mark-scoring by giving some commentary on every ratio as well as calculating them.

Part (b) is asking you not to describe the changes but to **explain why** they happened. It thus tests your imagination and your understanding of the most plausible reasons for changes – a share capital increase is caused by a share issue, but what sort of share issue? The question also tests your understanding of the **interaction** of various ratios; a decision to increase dividends may leave the dividend yield unchanged, but it may cause the dividend cover to fall. You also would gain credit by linking events (company buying back shares) with impact on market and share price (market becomes uncertain of company's intentions.)

Part (c) is another weighted average cost of capital calculation with the complications of preference shares and tax. Part (d) demonstrates why WACC should be used by companies for assessing investment. If you are unsure about this, think about the effect of the new funding and investments on the overall capital structure of the firm, and the implications of this for raising finance in the future.

(a)

	Data:	20X6	20X7	20X8	20X9
1	Equity earnings ($m)	200	225	205	230
2	Number of shares (m)	2,000	2,100	2,100	1,900
3	Price per share (cents)	220	305	290	260
4	Dividend per share (cents)	5	7	8	8
	Solution:				
5	Earnings per share (=1 ÷ 2)	10.0c	10.7c	9.8c	12.1c
	Dividend yield (= 4 ÷ 3)	2.3%	2.3%	2.8%	3.1%
	Dividend cover (= 5 ÷ 4)	2.0	1.5	1.2	1.5 times
	Price/earnings ratio (=3 ÷ 5)	22.0	28.5	29.6	21.5 times

Earnings per share

Earnings per share (EPS) shows the amount of profit after tax attributable to each ordinary share. Although a high EPS generally indicates success, care must be taken in interpreting the trend in EPS when there have been **share issues**, especially rights issues at heavily discounted prices or bonus issues, both of which result in a fall in EPS. Similar problems are encountered when warrants or convertible loan notes are issued.

Dividend yield

The **dividend yield** shows the ordinary dividend as a rate of return on the share value. The figures shown in this example are *after* basic rate income tax, whereas they are normally shown gross. The figure is of limited use because it shows **only part of the return** to the **equity investor**.

Dividend cover

The **dividend cover** shows how many times bigger the EPS is than the dividend per share. A **high dividend cover** shows that a **large proportion** of **equity earnings** is being **reinvested for growth**.

Price/earnings ratio

The **price/earnings ratio** (P/E ratio) shows how many times bigger the share price is than the EPS. In general, the bigger the EPS, the more the share is in demand, though care must be taken when making comparisons because whereas EPS is a historical result, the **share price** is **based** on **future expectations** and is affected by both risk and growth factors. Consequently, abnormal results can often arise from a crude use of P/E ratios.

(b) **Trends in 20X7**

In 20X7, **share capital was increased by 5%,** probably through a **rights issue**. Equity earnings increased more than proportionately, resulting in a 7% increase in EPS, indicating a successful year. **Demand** for the company's **shares rose swiftly**, either because of a **general stock market rise** or because of **high expectations** of KJI's future growth, and the share price rose by approximately 40%. This caused a **big rise in P/E** and allowed a 40% increase in dividend per share with no fall in dividend yield. The dividend cover fell, however, because the dividend increased much more than earnings.

Trends in 20X8

The company's **earnings and EPS fell in 20X8**, either because of normal cyclical business risks or possibly because the high 20X7 dividend left insufficient cash for reinvestment. However, the company gave a 'bullish' signal to the market by **increasing** its **dividend per share**, indicating future prospects of a swift recovery and increased growth. As a result, the **dividend yield increased** and, although the share price fell in line with earnings, there was no disproportionate drop in demand for the company's shares, as shown by the stability of the P/E.

Trends in 20X9

There was 12% **earnings growth** in 20X9. The company used some of its cash to **buy back ordinary shares**. This is possibly because it offered shareholders the choice between a cash and a scrip dividend. Share capital reduced by about 10%, resulting in a big increase in earnings per share. Although 20X9 was a successful year for earnings, **demand for the company's shares fell**, as shown by the drop in share price and P/E. It is possible that the market has become **uncertain** of the company's **future plans**, as a result of the share issue and share buy-back in quick succession.

(c) **Assumptions**

It is assumed that the **market prices** of the shares and loan notes are **quoted excluding dividend** and interest. Since the WACC is to be calculated based on market values, the cost of reserves can be ignored.

Cost of equity

The dividend valuation model taking into account growth will be used.

$$k_e = \frac{d_1}{p_0} + g$$

where:			
	k_e	=	cost of equity
	d_1	=	next year's dividends
	g	=	annual rate of growth in dividends
	p_0	=	market price of shares (ex div)
In this case:	k_e	=	$4/80 + 0.12$
		=	17.0%

Cost of preference shares

	k_{pref}	=	d/p_0
where:	k_{pref}	=	cost of preference shares
	d	=	preference dividend (9c)
	p_0	=	market price of shares (72c)
	k_{pref}	=	$9/72$
		=	12.5%

Cost of loan notes

It is assumed that the loan notes are irredeemable. The after tax cost to the company will be calculated.

$$k_{dnet} = \frac{i(1-T)}{p_0}$$

where:			
	k_{dnet}	=	cost of loan notes
	I	=	annual interest payment (14c)
	p_0	=	market price of loan notes (100c)
	T	=	rate of tax (33%)
	k_{dnet}	=	$\dfrac{14(1-0.33)}{100}$
		=	9.4%

Weighted average cost of capital (WACC)

	No in issue	Market price	Market Value
	$	$	$
Equity	10,400,000	0.80	8,320,000
Preference shares	4,500,000	0.72	3,240,000
Loan notes	5,000,000	1.00	5,000,000
			16,560,000

$$\text{WACC} = 17.0 \left[\frac{8,320}{16,560} \right] + 12.5 \left[\frac{3,240}{16,560} \right] + 9.4 \left[\frac{5,000}{16,560} \right]$$

$$= 13.8\%$$

(d) **Required rate of return**

It is not usually correct to regard the **required rate of return** for an individual project as the cost of the actual source of funds that will be used to finance it, even where the funds can be traced directly. Debt is cheaper than equity only because there is an **equity base** which takes the risk – if the equity funds were not there then the company could not borrow. Each year some profits should be retained to increase the equity base, thus allowing further borrowing to take place. The borrowing is not independent of equity funds, and thus it is appropriate to combine the two in arriving at the cost of capital to be used in project appraisal.

WACC

The WACC reflects the company's **long-term capital structure**, and therefore capital costs. The capital structure generally changes only very slowly over time, and therefore the marginal cost of new capital should be approximately equal to the WACC. The **WACC** is therefore a more appropriate yardstick for the evaluation of new projects.

(ii) Managers should be **discouraged** from attempting to **manipulate** their **accounting results**, since the truth will be realised quickly, and prices adjusted accordingly.

(iii) The company may concentrate on producing **constantly improving financial results** at the expense of the company's **responsibility** to **other stakeholders** in the business, such as its employees and the environment.

37 WEB Co

Text references. Cost of capital is covered in Chapter 15, capital structure theories in Chapter 16 and sources of finance in Chapter 12.

Top tips. In part (a) make sure you recognise that the debt is redeemable and use market values for the WACC. In the written parts of the question, you must focus on the question requirements and not just write everything you know about different sources of finance.

(a) **Cost of equity**

$$k_e = \frac{d_0(1+g)}{P_0} + g$$

$$= \frac{1(1+0.04)}{10.40} + 0.04$$

$$= 14\%$$

Cost of debt

Year		Cash Flow $	Discount Factor 10%	PV $	Discount Factor 5%	PV $
0	Market value	(100.84)	1.000	(100.84)	1.000	(100.84)
1-3	Interest	6.30	2.487	15.67	2.723	17.15
3	Capital repayment	100.00	0.751	75.10	0.864	86.40
				(10.07)		2.71

$$k_d = \left(5 + \left(\left(\frac{2.71}{2.71 - -10.07}\right) \times (10-5)\right)\right)$$

$$= 6.06\%$$

WACC

$$k_0 = k_e\left(\frac{V_E}{V_E + V_D}\right) + k_d\left(\frac{V_E}{V_E + V_D}\right)$$

$$V_E = 100 \times 10.40$$
$$= \$1,040 \text{ million}$$

$$V_D = 200 \times 1.0084$$
$$= \$201.68 \text{ million}$$

$$k_0 = 14\left(\frac{1,040}{(1,040 + 201.68)}\right) + 6.06\left(\frac{201.68}{(1,040 + 201.68)}\right)$$

$$= 12.71\%$$

(b) (i) **Cost of equity**

The **cost of equity** will **rise** if the company takes out extra loans. The **interest and debt repayment** burden will increase the risk that WEB will not be able to pay dividends, and also increase the risk that WEB will run into financial difficulties through not being able to meet its loan commitments. If liquidation occurs, debtholders will rank before equityholders. Equity investors will demand an increased level of return to compensate for this risk.

(ii) **Cost of debt**

According to the traditional view, the **cost of debt** will remain unchanged up to a certain level of gearing. Above that level it will increase, because of the financial risk that the company will not be able to meet its commitments, and hence interest or even principal lent may be jeopardised. In WEB's case the net assets are $50 million less than the level of net assets.

(iii) **Weighted average cost of capital**

According to the traditional view, the **weighted average cost of capital** will fall initially as debt capital is introduced, because debt at first has a lower cost than equity, being a lower-risk investment. Ultimately however the weighted average cost of capital will rise as risk levels increase, resulting in the rise in the cost of equity becoming more significant, and ultimately the cost of debt will rise. The **optimum level of gearing** is where **the company's weighted average cost of capital is minimised**.

(c)   **Bank loan**

A **bank loan** is a loan of a specific amount from a bank for a set period. **Repayment** may be in **instalments** or at the end of the **loan**, and **interest** will be payable on the amount outstanding. Security is likely to be in the form of a **floating charge** over the company's assets.

Loan notes

Loan notes are issued by the company, backed by a **written acknowledgement** of the debt given under seal containing **provisions** on **payment of interest** and the **terms of repayment of principal.** It may be held by more than one lender. Loan notes of listed companies can be **traded**, and they may be **redeemable** (repayable at a certain time), **convertible** (can be converted into share capital at a certain time) or **irredeemable.**

The cost of debt may differ because:

(i)   Loan note holders can **trade** the loan notes and may therefore accept a lower yield in return for **better liquidity**.

(ii)   The **security** that the bank demands may differ from the security given to the loan note holders. A lower rate of interest may be accepted in return for stronger security.

(iii)   The loan notes cover a **different period** from the bank loan. When the loan notes were issued, expectations about the **level of interest rates** and the **business and financial risks faced by WEB** may have been different.

(d)   **Convertibles**

Companies normally issue convertibles in the expectation that the **holders will exercise their options**. Convertibles can therefore be seen as a form of **delayed equity**.

(i)   They are **attractive** to the firm when the price of the ordinary shares is abnormally low at the date of issue, and at times when to issue a further tranche of equity would result in a significant drop in earnings per share.

(ii)   However they also carry the **risk** that the **share price will not rise in line** with expectations at the time of issue and that holders will not therefore convert.

(iii)   If the loan notes are dated, then the company must have funds in place to allow redemption on the due date.

(iv)   Convertibles also have a short-term benefit in that **interest payments** are **allowable against tax**.

Strategic implications of convertibles

Convertibles therefore may form part of the strategy of a company whose objective is to raise new equity, but which for various reasons does not wish to go directly to the market in the short term.

(i)   They are often preferable to straight loan notes since they **do not commit the company indefinitely** to the payment of large interest bills.

(ii)   They further allow the company to **widen the investment base** by attracting investors looking for a guaranteed short term income plus the possibility of a capital gain at a later date.

38 CAP Co

> **Text references.** The capital asset pricing model is covered in Chapter 15.
>
> **Top tips.** In (a) you should give a brief definition of the beta factor and what it measures. This will help you to explain the implications of a beta factor of less than one. Remember that preference shares do not count as equity for these purposes and should be ignored at this stage of the calculations.
>
> In (b) there are a number of valid approaches that can be used to find the cost of the loan notes. The most usual of these, using the internal rate of return, is described in the suggested solution. Using 5% as we have means you only need to calculate one rate. It is equally correct to use a higher and lower rate, say 7% and 4%, and then to use interpolation to find the discount rate at which the NPV approaches zero.
>
> In (c) you may find it helpful to think in terms of financial factors and factors affecting the level of business risk when structuring your answer.
>
> **Easy marks.** Limitations of CAPM should always represent straightforward marks.

(a)   The cost of equity can be found using the following formula:

$$E(r_i) = R_f + \beta_i (E(r_m) - R_f)$$

where $E(r_i)$ is the cost of equity capital – expected equity return
  R_f is the risk-free rate of return
  $E(r_m)$ is the return from the market as a whole
  β is the beta factor of the individual security

Here: R_f =   5% (annual yield on treasury bills)
  $E(r_m)$ =   15%
  β_i =   0.8
  $E(r_i)$ =   5% + (15% – 5%)0.8
    =   13%

The required rate of return on equity of CAP Co at 30 September 20X2 is therefore 13%.

Beta factor levels

The beta factor is a measure of **systematic risk**, that is, the element of risk that cannot be avoided by **diversification**. The beta factor measures the **variability in returns** for a given security in relation to the variation in returns for the market as a whole.

A beta factor of 1.0 means that if the market goes up by x%, all other things being equal, one would expect the return on the security to go up by x% as well. A beta factor of less than 1.0 means that the return on the security is likely to be less variable than the return on the market as a whole. A beta value of 0.8 means that if the market returns go up by 5%, the return on the security would only be expected to go up by 4% (5% × 0.8). Similarly, if the market returns fall by 5%, the return on the security would only be expected to fall by 4%.

(b)   **Weighted average cost of capital**

The weighted average cost of capital (WACC) is the **average cost** of the **company's finance** weighted according to the proportion each element bears to the total pool of capital. Weighting is usually based on market values, current yields and costs after tax. Where market values can be used, as in this case, reserves can be ignored.

Equity

The cost of equity has already been calculated at 13%.

The market value of equity (V_E) is the number of shares in issue multiplied by the market price (ex div):

$$V_E = 200m \times \$3$$
$$= \$600m$$

Preference shares

Preference shares are irredeemable. The interest on preference shares is not tax deductible. The cost of the preference shares (k_{Pref}) is therefore:

$$k_{pref} = D/p_0$$

where: D = annual dividend in perpetuity
         P_0 = current ex div price
     k_{pref} = 9%/0.90
         = 10%

The market value of the preference shares (V_P) is the number of shares in issue multiplied by the market price (ex div):

$$V_P = 50m \times \$0.90$$
$$= \$45m$$

Loan notes

The loan notes pay interest of 8%, which is allowable against tax. Tax is paid at the end of the year in which taxable profits arise, in other words, at the same time as the interest payment at the end of year 1.

Since the net cost of the interest is 5.6% (8% × 0.7), and the current market price of the notes is just above par, we will try an initial rate of return of 5%.

Year		Cash flow $	5% disc factors	Present value $	
0	Market value	(100.57)		1.00	(100.57)
1	Interest	8.00	0.952	7.62	
1	Tax saved	(2.40)	0.952	(2.28)	
1	Redemption	100.00	0.952	95.20	
Net present value					(0.03)

This net present value is virtually zero, and therefore the effective cost of the loan notes is 5%.

The market value of the loan notes (V_D) is the number of units in issue multiplied by the market price:

$$V_D = 250m \times \$100.57/100.00$$
$$= \$251.4m$$

WACC

	MV
Equity	600.0
Preference shares	45.0
Loan notes	251.4
Total	896.4

$$WACC = k_e \left[\frac{V_E}{V_E + V_P + V_D} \right] + k_{pref} \left[\frac{V_P}{V_E + V_P + V_D} \right] + k_d \left[\frac{V_D}{V_E + V_P + V_D} \right]$$

$$= 13 \left[\frac{600.0}{896.4} \right] + 10 \left[\frac{45}{896.4} \right] + 5 \left[\frac{251.4}{896.4} \right]$$

$$= 10.6\%$$

(c) **Factors affecting equity beta**

CAP Co's equity beta will be affected by factors that change the perceived **volatility in returns** to the ordinary shareholders. These will include **financial factors**, such as the **change in gearing**, and other factors related to effect of the new investment on the systematic risk of the company's activities.

Rise in gearing

Following the new issue of loan notes, the **gearing will rise**. This in turn is likely to affect the **volatility** of the returns to equity in relation to the market index. As a consequence, the beta may rise.

Effect of diversification

Since the returns on the campsite business are likely to have a very **low correlation** with those of the existing farming business, the effect of the new investment will be to **smooth out the earnings pattern**. This will reduce the volatility of the returns to equity. However the beta value will be affected by how the **campsite returns vary** in relation to **returns on the market portfolio**, and they may **vary more or less** than the **returns from the farming activities**. The equity beta will be the weighted average of the betas of the two sorts of activity.

Refinancing

As well as raising new debt, the company also has to redeem its existing debt in 20X3. If it replaces existing debt with similar debt, there will be little or no effect on the beta. However, if the debt is **replaced by equity** and gearing reduced, volatility of returns on equity and hence the **beta factor** are likely to fall.

Investor perceptions

This is a major diversification by CAP, and investors may perceive this to be a **risky strategy**. As a consequence in the short-term, the beta could rise to reflect this. Investors may feel that CAP managers **lack the skills required** to manage campsites, as managing camping sites is a very different job from farming. As a consequence this will increase the risk of the new investment, and hence the equity beta may rise. There are also **start-up costs** associated with the new investments. These may depress the profits in the first year of trading, which in turn may cause investors to perceive the new business to be riskier than it really is. The effect of this will be to cause a short-term rise in the beta value.

Industry

Events within the farming and tourism industries, and perceptions of how they are doing, may also affect the beta levels.

(d) **Diversification**

Under the CAPM, the return required from a security is **related** to its **systematic risk** rather than its total risk. Only the risks that **cannot** be **eliminated** by diversification are **relevant.** The assumption is that investors will hold a **fully diversified portfolio** and therefore deal with the unsystematic risk themselves. However, in practice, markets are **not totally efficient** and investors do not all hold fully diversified portfolios. This means that total risk is relevant to investment decisions, and that therefore the relevance of the CAPM may be limited.

Excess return

In practice, it is difficult to determine the excess return ($R_m - R_f$). **Expected rather than historical returns** should be used, although historical returns are used in practice.

Risk-free rate

It is similarly difficult to **determine the risk-free rate**. A risk-free investment might be a government security; however, interest rates vary with the term of the debt.

Risk aversion

Shareholders are risk averse, and therefore **demand higher returns** in compensation for increased levels of risk.

Beta factors

Beta factors based on historical data may be a **poor basis** for future **decision making**, since evidence suggests that beta values fluctuate over time.

Unusual circumstances

The CAPM is unable to forecast accurately returns for companies with low price/earnings ratios, and to take account of seasonal 'month-of-the-year' effects and 'day-of-the-week' effects that appear to influence returns on shares.

39 Question with student answer: MC

REPORT

To: Directors of MC
From: Independent Consultant
Date: May 20X0
Title: Valuation of MC

Introduction

This report will discuss the advantages and disadvantages of a flotation compared to the direct selling of shares.

It will analyse a range of potential share prices that could be used, explaining how they have been arrived at and any assumptions used or drawbacks to the method/

Finally an appropriate course of action will be recommended.

Flotation

Advantages

One of the key advantages of floating the company is that the profile and public image of the company may be raised, and arguably it could be viewed more favourably.

There is also the ability to increase growth through mergers or takeovers of other listed companies once MC has been floated.

Floating on the stock market rather than selling shares directly may lead to a much more diverse range of shareholders and therefore limit the dilution of control that may be experienced through a direct sale.

Disadvantages

There is substantial increased pressure for short-term results once a company is floated with shareholders demanding quick results which could be detrimental to the company's long-term prospects.

There are huge costs involved with floating a company. There are lawyers and accountants fees, as well as lots of criteria to meet and it can be very lengthy process taking up considerable time. There is also likely to be underwriting costs involved.

Direct sale

Advantages

This option would have much lower transaction costs, and it would also limit the restrictions and regulations placed on the company, such as those required by corporate governance.

Disadvantages

It may be difficult to find an appropriate buyer for the business that wishes to invest such a large amount. It is also likely to be more difficult to agree an appropriate price, as will be discussed later. On the stock market using an offer for sale. The company has a more straightforward method of determining the "right" price.

A new purchaser would undoubtedly have considerable control in the company and this could lead to managers being demotivated and could negatively affect staff morale and productivity.

Valuations

Assets method

Appendix A shows that based on the net assets in the business, the company can be valued at £6.00 per share.

This method is relatively straightforward and simple to calculate. However, the values used are book values and therefore due to the subjectivity and valuation in depreciation, may not provide a true and fair reflection of the company's real worth.

This method also does not reflect the value of human capital within the business. Many staff are the leading experts in their field and their expertise is helping the business to add value.

Overall, this method may be undervaluing the business.

P/E method

This method values a company based on its current earnings multiplied by the price earnings ratio.

MC is not listed and does not have a share price and this can therefore not properly be calculated.

An assumption has been made that MC's P/E ratio would be similar to that of a competitor and this results in a share price of £12.25.

Despite the P/E method being the most common approach, it is not prudent to use this figure due to considerable differences between MC and the competitor, such as a lower forecast growth rate, lower earnings and dividends per share last year and differences in the nature of operations, eg the competitor has no research capability.

NPV method

The NPV method values a company based on the discounted future value of dividends (although cash flows or profits after tax can be used).

This method has produced a value of £8.49 per share.

Theoretically this is the most superior method, with it reflecting the time value of money and reflecting all future cash flows. True of cash flow, not dividend method.

There are still several limitations of this approach though. A beta co-efficient was required during calculation and a proxy number from the competitor had to be used which is likely to be inaccurate for the previously stated reasons and due to different gearings.

Also constant growth had o be assumed which may change and the cost of equity was also a "rule of thumb" rather than completely accurate.

APPENDIX A

Valuations

Assets method

$$\text{Net asset value} = £60m$$

$$\text{Value per share} = \frac{£60m}{10m} = 600p$$

P/E method

Based on last year:

$$\text{Earnings} \times \text{P/E ratio} = £0.75 \times 10m \text{ shares} = £7.5 \times 16.3 = £122.25m$$

$$\text{Value per share} = £122.25m \div 10m = £12.25$$

$$\text{P/E ratio of competitor} = \frac{\text{Market price of share}}{\text{EPS}} = \frac{980}{60} = 16.3$$

NPV method

$$\frac{D_1}{k_e - g} = \frac{£0.55 \times 1.08}{0.15 - 0.08} = £8.49 \text{ per share}$$

$$\text{Total company value} = 8.49 \times 10m = £84.9m$$

$$K_{eg} = R_F + (R_m - R_F)\beta G$$

$$= 5\% + (12\% - 5\%) \times 1.25$$

$$= 13.75\%$$

Recommendations

If the Directors decide that a floatation is the most appropriate course of action then an offer for sale can be used to determine the relevant share price that will be accepted by the market, however as discussed earlier and floatation is by no means the easier or cheaper option.

If a direct sale is chosen then a price will need to be negotiated with the buyer, likely to at last 600p per share.

BPP answer

Text references. Business valuation is covered in Chapter 15 and equity issues in Chapter 12.

Top tips. This lengthy question addresses a number of areas of knowledge, including share valuation, and the issues surrounding a stock market flotation. The answer is required in a report format, and you should map out an appropriate structure that will allow you to address all the key issues as succinctly as possible.

Important points brought out by the discussion are when each method is useful and the **problems** with the figures used (for example balance sheets not including intangible assets, difficulties with figures of comparable companies).

Note that the discussion in (b) focuses on the aims of shareholders and management. A conclusion, recommending a method and price, would be essential even if the question had not required it.

Student answer. The student answer would have scored a very comfortable pass with 16 or 17 marks, although tackling the question in the wrong order would have irritated the marker. The direct comparison that BPP uses to answer (b) is a better technique than discussing each in turn.

It is reasonable, if pessimistic, to use the competitor's P/E ratio, although BPP's answer explains why a more optimistic answer may be better and suggests a possible figure, which the student doesn't do; doing a calculation and then saying it's not a very good guide is a limited approach, when you could do better.

The main weakness in the student answer is the confusion of the dividend valuation model with the cash flow (NPV) model; the two may give very different results depending on the company's dividend policy.

Easy marks. Knowing the advantages and limitations of each valuation method always earns marks in this question.

Marking scheme

		Marks
(a)	3-4 marks for each method discussed. Max 10 for discussions not supported by calculations	16
(b)	Up to 2 marks for each advantage/disadvantage/point of comparison	6
(c)	Reasonable conclusions based on previous analysis	$\underline{3}$
		$\underline{\underline{25}}$

To: Board of Directors, MC
From: Independent Consultant
Date: 31 December 20X0
Re: Valuation of MC

Introduction

This report deals with the alternative methods available for the valuation of the shares in the company. It also seeks to highlight some of the key issues to be addressed in arriving at an appropriate valuation for this type of company, and looks at the relative merits of public flotation versus an outright sale of the business.

(a) **Company valuation**

There are four main valuation techniques that could be appropriate in this situation:

- Net assets basis
- Price/earnings ratio
- Dividend valuation model
- Discounting the future earnings stream

These will be discussed in more detail below.

(i) **Net assets basis**

This method arrives at a price for the business on the basis of the **market value** of the **asset base**. It is most commonly used to arrive at a **break-up value** for businesses with a significant amount of fixed assets. However, it is **less appropriate for service businesses**, and in particular for those in which the majority of the value is in the form of human and/or intellectual capital. In the latter type of company, a net assets valuation can be attempted if the intangibles are included as assets in the balance sheet. However, a significant part of the value of MC resides in its research division, and this is not reflected at all in the company's present balance sheet.

Although it could be argued that items such as brands should be included in the balance sheet so as to make the market more aware of the true value of the company, in reality it is extremely difficult both to **arrive** at and to **retain** an appropriate measure of these types of items.

A further argument against the incorporation of this type of intangible is that if the company is **publicly quoted**, and if the market shows **semi-strong or strong form efficiency**, then the market price of the shares should reflect this information in any case.

In view of these points, there is little point in attempting a net assets valuation for MC at the present time. The inappropriateness of this can be illustrated with reference to the competitor, which would have a theoretical net assets based valuation of £75m as compared with a market capitalisation of £196m (£9.80 share price × 20m shares in issue).

(ii) **Price/earnings ratio**

This method **compares the earnings information** of the company with that of other **companies of similar size** and characteristics that operate in the same markets, to arrive at an appropriate market price for the shares. The information that has been provided for the quoted competitor will be used to arrive at an initial price, but this will need to be adjusted to reflect the fact that the competitor lacks MC's research capability.

The **price/earnings (P/E) ratio** is calculated by **dividing the market price of the shares** by the **earnings per share**. The competitor has a P/E ratio of 16.3 (980p/60p). Although this is likely to be above the average for quoted industrial companies as a whole, it does not appear to be unreasonably high for the medical sector. Given that MC is forecasting better growth prospects than the competitor, and also has a research capability, it seems reasonable to value the company on a P/E of around 18 times. This would value MC at £135m (18 × 75p × 10m shares in issue). However, if the shares were to be offered on the open market, it would be prudent to price them at a discount to this to reflect the fact that the company would be a new entrant to the stock market, despite an eleven year trading history. Pricing at a discount will also make the issue more attractive to investors and thereby help to obtain a good take-up of shares.

Valuation on a P/E of 18 implies a price of £13.50 per share. If the shares were to be offered at a discount of, say, 15%, this would result in an offer price of around £11.50 per share, and a market capitalisation of £115m.

(iii) **Dividend valuation model**

The dividend valuation model has the central assumption that the **market value** of shares is **directly related** to the **expected future dividends** on those shares. It can be expressed as:

$$P_0 = \frac{d_0(1+g)}{(k_e - g)}$$

Since the shares are not yet quoted, it is **not possible to say** exactly what the **shareholders' net cost of capital** is likely to be. However, given the comments about comparability above, it might be reasonable to use the competitor's data to obtain an estimate.

$$\beta_u = \beta_g \left[\frac{V_E}{V_E + V_D (1-t)} \right] \text{ can be used as debt is risk-free, and } \beta_d = 0$$

$$\beta_u = 1.25 \left[\frac{80}{80 + 20(1-0.3)} \right]$$

$$= 1.064$$

Regearing for MC

$$\beta_g = \beta_u \times \left[\frac{(V_E + V_D (1-t))}{V_E} \right]$$

$$= 1.064 \left[\frac{90 + 10(1-0.3)}{90} \right]$$

$$= 1.147$$

Substituting in CAPM

$$k_e = 5\% + (12 - 5) \, 1.147$$
$$= 13.03\%, \text{ say } 13\%$$

This cost of equity can now be used in the dividend valuation model to estimate the market value of MC:

$$P_0 = \frac{d_0 (1+g)}{(k_e - g)}$$

$$P_0 = \frac{(55p \times 10m) \times (1 + 8\%)}{(13\% - 8\%)}$$

$$P_0 = £118.8m$$

The dividend valuation model values the company at £118.8m, or £11.88 per share. This assumes a growth rate of 8%, however in reality the **potential growth** rate may be **higher** since the company is currently evaluating investments at a discount rate that is above the estimated cost of capital. This means that it may be turning down investments that would in fact add value to the company.

The same method of valuation can be applied to the competitor for comparative purposes:

$$P_0 = \frac{(50p \times 20m) \times (1 + 7\%)}{(13.75\% - 7\%)}$$

$$P_0 = £158.5m \text{ or } £7.92 \text{ per share}$$

(iv)   **Discounting the future earnings stream**

This method involves **discounting the future long-term earnings stream** at the shareholders' cost of capital to **arrive at a value for the company**. However, there is insufficient information available to use this approach here; much more information about the long-term cash flow projections and estimates of terminal values is needed before this method could be attempted.

(b)   **The relative advantages of flotation and direct sale**

The following points should be considered when deciding which option is to be preferred.

(i)   **Aims of existing owners**

The **aims of the existing owners** are important in determining the best course of action. If a significant number of the existing consortium wish to **maintain control** over the business in the future, then they are more likely to be able to achieve this if the company is floated rather than sold.

(ii)   **Market for shares**

Flotation will create a **wider market** for the **company's shares**. This has the twin benefits that it will be **easier** for the company to **raise additional capital** to finance expansion, and that the existing shareholders will be able to realise all or part of their holding. However, if MC is to achieve a good price, the existing owners should aim to retain the major part of their holding for a reasonable period following the flotation.

(iii)   **Share option schemes**

Flotation will allow the company to offer **share option schemes** to its employees, which should **assist** in the **recruitment** and **retention of good staff**. This is particularly important in a company such as MC, where a significant part of the value in the company is linked to the knowledge base and research capability. Retaining a high proportion of the key staff will be vital to the success of any change in ownership, and must be taken into account in the structuring of either the sale or the flotation.

(iv)   **Costs of flotation**

Flotation will be an **expensive process** and will mean that the company has to comply with the stringent Stock Exchange regulations. It will put extra administrative burdens on the management and will cost more to organise than would a direct sale of the business.

(c)   **Conclusions and recommendations**

(i)   **Sale price**

The calculations suggest that the company should achieve a **sale price** of at least £120m. This compares with a **market capitalisation** of the **competitor** of £196m. Since MC has better growth prospects and also has a research base, which the competitor lacks, it may be able to achieve a better price than this, but £120m should be regarded as the base price in any negotiations.

(ii)   **Stock market quotation**

It is also recommended that the company should opt for a **Stock Market quotation** rather than for a direct sale. Given the current state of the market for this type of stock, it should be able to achieve a good price, and flotation will also give flexibility to the owners in allowing them to realise a part of their investment, while at the same time retaining control over the future direction of the business.

40 OA & ML

> **Text references.** Business valuations are covered in Chapter 17.
>
> **Top tips.** Read the question in (a) carefully – you are required to provide critical comment on each of the valuation methods used, not just that in part (iii). The calculations in (a)(iii) can appear confusing. You must work out which figures and discount rates are real rates excluding inflation, and which are nominal rates including inflation. You must be particularly careful with the consultancy fees; firstly, you will need to adjust for tax, and then for inflation. Although the fee is fixed at £100,000 per year, and does not increase with inflation, the amount that the directors receive will be reducing each year in real terms due to the effects of inflation. Therefore, if you choose to base your calculations on real rather than inflated figures (which is the quickest approach) you will need to deflate these figures before discounting.
>
> Part (b) is a straightforward explanation that can be written even if you do not complete all of part (a).

(a) (i) **P/E ratio**

Since ML operates in a different industry, the comparative P/E ratio valuation must be based upon the average P/E ratios in that industry. The P/E ratio of 7:1 will therefore be used.

Current share price	370 pence
Earnings yield	19.2%
Earnings per share	71.04 pence (370 × 19.2%)
Price per share	497.28 pence (71.04 × 7)
Value of ML	**£24.864m** (£4.9728 × 5m shares)

Problems with calculations

The problem with this approach is that P/E ratios are based on historic performance, and take no account either of the likely impact of the takeover on the performance of the company, or of its current earnings projections.

Comparability of companies

In this case, there is a further problem in that it is not known whether the recently taken over companies on which the ratio is based were sufficiently similar to ML in terms of size, rate of growth, type of activities and overall level of risk. It may well be that the average should be adjusted to take into account the particular situation of ML.

(ii) **Dividend valuation model**

The dividend valuation method (including growth) for share valuation is:

$$p_0 = \frac{d_0(1+g)}{k_e - g}$$

In the case of ML:

$d_0 = £842,000$

$g = 8\%$, assuming that this rate of dividend growth will continue

$k_e =$ can be estimated using the Capital Asset Pricing Model (CAPM):

$$E(r_i) = R_f + \beta_i (E(r_m) - R_f)$$

where
$$E(r_i) = \text{cost of equity}$$
$$R_f = \text{risk free rate of return (6\%)}$$
$$\beta_i = \text{beta factor (0.8)}$$
$$E(r_m) = \text{market rate of return (14\%)}$$
$$E(r_i) = 6\% + 0.8(14\% - 6\%) = 12.4\%$$

$$p = \frac{£842,000(1 + 0.08)}{(0.124 - 0.08)} = £20.667m$$

Weakness of dividend valuation model

The main weakness of this approach is the **method used** to **estimate the growth** rate. This assumes that the **historic rate of dividend growth** will **continue** at a constant rate into the future, but the current rate of dividend growth is different from that of OA, and could well change following the acquisition. However, the model does attempt to relate the share price to the future stream of earnings from the business, and in this sense is more realistic than the comparative P/E ratio basis of valuation.

(iii) **Operating cash flows**

The first stage is to estimate what the operating cash flows will be following the acquisition.

	£'000
Current pre-tax operating cash flow	5,300
Post acquisition adjustments:	
Annual wage savings	750
Advertising/distribution savings	150
	6,200
Taxation (33%)	2,046
Annual post tax cash flow	4,154

The other cash flows to be taken into account are:

		£'000
Year 0:	Redundancy costs (after tax)	(1,200)
	Sale of land and buildings (after tax)	800
Years 1-3:	Consultancy payments of £201,000 (£300,000 × 0.67) per year after tax	

Discount rate

The discount rate used will be the existing weighted average cost of capital (WACC) for ML, although it must be recognised that this could be **different** after the **acquisition** since OA is a much larger company and its shares are quoted on the main market rather than the AIM. The cost of equity has already been calculated above as 12.4%, and the cost of debt is 11% as per the balance sheet. The following expression will be used.

$$WACC = k_{eg} \frac{V_E}{(V_E + V_D)} + k_d(1 - T)\frac{V_D}{(V_E + V_D)}$$

where: k_{eg} = cost of equity in geared company
k_d = cost of debt
T = tax rate (33%)
V_E = market value of equity (5m × £3.70 = £18.5m)
V_D = market value of debt (£3.5m)

$$WACC = 12.4\% \frac{18.5}{(18.5 + 3.5)} + 11\%(1 - 0.33)\frac{3.5}{(18.5 + 3.5)}$$

WACC = 11.60%

This discount rate has been calculated on the basis of market values, and therefore will incorporate **inflation**. The cash flows (with the exception of the consultancy fees) all exclude inflation, and therefore either the **nominal discount rate** that has been calculated must be **adjusted to the real rate**, or the **cash flows** must be **adjusted to include inflation**.

If we adjust the discount rate to exclude the expected 2.4% rate of inflation: 1.116 ÷ 1.024 = 1.0898, ie the real discount rate to be used is 8.98%, say 9.0%.

PV of cash flow

The present value of the cash flows can now be found.

	Year 1 £'000	Year 2 £'000	Year 3 £'000	Total £'000
Gross payment to directors (after tax)	201	201	201	
11.6 say 12% discount factors	0.893	0.797	0.712	
PV cash flow	179	160	143	(482)
Ongoing cash flows for 10 years at 9% (4,154 × 6.418)				26,660
Income from land and buildings				800
Redundancy costs				(1,200)
Total PV of relevant operating cash flows				25,778

Problems with calculations

Although this is theoretically the best method of valuation to use, the calculations are in reality quite crude. Any likely **changes** in the pattern of the **cash flows** following the acquisition are **ignored**, as are any strategic plans that the company may have for such a long time frame. Ten years is a long period over which to estimate cash flows, inflation rates and discount rates, and there will inevitably be a large margin for error in the figures.

End of period

In addition, the question of what happens at the end of the ten year period is not addressed. Is there an **appropriate terminal value** that could be used in the calculations to reflect the ongoing value of ML as a business?

(iv) **Comparison with offer price**

Two of the valuation methods used, including the present value of the operating cash flows (which is possibly the best of the three approaches) give a valuation greater than the proposed offer price of £22m. If OA can successfully complete negotiations at this price, and if the acquisition of ML would be in line with OA's long-term strategic objectives, then it is **recommended** that the **offer** should go ahead.

(b) **Behavioural finance** is an alternative view to the efficient market hypothesis. Speculation by investors and market sentiment is a major factor in the behaviour of share prices. Behavioural finance attempts to explain the market implications of the **psychological** factors behind investor decisions and suggests that **irrational investor behaviour** may significantly affect share price movements. These factors may explain why share prices appear sometimes to over-react to past price changes.

41 BiOs

Text references. Business valuation techniques are covered in Chapter 17. Venture capital is discussed in Chapter 12.

Top tips. Questions or parts of questions like (a) are typical business valuation questions. You could have calculated a more precise P/E ratio based on forecast growth rates but this would be complicated and unnecessary. (b) brings out the sort of knowledge you need to have about different finance sources. However the last paragraph brings out the possibility that there is not a 'right' answer; it may be that what is most **suitable** for the **company** (delaying listing?) may not be so **acceptable** to **shareholders** who wish to realise their investments.

Easy marks. The discussion of the advantages and disadvantages of a stock exchange listing is a standard one that you must be able to reproduce.

(a)   **Range of values for the company**

   Valuation methods

   A company can be valued in terms of:

   - The **underlying value** of its assets
   - Its **ability to generate future profits** and cash flows (economic value).

   Net asset valuation

   Asset values are mainly of relevance if the company is to be broken up for disposal. BiOs' net asset value is **$395,000**, which, we are told, reflects the realisable value of its assets. This gives a 'floor level' value for the company, but is far too low to be of relevance to negotiations with the investment bank, because:

   - The company is a **going concern** and is not about to be broken up.
   - As BiOs is a consultancy company, most of its **assets** (know-how, skills, contacts) are **intangible** and their value is not included in the net asset value.

   It is more relevant to estimate the **economic value** of BiOs, which can be done in a number of ways.

   Price/earnings (P/E) ratio method

   In this method, which gives a quick approximation to economic value, equity earnings are multiplied by a suitable P/E ratio taken from quoted companies in the same industry.

   BiOs' earnings in 20X3   = 756c × 100,000 shares
                             = $756,000

P/E ratio	12	18	90
Valuation ($'000)	9,072	13,608	68,040

   The problem with P/E ratios is that they are affected significantly by the expected growth rate of the company. In the industry examined, P/Es vary between 12 and 90. Given that BiOs is predicted to **grow fast**, we would expect its value to be in the top half of this range, at least, but the P/E ratio method does not adequately allow for the growth rate in the computation.

   This approach to valuation is therefore relevant but simplistic and subject to large margins of error.

   Present value of future cash flows

   This method estimates a stream of future cash flows rather than just one profit figure and discounts the cash flows at a **cost of capital** suitable for the risk of the company's operations.

   Using the assumptions that profit after tax equals cash flow, that this will grow in years 2 and 3 at 30% per annum, followed by 10% per annum after that, and that the industry average cost of capital is suitable, we can estimate the company's value as follows:

20X3 = year 0, 20X4 = year 1 etc.

	$'000	12% factor	PV $'000
20X4 earnings	1,487	0.893	1,328
20X5 earnings: 30% higher	1,933	0.797	1,541
20X6 earnings : 30% higher	2,513	0.712	1,789
			4,658
20X7 to perpetuity: 10% growth (Working)	2,764		98,398
Present value of future cash flows:			103,056

Working

20X7 cash flow = 2,513 × 1.1 = 2,764. Present value (at 20X6) of the perpetuity from year 4 onwards, growing at 10% per annum = 2,764/(12% − 10%) = 138,200. To find the PV as at year 0, discount by the 3 year factor: 138,200 × 0.712 = 98,398.

The value of BiOs by this method is **$103 million**. Although there is a substantial margin of error on this valuation estimate, the method is considerably more useful than the P/E approach because it allows for **earnings growth estimates**. The company's growth projections are dependent on the ability to find skilled consultants, who are in short supply.

Conclusion

On the basis of the figures given, the company's value is probably in the range $65 million to $130 million. Further information is needed on the following areas:

- The **assumptions** on which earnings forecasts are based, in particular the assumption that staffing resources can deliver the **predicted growth rates**

- The **company's cost of capital** would help to make a more accurate assessment.

(b) **Advantages of using venture capital**

Venture capital funding

Venture capital funds specialise in financing **early stage**, **risk-oriented ventures** like BiOs. They will offer finance and assistance once a company has started to generate revenue and shows that it has high growth prospects. The funds offered are typically for **five to seven years**. At the end of this period it is presumed that the company will have grown and will be looking for more permanent sources of funds, at which point the venture capital fund will seek an exit route.

Exit route

The most profitable exit route for a venture capital company is when the company in which it has invested achieves a **stock exchange listing** (see below). Alternatives are to sell their shares to another investor (which might be another venture capital fund, but could be a potential acquirer of BiOs) or back to the original owners.

Disadvantages of using venture capital

Selection of investments

Extensive research is carried out on potential companies for **venture capital investment** and only a very small percentage of applications are accepted. The fact that BiOs has been approached by the marketing department of an investment bank is no guarantee that a venture capital fund will find the company an acceptable proposition.

Participation of venture capitalist

The venture capital fund becomes an equity participant in the company through a structure typically comprised of a combination of a substantial proportion of shares, warrants, options, and convertible securities. It also provides a representative who sits on the **company's board**, offers strategic advice to the management team and assures that the fund's interests are considered. If the directors of BiOs would not welcome this level of **investor involvement**, they should not consider venture capital.

Stock market flotation

The alternative under consideration by BiOs is to continue with existing sources of funds and to go for a stock exchange flotation within two to three years. To achieve a listing, the company needs to demonstrate that, in addition to good growth prospects, it has a **strong management team**, **strong financial controls** and **good management reporting systems**. These last factors will probably need improvement, as most of BiOs' administration systems are currently outsourced.

Advantages of obtaining a stock exchange listing

- Existing owner directors can **realise** some or all of **their investment**
- **New equity finance** is easier to raise
- The company's **status** is **raised**
- The company's shares can be used as **consideration for an acquisition**

Disadvantages of obtaining a stock exchange listing

- **Accountability is increased**: directors must be seen to be accountable to outside shareholders and there is more scrutiny over the company's activities
- **Costs** are incurred for the initial flotation and as ongoing annual fees

The choice

Whichever method is adopted, the end result is probably a **stock exchange flotation**. The directors of BiOs need to decide whether they are happier reaching this end with funding and advice from a venture capital company or whether they are better off seeking an **earlier listing** and thus encouraging equity investors through the stock market. To make their decision they need first to consider their **personal and business objectives**, for example do they wish to realise their wealth in the shortest time or to develop a dominant force in their market sector.

42 BST

Text references. Business valuation is covered in Chapter 17 and market efficiency in Chapter 18.

Top tips. In (a), you are not told what methods to use so you have to identify relevant information. You are given the net assets value, given all the information for the price-earnings, market capitalisation calculation, and given an indication of future growth that you can use in the dividend valuation model calculation.

Key factors in (b) are quality of forecasts, assets being purchased, effect on dividend policy and post-acquisition savings.

Part (c) is a straightforward discussion of factors affecting share prices.

(a) **Methods of valuation and range of values for SM**

Net assets

The book value of SM's **net assets attributable to equity shareholders** is $45 million. This figure may need to be adjusted for **increased or decreased market values** of assets, particularly SM's property holding. However in any case, for a going concern, the book value of assets is a poor indicator of their economic value, which depends on their **income-generating capacity,** rather than their historical cost or realisable value. Here also SM has a **franchise** generating earnings that will not be reflected in the balance sheet.

Price/earnings model

SM's existing earnings per share is $1.53, and number of shares is 1.5 million, giving total equity earnings of $2.295 million. Taking the 5% growth figure given, next year's earnings would be **$2.410 million.**

However, the managing director is estimating $4 million for next year. This figure cannot be accepted at face value and would need to be substantiated.

In the absence of any better information, BST's P/E ratio could be applied to these earnings figures. This is 1237/112.5 = 10.996, say 11.

The range of values for SM's valuation would be between $2.410 million × 11 and $4 million × 11 ie between **$26.5 million and $44 million.**

This valuation is dependent upon the **P/E ratio.** Arguably a lower ratio should be used as SM is unquoted, but it is difficult to say how much lower. Also BST's ratio may not be typical of the industry.

Dividend valuation model

Again there is a range of values depending on whether the MD's forecast earnings are believed.

Last year's total dividends were 1.5m × 100 cents = $1.5 m. A 5% increase next year would give $1.575 million. The cost of equity for similar firms is 10% and the expected growth rate 5%.

So on this basis the expected company value = $1.575m/(0.1 − 0.05) = **$31.5 million.**

SM 's dividend payout ratio (dividend/earnings) is 100 /153 = 0.654.

Based on the MD's forecast earnings of $4 million, next year's dividend would be $4m × 0.654 = **$2.616 million.**

The forecast company value would be $2.616 million/(0.1 − 0.05) = $52.3 million.

The **drawbacks** of this method are:

(i)   The assumption that SM's **cost of equity** is the **same as similar firms** may be misleading.

(ii)   The **assumption of constant dividend growth** at that rate may be **misleading.** Dividend policy may change on takeover.

(iii)   Share price is **not normally** just **a function of dividend policy;** future expected earnings are also a key factor.

Summary

Based on valuation of assets and income earning capacity, SM appears to have a value **anywhere between $25 million and $£52 million**. The higher earnings-based figures are heavily dependent on the MD's forecast of next year's earnings that may well be overstated. Because the net asset value is towards the top end of the valuation range, BST could probably look at a value of between **$40 million and $45 million,** but will need to carry out further investigations on likely asset values.

(b)   **Financial factors that may affect the bid**

Financial factors relating to BST

(i)   Like SM, the **forecast of next year's earnings** may be **overstated.** Current earnings = $1.125 × 25 million = $28.125 million. 4% growth (given) gives $29.25 million, but BST's forecast for next year is $35 million.

(ii)   The **total market value of the company's shares** is **below the net asset value.**25m shares × $12.37 = $309.25.m that is below the $350m net asset value. This may indicate that the company possesses **under-utilised assets**, or alternatively that its assets are overstated in value. On the face of it, the company would be better broken up than operating as a going concern. All these factors will be of interest to any of SM's shareholders who would be considering receiving BST shares. It will also interest the market and BST's low market value may mean that it becomes a takeover target itself.

(iii) BST has a fairly **high gearing ratio.** If BST lacks cash and has to borrow more in order to buy out those 50%+ shareholders of SM who do not wish to have BST shares, this may have the effect of increasing the company's cost of capital.

(iv) BST has a **lower dividend payout ratio** than SM. This may discourage some of SM's shareholders from accepting BST's shares.

(v) **Strategically** it is **unclear** why BST is buying SM; whilst BST may be trying to diversify, SM may not be a big enough acquisition to make it worth diversifying. There may be better investment opportunities.

Relevant financial factors relating to SM

(i) Next year's **forecast earnings** may be **overstated.** However, some of the directors may be taking **higher salaries** than **realistic market levels,** and the ongoing future profitability of the company may be higher if these people are replaced with lower cost managers.

(ii) Like BST, **asset value is high.** The net asset valuation is in fact higher than some of the other valuations, and SM's shareholders are unlikely to accept an offer below net asset value.

(iii) The company is **ungeared,** which is advantageous, as it enables BST to borrow to fund part of the acquisition.

(iv) The **'quality' of SM's earnings** is probably **higher** than BST's, as it operates in up-market areas.

(v) Selling SM to a listed company represents a good way for SM's shareholders to **realise the value of their investment**. However, many of the shareholders are likely to lose their jobs and may find it difficult to find equivalent positions. The bid may therefore be opposed by a substantial number of shareholders.

(vi) There are likely to be many areas where **costs can be saved** as a result of the acquisition of SM. This may make it worthwhile for BST to pay a higher price for SM.

(vii) BST is likely to have **good access to SM's business documentation** as SM has contacted BST. This should enable BST to calculate a more accurate valuation.

(c) The **fundamental theory of share values** states that the realistic market price of a share can be derived from a valuation of estimated future dividends. The value of a share will be the discounted present value of all future expected dividends on the shares, discounted at the shareholders' cost of capital.

If the fundamental analysis theory of share values is correct, the price of any share will be **predictable**, provided that all investors have the same information about a company's expected future profits and dividends, and a known cost of capital.

However, share prices are also affected by a number of other factors.

Marketability and liquidity of shares

In financial markets, **liquidity** is the **ease of dealing** in the shares, how easily can the shares can be bought and sold without significantly moving the price?

In general, large companies, with hundreds of millions of shares in issue, and high numbers of shares changing hands every day, have good liquidity. In contrast, small companies with few shares in issue and thin trading volumes, can have very poor liquidity.

The **marketability** of shares in a private company, particularly a minority shareholding, is generally very limited, a consequence being that the price can be difficult to determine.

Shares with restricted marketability may be subject to sudden and large falls in value and companies may act to improve the marketability of their shares with a **stock split**. A stock split occurs where, for example, each ordinary share of $1 each is split into two shares of 50c each, thus creating cheaper shares with **greater marketability**. There is possibly an added psychological advantage, in that investors may expect a company which splits its shares in this way to be planning for substantial earnings growth and dividend growth in the future.

As a consequence, the market price of shares may benefit. For example, if one existing share of $1 has a market value of $6, and is then split into two shares of 50c each, the market value of the new shares might settle at, say, $3.10 instead of the expected $3, in anticipation of strong future growth in earnings and dividends.

Availability and sources of information

An efficient market is one where the prices of securities bought and sold reflect all the **relevant information** available. Efficiency relates to how quickly and how accurately prices adjust to new information. Information comes from financial statements, financial databases, the financial press and the internet.

It has been argued that shareholders see **dividend decisions** as passing on **new information** about the company and its prospects. A dividend increase is usually seen by markets to be good news and a dividend decrease to be bad news, but it may be that the market will react to the difference between the actual dividend payments and the market's **expectations** of the level of dividend. For example, the market may be expecting a cut in dividend but if the actual decrease is less than expected, the share price may rise.

Market imperfections and pricing anomalies

Various types of anomaly appear to support the views that irrationality often drives the stock market, including the following.

- **Seasonal month-of-the-year effects**, day-of-the-week effects and also hour-of-the-day effects seem to occur, so that share prices might tend to rise or fall at a particular time of the year, week or day.

- There may be a **short-run overreaction** to recent events. For example, the stock market crash in 1987 when the market went into a free fall, losing 20% in a few hours.

- Individual shares or shares in small companies may be neglected.

Market capitalisation

The market capitalisation or **size** of a company has also produced some pricing anomalies.

The return from investing in **smaller** companies has been shown to be **greater** than the average return from all companies in the long run. This increased return may compensate for the greater risk associated with smaller companies, or it may be due to a start from a lower base.

Investor speculation

Speculation by investors and market sentiment is a major factor in the behaviour of share prices. **Behavioural finance** is an alternative view to the efficient market hypothesis. It attempts to explain the market implications of the **psychological** factors behind investor decisions and suggests that **irrational investor behaviour** may significantly affect share price movements. These factors may explain why share prices appear sometimes to over-react to past price changes.

43 COE

> **Text references.** Market efficiency is covered in Chapter 18 and business valuation in Chapter 17.
>
> **Top tips.** The facts in this question take a bit of untangling and it is easy to make a mistake. You may find it helpful to tabulate what happens when, right up to 20X8, in order to avoid making a silly mistake.
>
> Do not waste a lot of time in (a) by giving a detailed description of the semi-strong form of the efficient markets hypothesis. It is more important to demonstrate your understanding of what the EMH means in practice.
>
> In (b), there is more than one way to calculate the value of the company using the dividend valuation model. It would be equally correct to value the entire dividend stream in two stages – 20X3 to 20X8, and 20X9 onwards.

(a)   **Characteristics of semi-strong efficient market**

In a semi-strong efficient market, current share prices reflect:

(i)   All **relevant information** about **past price movements** and their implications

(ii)   All **knowledge** that is **available publicly**

Under these conditions, the market would respond as follows to the development of kryothin:

Pre 1.3.20X2 The company's share price will begin to rise as the market obtains knowledge of the research and development activities being carried on by the company, and as the company is granted patents.

1.3.20X2 The share price rises in anticipation of the company being able to market the drug in the UK.

The extent of the price rise will depend on the market's assessment of the chances of government approval being obtained; if the market had been totally certain that approval would be obtained, the share price would not rise at all.

Apr/May 20X2 The share price continues to rise as other countries approve the drug and its potential market grows. Again the extent of the increase will partly depend on how certain the market had been of the drug being approved.

1.1.20X3	The share price reflects the published dividend forecasts in respect of kryothin.
2.1.20X3	The share price adjusts to reflect the method of financing used.
20X3 – 20X7	The share price gradually falls to reflect the reduced 'premium' earnings remaining from kryothin.
20X8 onwards	The share price stabilises at a level that reflects the fact that there are no further premium earnings available from the drug.

(b)   **Option 1**

Calculate the value of the company at 1.1.20X3

At this time, there are two components to the expected dividend stream:

(i)   £19m per year in perpetuity

(ii)   £13.2m per year for the five years from 20X3 to 20X8.

The **dividend valuation model** can be used to find the value of the company using these dividend payments, taking the cost of equity as 10%.

$P_0 = D/k_e$

where P_0 = market capitalisation

            D = annual dividend payment in perpetuity

            k_e = cost of equity

Using the first element of the dividend stream:

P_0 = £19m/10%

    = £190m

Taking the second element of the dividend stream, this can be valued as follows:

$$P_0 = \frac{D}{(1+k_e)} + \frac{D}{(1+k_e)^2} + \ldots + \frac{D}{(1+k_e)^5}$$

$$= \frac{13.2}{(1+0.1)} + \frac{13.2}{(1+0.1)^2} + \ldots + \frac{13.2}{(1+0.1)^5}$$

$$= 13.2 \times 3.791$$

$$= £50m$$

At 1 January 20X3, therefore, the total value of the company on the basis of the projected dividend stream is:

	£m
First element of dividend stream	190
Second element of dividend stream	50
Less required investment	(80)
Net value	160

There are 20m shares in issue, and therefore the share price at this date should be **£8.00 per share.**

To raise the additional £80m, it is necessary to issue a further 10m shares at £8.00 per share.

On 2.1.20X3, therefore, there are 30m shares in issue. The total market capitalisation will now be £240m, due to the inflow of the additional £80m. The share price will therefore be £240m ÷ 30m = **£8.00 per share.**

There is therefore **no change in the share price** following the issue, as predicted by the semi-strong form of the efficient markets hypothesis. This is because the information has already been taken into account by investors.

Option 2

In this case, the **dividend stream** will be reduced by the amount of the annual interest payments.

Since the corporate bonds are irredeemable, this means that the first element of the dividend stream calculated above will reduce by £80m × 7% = £5.6m per year.

This part of the dividend stream will therefore be £19m − £5.6m = £13.4m per year. This can be valued as follows:

P_0 = £13.4m/10%

    = £134m

The market value of the company will therefore be:

	£m
First element of dividend stream	134
Second element of dividend stream	50
	184

There will still be 20m shares in issue, so the share price will be £184m ÷ 20m = **£9.20 per share.**

(c)   **Main assumptions of dividend valuation model**

    (i)   The dividends from projects for which the funds are required will be of **the same risk type or quality** as dividends from existing operations.

    (ii)   There would be **no increase** in the **cost of capital**, for any other reason besides (i) above, from a new issue of shares.

(iii) All shareholders have **perfect information** about the company's future, there is no delay in obtaining this information and all shareholders interpret it in the same way.

(iv) **Taxation** can be **ignored**.

(v) All shareholders have the **same marginal cost of capital**.

(vi) There would be **no issue expenses** for new shares.

These assumptions will not always hold in practice.

44 Collingham Co

Text references. Equity finance is covered in Chapter 12 and the efficient market hypothesis in Chapter 18.

Top tips. Your answer to (a) needs to go beyond raising new finance and easier access to capital. You must give explanations of reasons given.

In (b) it is helpful to tabulate a comparison of Collingham's ratios with the industry averages. These can then form the basis for a discussion of the profitability, liquidity and financial security of the company. Define clearly the way in which the ratios are calculated.

In (c) you can discuss the ways in which Collingham could seek to remedy the deficiencies revealed by your earlier analysis. Take into account the effect of your suggestions on all the performance indicators since changes in one area can impact on reported performance in others.

In (d) you need to define market efficiency and strong form efficiency first. Points from the definition can then be used to support your reasoning on the possible effects of the hypothesis on managers' behaviour.

(a) **Reasons for seeking listing**

A company such as Collingham may seek a stock market listing for the following reasons.

(i) **Access a wider pool of finance**

Companies that are growing fast may need to raise larger sums than is possible privately. Obtaining a listing widens the potential number of equity investors, and may also result in an improved credit rating, thus reducing the cost of additional debt finance.

(ii) **Improve the marketability of the shares**

Shares that are traded on the stock market can be bought and sold in relatively small quantities at any time. This means that it is easier for existing investors to realise a part of their holding.

(iii) **Allow capital to be transferred to other ventures**

Founder owners may wish to liquidate the major part of their holding either for personal reasons or for investment in other new business opportunities.

(iv) **Improve the company image**

Quoted companies are commonly believed to be more financially stable, and this may improve the image of the company with its customers and suppliers, allowing it to gain additional business and to improve its buying power.

(v) **Facilitate growth by acquisition**

A listed company is in a better position to make a paper offer for a target company than an unlisted one.

(b) The performance and financial health of Collingham in relation to that of the industry sector as a whole can be evaluated by comparing its financial ratios with the industry averages, as follows.

Collingham Co	*Industry average*
Return on (long-term) capital employed Operating profit (PBIT): Equity + long-term debt $10m: ($28m + $5m) = 30.3%	22%
Return on equity Profit attributable to ordinary shareholders: Equity $6m: $28m = 21.4%	14%
Operating profit margin Operating profit : Sales $10m: $80m = 12.5%	10%
Current ratio Current assets: Current liabilities $23m: $20m = 1.15:1	1.8:1
Acid test Current assets excluding inventory: Current liabilities $13m: $20m = 0.65:1	1.1:1
Gearing Long-term debt: Equity ($5m + $5m): $28m = 35.7%	18%
Dividend cover Profit attributable to equity: Dividends $6m: $0.5m = 12 times	2.6
Interest coverage Profit before interest and tax (PBIT): Interest $10m: $3m = 3.33 times	5.2

These ratios can be used to evaluate performance in terms of profitability, liquidity and financial security.

Profitability

Collingham's return on capital employed, return on equity and operating profit margin are all significantly above the industry averages. Although the first two measures could be inflated due to assets being shown at low book values, the profit margin indicates that Collingham is managing to make good profits, which could be due to successful marketing, a low cost base or to its occupation of a particularly profitable niche in the market.

Liquidity

Both the current and the quick (acid test) ratios are well below the industry averages. This suggests that Collingham is either short of liquid resources or is managing its working capital poorly. Three key working capital ratios are:

Receivable days:	365 × 10/80	=	45.6 days
Inventory turnover:	365 × 10/70	=	52.1 days
Payment period:	365 × 15/70	=	78.2 days

Although the industry averages are not known, these ratios appear to be very good by general standards. It therefore appears that Collingham has become under-capitalised, perhaps through the use of working capital to finance growth.

Financial security

Gearing is high in comparison with the rest of the industry, and 50% of the debt is in the form of overdraft which is generally repayable on demand. This is therefore a risky form of debt to use in large amounts. The debenture is repayable in two years and will need to be refinanced since Collingham cannot redeem it out of existing resources. Interest coverage is also poor, and this together with the poor liquidity probably account for the low payout ratio (the inverse of the dividend cover).

Conclusion

In summary, profit performance is strong, but there are significant weaknesses in both the liquidity and the financial structure. These problems need to be addressed if Collingham is to be able to maintain its record of strong and consistent growth.

(c) (i) **Restructuring balance sheet**

Restructuring its balance sheet prior to flotation will help to make Collingham appear a sounder prospect to potential investors who know little about its past performance. Methods available include the following.

Disposal of surplus assets

This will improve both **gearing** and **liquidity**.

Non-current asset revaluation

Land and buildings may well be shown in the accounts at values that are significantly below the **current market valuation**. Adjustment to market values will **improve the gearing ratio** and the value of shareholders' funds, although the effect of this will be to depress the reported return on capital employed and return on equity. However, since these are currently well above industry averages this should not present too much of a problem.

Liquidity improvement

Although there does not appear to be much scope for tightening the control of working capital, Collingham may be able to improve its cash flow by other means, for example by **reducing overheads** and **delaying the purchase of additional non-current assets.**

Sale and leaseback

If Collingham owns valuable freehold premises it may be able to **release cash** by **selling** them and **exchanging the freehold** for an operating lease. This would improve both the liquidity position and the reported return on capital employed although the gearing would be little affected.

Share split

On the basis of the industry average P/E of 10, the shares would be **priced** at $9.75 (= 13 × $6m/8m). A highly priced new issue is likely to deter potential small investors. This problem could be overcome by reducing the nominal value of the shares by means of a share split.

(ii) **Improved dividends**

Following the flotation, Collingham is likely to come under pressure to improve the **payout ratio** and **dividend performance** of the shares. If it wishes to maintain a good share price and the ability to raise further finance in the future then it would be well advised to consider this seriously. It could also work towards **lowering the gearing ratio**, perhaps by using a part of the issue proceeds to redeem some or all of the loan notes. However this should not appear to be the prime reason for the float or the attractiveness of the issue will be diminished.

(d)   **Market efficiency**

An efficient stock market is one in which:

(i)   the prices of securities traded **reflect** all the **relevant information**, which is **available** to the buyers and sellers. Share prices **change quickly** to reflect all new information about future prospects.

(ii)   **no individual dominates** the market.

(iii)   **transaction costs** of buying and selling are **not so high** as to **discourage trading** significantly.

Strong form efficiency

The efficient markets hypothesis exists in a number of forms, which relate to the nature of the information available to investors. Strong form efficiency means that share prices **reflect all information** available from:

(i)   past price changes
(ii)   public knowledge or anticipation
(iii)   insider knowledge available to specialist or experts such as investment managers

Impact of strong form efficiency

If the stock market is believed to operate with strong level efficiency, this might affect the behaviour of the finance directors of publicly quoted companies in the following ways.

(i)   **Share price implications**

Managers are likely to be aware that **share prices** will **change quickly** to reflect decisions that they take. This means that all financial decisions are likely to be evaluated in the light of their **potential impact** on the **share price**. A contrary view is that management should concentrate simply on **maximising** the **net present value** of its investments and need not worry about the **effect** on **share prices** of financial results in the published accounts. **Investors** will make **allowances** for low profits or dividends in the current year if higher profits or dividends are expected in the future.

(ii)   **Deterrent to manipulation**

Managers should be **discouraged** from attempting to **manipulate** their **accounting results**, since the truth will be realised quickly, and prices adjusted accordingly.

(iii)   **Priorities**

The company may concentrate on producing **constantly improving financial results** at the expense of the company's **responsibility** to **other stakeholders** in the business, such as its employees and the environment.

45 Marton Co

Text references. Working capital management is covered in Chapters 4, 5 and 6. Foreign currency risk is covered in Chapter 19.

Top tips. This is a wide-ranging question on management of receivables, both domestic and foreign and makes an excellent revision question for the subject. In part (b) the emphasis should have been on the specific services offered by *overseas* as opposed to domestic factors.

(a)   **Relative costs and benefits of the two proposals for reducing UK receivables**

Option 1: factoring

> **Top tips.** A 'with recourse' service implies that the factor does not guarantee against bad debts. Marton can therefore choose whether it takes up the credit insurance facilities or not. Unfortunately the question does not give any information about the current or expected level of bad debts which would be useful in making this decision. We have assumed that the insurance is taken up, but we cannot put in any figure for bad debts saved.
>
> The question gives no indication of the level of bad debts which are being borne at the moment. It is therefore impossible to say whether the credit insurance is worthwhile or not. If the credit insurance is compulsory, then the factoring agreement is non-recourse, not with-recourse.

UK sales are £20 million in 365 days.

If the **receivable collection period** is reduced by 15 days, the reduction in receivables will be:

15/365 × $20 million = £821,918.

The cash inflow is used to reduce the overdraft, giving an annual interest saving of:

13% × £821,918 = £106,849.

Thus:

	£	£
Administrative savings		200,000
Annual interest saved		106,849
Total savings		306,849
Factor's service charge: 1% × $20 million	200,000	
Credit insurance (if taken)	80,000	
		280,000
Net benefit to profit before tax		26,849

Option 2: prompt settlement discounts

The effect of the discount scheme is that 50% of UK receivables will pay faster than before. The remaining 50% are unchanged.

Before the discount scheme is in place, 50% of UK receivables is 50% × £4.5 million = £2.25 million.

After the scheme is introduced:

Customers		Sales value £'000		Receivables £'000
Paying within 10 days:	20%	4,000	4,000 × 10/365	109,589
Paying within 20 days:	30%	6,000	6,000 × 20/365	328,767
	50%	10,000		438,356

After the discount scheme gets going, the value of receivables for 50% of the sales will be reduced from £2,250,000 to £438,356. The remaining receivables will be unchanged.

Reduction in receivables = £2,250,000 – £438,356 = £1,811,644.

Again, the resulting cash inflow is used to reduce the overdraft, saving interest:

		£	£
Annual interest saving:	13% × £1,811,644		235,514
Cost of discount:			
Customers paying within 10 days	20% × £20m × 3%	120,000	
Customers paying within 20 days	30% × £20m × 1.5%	90,000	
			210,000
Net gain			25,514

> **Top tips.** Because there will be a transition period during the first few months while receivables move from £2,250,000 down to £438,356, the annual interest saving figure is slightly overstated. In this style of question you are not expected to calculate the accurate interest saving figure by looking at receivables month by month.

On the basis of the above figures, the factoring option appears to be marginally better. Two other considerations weigh in favour of factoring:

(i) **Need for credit insurance**

It is not obvious that the **credit insurance** is required. An examination of the current level of bad debts is needed. If the credit insurance can be avoided, there is a clear advantage to the factoring agreement.

(ii) **Risk**

Risk is far lower for the **factoring** scheme than the discount scheme. The estimates of proportions of receivables taking the discount in the prompt payment scheme are subject to extreme uncertainty and the vagaries of human nature. For example, some large customers may insist on the discount and then pay late. By contrast, all the key elements of the factoring scheme are negotiable 'up front' and can be written into the contract. For example, if the factor does not pay within the agreed period, the service fee is reduced or avoided.

(iii) **Customer confidence**

The disadvantage of factoring, that it supposedly reduces customer confidence, is probably not significant. The customers most likely to be 'put off' are those who are aiming to take more credit than they are entitled to do.

Conclusion

It is therefore recommended that the factoring services are used.

(b) **Overseas factoring**

For a company with annual overseas credit sales of at least £250,000, **overseas factors** offer the same basic facilities as domestic factors. Broadly, these facilities are the collection of debts, sales ledger management and provision of flexible finance based on the size of the sales ledger.

Non-recourse factoring

Non-recourse factoring means that the factor will bear the risk of bad debts. With recourse means that the factor can return to the principal and say that a debt is irrecoverable. For overseas sales especially, non-recourse factoring is preferable and can be a cheaper alternative than using documentary letters of credit.

Additional services

Overseas factors offer two additional services which are valuable to firms without much experience of exporting:

(i) **Handling export sales documentation**
(ii) Providing a **credit rating service** on potential overseas customers

(c) (i) **Losses** on sales receipts will be **sustained** if the dollar weakens relative to sterling, ie if there are more dollars to each pound.

		£
Current export sales in £		5,000,000
Spot exchange rate $/£	1.45	
Current $ value of export sales at spot rate 1.45 $/£	$7,250,000	
Maximum forecast $/£	1.60	
£ value of $7.25 million at 1.60 $/£		4,531,250
Maximum exchange loss if no hedge used		(468,750)

(ii)

		£
Agreed forward rate for $/£	1.55	
Selling $7.25m forward at 1.55 $/£ gives		4,677,419
Best possible result is when $/£ strengthens to	1.30	
£ value of $7.25 million at 1.30 $/£		5,576,923
Maximum opportunity cost		(899,504)

(iii)   **Hedging**

Hedging foreign currency risk means taking action to reduce that risk in the sense that the cash flow is made more predictable and the chance of a large unexpected currency loss is eliminated.

Benefits and drawbacks

The advantage of predictable cash flows is that cash planning is made easier and it is easier to raise loans. However, it must be recognised that in eliminating the chance of a large loss, the company loses the chance of currency gains and can also pay a high price to bankers in the long run unless it is dealing in very large sums of foreign currency.

Forward contracts

A popular currency hedge is the forward contract of the type described in this question. However the forward rate given (1.55 $/£) appears to be very expensive compared with the most likely value of the future $/£ spot rate estimated by the company's advisors (1.45 $/£). This estimate must be investigated further, as it may be inaccurate. In general, it is likely to be better to confine forward contracts to high value dollar sales, bearing the risk on lower value invoices.

Borrowing in dollars

If Marton's dollar receivables are fairly constant in value, an alternative and better hedging technique would be to **switch some of its borrowing** from sterling to US dollars (ie take out a US dollar overdraft). The amount of borrowing should be roughly equal to the value of dollar receivables. Any loss on the receivables is then countered by an equal and opposite gain on the overdraft and vice versa.

46 SDT

Text references. Foreign currency risk is covered in Chapter 19.

Top tips. Note the requirements in (a) require **critical** commentary, which should have indicated to you the need to explain why the director's views were wrong.

The main problem in (b) appears to have been identifying which figure you had to calculate, indicating you needed to read the question carefully. The greater of the two relevant exchange rates is used in every calculation, as in each case SDT is receiving the foreign currency, and is having to pay the higher amount to obtain each £ that it wants.

(c) is a straightforward look at the higher risks that mean a higher return is required. (d) can bring in debtor management as well as option forward contracts.

(a)   The main problems with the Managing Director's views are:

(i)   **Conditions for efficiency**

The conditions for efficiency are **market liquidity**, **full information** and **freely floating currencies**. In practice liquidity and information available varies between currencies. Many currencies are at most subject to managed floating, floating within limits decided (possibly in secret) by governments.

However conditions for efficiency will apply more to the major currencies in the scenario, and gains and losses from each individual currency may be equally likely.

(ii) **Limited range of currencies**

Although the managing director is correct in saying that the risk is diversified, it is not diversified across all currencies. It is possible that the £ may move in an **adverse direction** against each of the three currencies, if for example the UK's inflation rate was higher than other major nations or because of interdependence between the economies. In fact the currencies quoted are known as the Triad because the countries are similar markets, so in practice there might be **positive correlation between the three** and hence diversification over them will increase the risk of losses.

(iii) **Hedging sales only**

Foreign exchange risk is enhanced because it is only in one direction, for **sales**. As purchases are all in £, there is no matching of sales and purchases in the same currency which will limit foreign exchange risk.

Currency hedging may be beneficial for the following reasons, although it will incur costs:

(i) **Risk limitation**

Hedging risk can mean that the amounts SDT receives can be **fixed**, and SDT is not **subject to adverse fluctuations**. In an efficient market, prices respond to new information, so shocks may have unexpected effects on exchange rates.

(ii) **Size of possible losses**

Because SDT exports over 90% of its production, **potential losses** from adverse events could be **very large**.

(iii) **Improved forecasting**

Fixing the amounts to be received will also help **internal forecasting and budgeting procedures**.

Conclusion

Bearing these considerations in mind, SDT needs to consider hedging risk

(b) (i) (1) **A**

Contribution = $(9,487,500/200.032) - (2.75 \times 9,487,500/632.50)$

= 47,430 − 41,250
= £6,180

B

Contribution = $(82,142/1.7775) - (4.80 \times 82,142/10.2678)$

= 46,212 − 38,400
= £7,812

Euro

Contribution = $(66,181/1.4784) - (6.25 \times 66,181/12.033)$

= 44,765 − 34,375
= £10,390

(2) **A**

Contribution = $(9,487,500/202.63) - 41,250$

= 46,822 − 41,250
= £5,572

B

Contribution = (82,142/1.7750) – 38,400

= 46,277 – 38,400
= £7,877

Euro

Contribution = (66,181/1.4680) – 34,375

= 45,082 – 34,375
= £10,707

(ii) **Hedging**

$$\text{Contribution to sales ratio} = \frac{6,180 + 7,812 + 10,390}{47,430 + 46,212 + 44,765} = 17.62\%$$

Not hedging

$$\text{Contribution/sales ratio} = \frac{5,572 + 7,877 + 10,707}{46,822 + 46,277 + 45,082} = 17.48\%$$

Hedging leads to a higher contribution per sale than not hedging and accordingly SDT should hedge its foreign exchange exposure.

(c) **Reasons for generating higher rates of return**

Businesses will try to generate higher contributions from export sales as they appear to be riskier than domestic sales.

Foreign exchange risk

Foreign exchange risk will mean that the **receipts** are **uncertain**, unless the exports are **invoiced** in the **domestic currency**.

Physical risk

Because of the greater distances, there may be an increased risk of the goods being **lost, damaged or stolen in transit**, or the documents accompanying the goods going astray.

Credit risk

There may be a higher risk in allowing customers credit because **researching** their suitability is more difficult than domestic customers. Payments may be **slower** from **overseas customers**, and it may be difficult and costly to monitor and pursue customers who fail to pay promptly or at all.

Trade risk

Because of the large distances travelled, there may be a risk that the customers **do not accept** the **goods** when delivered, or that the order is cancelled in transit.

Political risk

Overseas governments may impose a **variety of rules and restrictions**, including **higher quality standards** than are imposed in the company's own domestic market.

Risk mitigation

The effects of all these risks can be mitigated by **hedging techniques** for foreign exchange currency, **insuring** against the **risks** or reducing the risk of problems by, for example, using **credit reference agencies** to report on customers. However all of these will have a cost, and increased sales revenues will cover those costs.

Investment

If costs of investment are **higher abroad** than at home, increased revenues will be required to cover these. This includes not only capital costs, but also costs of investing in administration and specialist trading and treasury staff.

(d) **Risk**

The risk is that SDT will be forced to **buy currency at a poorer spot rate**, in order to be able to sell it to the bank at the forward rate. If the customer subsequently fulfils the contract, SDT may not be able to recoup the loss it has made. Alternatively SDT may take out another forward contract up until the time that the customer is expected to pay, but this may be on poorer terms than the original contract. **Transaction costs** will also be incurred.

Risk reduction procedures

(i) The risk can be avoided by taking out **insurance** against the possibility of the customers failing to fulfil their obligations, although a premium will be payable.

(ii) SDT could **reduce the risk of the customers paying late** by offering a discount for payment on time; the cost then would be the amount of the discount. Alternatively SDT could specify **penalties** for late payment; this would reduce the cost for SDT if payment was late.

(iii) SDT could take out an **option forward contract** that would give it some leeway as to the date the contract will be fulfilled. However there would be **increased transaction costs**, and SDT would have to accept the worst exchange rate over the period the option could be exercised.

47 RET

Text references. Foreign currency risk is covered in Chapter 19.

Top tips. In (a) the first stage is to net off the receipts and payments. In Part (b), you use the lower rates for the forward market hedges as the US company is seeking Euros, and will get fewer Euros for each dollar it pays. For the receipts, you use the higher rate, as the company is trying to dispose of kroners and obtain dollars, and will need to provide more kroners to obtain dollars.

In part (c), with the money market hedge, you invest in the foreign currency to obtain money to fulfil a payment requirement, but you have to borrow in your own currency. You invest a lower amount now in that foreign currency to obtain the interest and add capital and interest together at the end to obtain the payment you require. However you have to pay back the borrowing plus the interest charged in your own currency.

If you are going to obtain a receipt in a foreign currency, you borrow the lower amount, and the receipt will cover what you borrowed plus the interest. The amount you borrow is converted into your own currency for investment and that amount plus the interest is your ultimate benefit.

The advantages and disadvantages in (d) are very important. You need to consider certainty of receipt, timing, costs, availability, complexity and any risks.

Part (e) involves a straightforward description of foreign currency risk management techniques.

(a)

Receipts	Payments
Two months	€393,265
Three months Kr8.6m	491,011 + 890,217 − 60,505 − 1,997,651
	= €676,928

(b) **Forward market hedge**

Two months

Payment $\dfrac{€393,265}{1.433} = \$274,435$

Three months

Payment $\dfrac{€676,928}{1.431} = \$473,045$

Receipt $\dfrac{Kr8,600,000}{10.83} = \$794,090$

(c) **Money market hedge**

- Two months payment

  We need to invest now to match the €393,265 we require in two months.

  Amount to be invested $= \dfrac{€393,265}{1+\dfrac{0.035}{6}}$

  $= €390,984$

  Converting at spot rate $\dfrac{390,984}{1.439} = \$271,705$

  To obtain \$271,705, we have to borrow \$271,705 for two months.

  Amount to be borrowed $= 271,705 \times \left(1+\dfrac{0.075}{6}\right)$

  $= \$275,101$

- Three months payment

  Again we need to invest

  Amount to be invested $= \dfrac{€676,928}{1+\dfrac{0.035}{4}}$

  $= €671,056$

  Converting at spot rate $\dfrac{671,056}{1.439} = \$466,335$

  Borrowing \$466,335 for three months

  Amount to be borrowed $= 466,335 \times \left(1+\dfrac{0.075}{4}\right)$

  $= \$475,079$

- Three months receipt

  We need to borrow now to match the receipt we shall obtain.

  Amount to be borrowed $= \dfrac{Kr8,600,000}{\left(1+\dfrac{0.08}{4}\right)}$

  $= Kr8,431,373$

  Converting at spot rate $\dfrac{8,431,373}{10.71} = \$787,243$

  Amount to be invested $= 787,243 \times \left(1+\dfrac{0.055}{4}\right)$

  $= \$798,068$

(d) **Advantages of forward contracts**

(i)   The contract can be **tailored** to the user's **exact requirements** with quantity to be delivered, date and price all flexible.

(ii)   The trader will **know in advance** how much money will be received or paid.

(iii)   **Payment** is **not required** until the contract is settled.

Disadvantages of forward contracts

(i)   The user may **not** be able to negotiate **good terms**; the price may depend upon the **size** of the **deal** and how the user is rated.

(ii)   Users have to **bear** the **spread** of the contract between the buying and selling price.

(iii)   Deals can only be **reversed** by going back to the original party and offsetting the original trade.

(iv)   The **creditworthiness** of the other party may be a problem.

Advantages of currency futures

(i)   There is a **single specified price** determined by the market, and not the negotiating strength of the customer.

(ii)   **Transactions costs** are generally **lower** than for forward contracts.

(iii)   The exact date of **receipt** or **payment** of the currency does not have to be **known**, because the futures contract does not have to be closed out until the actual cash receipt or payment is made.

(iv)   **Reversal** can easily take place in the market.

(v)   Because of the process of **marking to market**, there is no default risk.

Disadvantages of currency futures

(i)   The **fixing** of **quantity** and **delivery dates** that is necessary for the future to be traded means that the customer's risk may not be fully covered.

(ii)   Futures contracts may **not** be **available** in the **currencies** that the customer requires.

(iii)   The procedure for converting between two currencies, neither of which is the US dollar, can be **complex.**

(iv)   **Volatile trading conditions** on the futures markets mean that the potential loss can be high.

(e)   **Currency of invoice**

One way of avoiding exchange risk is for an exporter to **invoice his foreign customer in his domestic currency**, or for an importer to arrange with his **foreign supplier to be invoiced in his domestic currency**. However, although either the exporter or the importer can avoid any exchange risk in this way, only one of them can deal in his domestic currency. The other must accept the exchange risk, since there will be a period of time elapsing between agreeing a contract and paying for the goods (unless payment is made with the order).

Matching receipts and payments

A company can reduce or eliminate its foreign exchange transaction exposure by **matching** receipts and payments. Wherever possible, a company that expects to make payments and have receipts in the same foreign currency should plan to **offset its payments against its receipts in the currency**. Since the company will be setting off foreign currency receipts against foreign currency payments, it does not matter whether the currency strengthens or weakens against the company's 'domestic' currency because there will be no purchase or sale of the currency.

The process of matching is made simpler by having **foreign currency accounts** with a bank. Receipts of foreign currency can be credited to the account pending subsequent payments in the currency.

(Alternatively, a company might invest its foreign currency income in the country of the currency – for example it might have a bank deposit account abroad – and make payments with these overseas assets/deposits.)

Matching assets and liabilities

A company which expects to receive a substantial amount of income in a foreign currency will be concerned that this currency may weaken. It can hedge against this possibility by borrowing in the foreign currency and using the foreign receipts to repay the loan. For example, US dollar debtors can be hedged by taking out a US dollar overdraft. In the same way, US dollar trade creditors can be matched against a US dollar bank account which is used to pay the creditors.

A company which has a long-term foreign investment, for example an overseas subsidiary, will similarly try to **match its foreign assets** (property, plant etc) by a **long-term loan in the foreign currency**.

Leading and lagging

Companies might try to use:

- **Lead payments** (payments in advance)
- **Lagged payments** (delaying payments beyond their due date)

in order to take advantage of foreign exchange rate movements. With a lead payment, paying in advance of the due date, there is a **finance cost** to consider. This is the interest cost on the money used to make the payment, but early settlement discounts may be available.

48 BS

> **Text references**. Foreign currency risk is covered in Chapter 19.
>
> **Top tips**. In (a) don't forget to convert the transaction costs at today's spot rate. (a) (ii) needs to be read carefully; the term annual rate for **three months' borrowing** indicates that the rate given just needs to be divided by 4 rather than the principles of compound interest be applied. Remember that you want $200,000 in three months time, so what you are effectively doing is calculating the present value of that amount now.
>
> (b) is only worth five marks and is asking for two sets of points; this indicates that the examiner doesn't want very much more than two lists. Within those lists you can however give indications of what is important to BS.
>
> Part (c) requires a full discussion of causes of exchange rate fluctuations not just a list of factors.

(a) (i) Since both the receipts and payments are expected to occur **on the same date**, BS plc need only hedge the net amount, ie a receipt of $200,000 ($450,000 – $250,000). To hedge this transaction, a three-month forward contract to sell dollars will be required.

The **transaction cost** will be paid immediately in US$. BS must therefore **buy dollars now** to cover this at the spot rate of $1.6540/£.

The net receipt can now be calculated:

	£
Sterling proceeds in 3 months' time: $200,000 ÷ 1.6513	121,117
Transaction costs: $200,000 × 0.2% ÷ 1.6540	(242)
Net receipt	120,875

(ii) Since the company is expecting to receive dollars, to effect a money market hedge it will need to **borrow dollars now** in anticipation. The sum to be borrowed must be just enough so that the receipt in three months' time will repay the loan and the interest due for the period.

The money will be borrowed in the US at an annual rate of 6%. This equates to a three month rate of 1.5% (6%/4). The amount to be borrowed in dollars is therefore $200,000 ÷ 1.015 = $197,044. These dollars will be sold now at the spot rate of $1.6590/£ to realise £118,773.

This **sterling amount** can now be invested in the UK at an annual rate of 6.5%. This equates to a three-month rate of 1.625%. The value of the deposit at the end of the three month period when the dollar loan is repaid will be £118,773 × 1.01625 = £120,703.

The transaction cost will be the same as for the forward market hedge. The net receipt under this method will therefore be £120,703 − £242 = **£120,461**.

The receipts are highest if the **forward market hedge** is used, and this will therefore be the **preferred method**.

(b) **Factors to consider**

(i) The **relative costs** of the different options

(ii) The **ability of the staff** to **manage the techniques**, given that there is not a specialist treasury department

(iii) The **attitude of the company to risk**

(iv) The **size of the transaction** in relation to the company's overall operations, and therefore the scale of the risks involved

(v) The **perceived level of risk** attached to the currencies in question

Alternative options to minimise risk

(i) **Operating bank accounts in foreign currencies.** This is only an option if the company has regular transactions in the currencies in question.

(ii) The **use of multilateral netting**. This will only be possible if there are a large number of foreign currency transactions.

(iii) The company could consider the **use of swaps and option contracts**.

(iv) The company could consider the **cost and viability** of insisting that more of its contracts are denominated in sterling.

(c) **The causes of exchange rate fluctuations**

Currency supply and demand

The exchange rate between two currencies – ie the buying and selling rates, both 'spot' and forward – is determined primarily by supply and demand in the foreign exchange markets. Demand comes from individuals, firms and governments who want to buy a currency and supply comes from those who want to sell it.

Supply and demand for currencies are in turn influenced by:

- The rate of inflation, compared with the rate of inflation in other countries
- Interest rates, compared with interest rates in other countries
- The balance of payments
- Sentiment of foreign exchange market participants regarding economic prospects
- Speculation
- Government policy on intervention to influence the exchange rate

Interest rates

The difference between spot and forward rates reflects differences in interest rates. If this were not so, then investors holding the currency with the lower interest rates would switch to the other currency for (say) three months, ensuring that they would not lose on returning to the original currency by fixing the exchange rate in advance at the forward rate. If enough investors acted in this way (known as arbitrage), forces of supply and demand would lead to a change in the forward rate to prevent such risk-free profit making.

The principle of **interest rate parity** links the foreign exchange markets and the international money markets.

Inflation

Purchasing power parity theory predicts that the exchange value of foreign currency depends on the relative purchasing power of each currency in its own country and that spot exchange rates will vary over time according to relative price changes.

In the real world, exchange rates move towards purchasing power parity only over the long term.

Countries with relatively **high** rates of inflation will generally have high nominal rates of interest, partly because high interest rates are a mechanism for reducing inflation, and partly because of the **Fisher effect**: higher nominal interest rates serve to allow investors to obtain a high enough real rate of return where inflation is relatively high.

According to the international Fisher effect, interest rate differentials between countries provide an unbiased predictor of future changes in spot exchange rates. The currency of countries with relatively high interest rates is expected to depreciate against currencies with lower interest rates, because the higher interest rates are considered necessary to compensate for the anticipated currency depreciation. Given free movement of capital internationally, this idea suggests that the real rate of return in different countries will equalise as a result of adjustments to spot exchange rates.

Four-way equivalence

The four-way equivalence model states that in equilibrium, differences between forward and spot rates, differences in interest rates, expected differences in inflation rates and expected changes in spot rates are equal to one another.

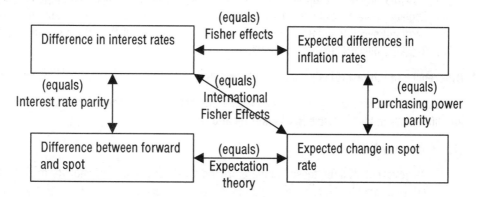

49 Interest rates

Top tips. (a) emphasises that as well as knowing what different sorts of instrument are, you need to be able to discuss their **risk, marketability** and **length.**

You should go through (b) very carefully, as the points are very important. (c) develops the issue of how changes in the cost of capital affect financial policy. Note that changes in the cost of capital will affect **investing** decisions (because the weighted average cost of capital is lower and returns are increased due to a rise in demand), and **financing** decisions (because of changes in the relative attractiveness of different sources of finance). The last paragraph demonstrates how investing and financing decisions may be interlinked.

Although you are not asked specifically to draw a yield curve in (d), it is difficult to explain it without illustration.

(a) (i) **Nature of instruments**

   (1) **Sterling certificates of deposits (CDs)**

   These are securities issued by a bank, acknowledging that a certain amount of **sterling** has been deposited with it for a **certain period of time** (usually, a short term). The CD is issued to the depositor, and attracts interest. The depositor will be another bank or a large commercial organisation. CDs are traded on the money market and so if a CD holder wishes to obtain immediate cash, he can sell the CD on the market at any time. This second-hand market in CDs makes them attractive, flexible investments for organisations with excess cash.

   (2) **Local authority bonds**

   These are **short-term securities** issued by local authorities to raise cash. They carry **interest**, and are **repayable on maturity**. They are traded secondhand in the money market, and so, like CDs, are a flexible investment for organisations with excess cash.

   (3) **Finance house deposits**

   These are **non-negotiable time deposits** with finance houses (usually subsidiaries of banks). Finance houses specialise in lending money, and have to raise the funds (much of them from the money market) for re-lending.

   (4) **Treasury bills**

   These are short-term debt instruments issued by the Bank of England, to raise **cash** for the **government's spending needs.** The bills are **sold by tender**, each week, at a price which is at a discount to their nominal value. They are **redeemable at their nominal value**, and so there is an implied rate of interest on the bill.

   Treasury bills are **bought initially** by **money market organisations** with which the Bank of England has a special relationship, mainly the discount houses. The discount houses then carry out secondhand trading in Treasury bills (and other bills) on the discount market. Treasury bills are therefore negotiable.

(ii) **Differences in interest rates between instruments**

   Some money market instruments carry a higher interest rate than others. The main reasons for this are differences in their **relative marketability and risk.**

   (1) **Treasury bills**

   As **government debt**, these are therefore the most secure form of short-term debt available. **Interest rates** on Treasury bills should therefore be **lower** than on other money market instruments. Interest rates at which the Bank of England deals in bills in the money market usually set the level of interest rates for all other money market instruments.

   (2) **Finance house deposits**

   As these are **not negotiable**, they are **less marketable** than the other money market instruments in the list. For this reason, **interest rates** on them are slightly **higher**. Similarly, CDs are more marketable than ordinary money market bank deposits, which are for a given (short) term; thus CD interest rates will be slightly lower than LIBID (the London inter-bank bid rate).

   Differences in interest rates over time

   Interest rates over time are affected by the **supply and demand of funds**, and by **expectations of future changes** in interest rates. Broadly speaking, interest rates on longer-term investments will be higher. In the data given, we see that interest rates are increased with the term of the deposit/bond/bill.

Expectations of fall in interest rates

However, when there are **expectations** of a **future fall** in interest rates, because yields on long term debt will be lower than yields on shorter term debt.

(b) ## Implications of a fall in interest rates for a typical company

(i) The **cost of floating rate borrowing will fall**, making it more attractive than fixed rate borrowing. For most companies with borrowings, interest charges will be reduced, resulting in higher profitability and earnings per share.

(ii) The **value of the company's shares will rise,** both because of the higher level of company profitability and also because of the lower alternative returns that investors could earn from banks and deposits, if interest rates are expected to remain low in the longer term.

(iii) The **higher share value results in a lower cost of equity capital**, and hence a lower overall cost of capital for the company. Investment opportunities that were previously rejected may now become viable.

(iv) As interest rates fall, consumers have **more disposable income.** This may increase demand for the company's products. Falling returns on deposits may, however, encourage many people to save more, rather than spend.

(c) ## Change in cost of capital

As explained above, if interest rates are expected to remain low in the longer term, the company's **overall cost of capital** will **fall**. The discount rates used in investment appraisal will therefore be lower, making **marginal projects** more **profitable**, with a resulting increase in the company's investment opportunities.

Investment policy review

The **cash flows** from all **possible investments** should be reviewed in the light of falling interest rates and the possible effects on consumer demand and the sterling exchange rate. These cash flows should then be **appraised** at the **new lower discount rates** and the project portfolio ranked and reviewed. The company's investment plans are likely to be expanded, unless constrained by other factors such as lack of skills or management time.

Introduction of debt

When interest rates are expected to fall in the future, an ungeared company may be tempted to **introduce debt** into its capital structure. If fixed interest rates are high at the moment, **floating rate debt** may be **more attractive**, because it allows the company to take advantage of falling interest rates.

Setting gearing level

New projects may be financed entirely by borrowings until an appropriate gearing level is reached. As gearing is increased, the company's **cost of capital** is usually **reduced** because of the **tax relief** on debt interest but, if gearing is increased to too high a level, increased risks of bankruptcy arise, causing the cost of capital to rise.

Choice of projects

If the company is tempted to increase its debt financing substantially, this may affect which investment projects are undertaken, as some projects are more suitable for debt financing than others. Generally, a project with significant tangible assets and stable cash flows will be most suitable for financing by debt.

50 QW

> **Text references**. Interest rate risk is covered in Chapter 20.
>
> **Top tips.** This is a completely discursive question which covers a broad range of issues. Part (a) is a straightforward explanation of interest rate risk, which you should be completely happy with.
>
> Part (b) gives you the chance to explain the purposes of derivatives in detail, showing the possible costs and the effects on risks. Your answer to (c) should concentrate on the main points of comparison (costs, flexibility, what each instrument achieves).

(a)   **Interest rate risk** is faced by companies with floating and fixed rate debt. It can arise from **gap exposure** and **basis risk.**

Interest rate risk relates to the sensitivity of profit and cash flows to changes in interest rates. An organisation will need to analyse how profits and cash flows are likely to be affected by forecast changes in interest rates and decide whether to take action.

Floating interest rate debt

The most common form of interest rate risk faced by a company is the volatility of cash flows associated with a high proportion of floating interest rate debt. Floating interest rates, of course, change according to general market conditions.

Some of the interest rate risks to which a firm is exposed may cancel each other out, where there are both assets and liabilities with which there is exposure to interest rate changes. If interest rates rise, more interest will be payable on loans and other liabilities, but this will be compensated for by higher interest received on assets such as money market deposits.

Fixed interest rate debt

A company with a high proportion of fixed interest rate debt has a commitment to fixed interest payments. If interest rates fall sharply, the company will suffer from a loss of competitive advantage compared with companies using floating rate borrowing whose interest costs and cost of capital will fall.

Gap exposure

The degree to which a firm is exposed to interest rate risk can be identified by using the method of gap analysis. Gap analysis is based on the principle of grouping together assets and liabilities which are sensitive to interest rate changes according to their maturity dates. Two different types of 'gap' may occur.

A negative gap occurs when a firm has a larger amount of interest-sensitive liabilities maturing at a certain time or in a certain period than it has interest-sensitive assets maturing at the same time. The difference between the two amounts indicates the net exposure.

There is a **positive gap** if the amount of interest-sensitive assets maturing in a particular time exceeds the amount of interest-sensitive liabilities maturing at the same time.

With a negative gap, the company faces exposure if interest rates rise by the time of maturity. With a positive gap, the company will lose out if interest rates fall by maturity.

Basis risk

It may appear that a company which has size matched assets and liabilities, and is both receiving and paying interest, may not have any interest rate exposure. However, the two floating rates may not be determined using the same basis. For example, one may be linked to LIBOR but the other is not.

LIBOR or the London Inter-Bank Offered Rate is the rate of interest applying to wholesale money market lending between London banks.

This makes it unlikely that the two floating rates will move perfectly in line with each other. As one rate increases, the other rate might change by a different amount or might change later.

(b) **Financial derivatives**

Financial derivatives are **traded products** that have developed from the securities and currency markets. Examples of derivative products include futures and options in currencies and interest rates.

There are two main purposes for which these products might be used:

1 **Hedging against known risks**

This can best be explained by means of an example. The company might have a **commitment** to **make a payment** in a foreign currency on a **specific date in three months' time**. It knows the amount of the sum to be paid in foreign currency, but it cannot know what the exchange rate will be at that time. It therefore faces the risk that if the home currency depreciates against the foreign currency, the size of the payment in sterling will be greater than if the payment were made now. This risk could be **hedged** by using a derivative. Such a transaction would have a **commission cost associated** with it, but it would **limit the risk** faced by the company.

2 **Speculation**

Derivatives can also be used to **gamble** on **expectations of movements** in interest and exchange rates. For example, the investor might believe that sterling would weaken against the dollar, and therefore buy dollars futures. These dollars would then be sold on the spot market once the expected movement in rates had taken place. The transactions are made purely with the **motive of making a profit**, and are not linked to any underlying business transactions. They are therefore very risky.

Since QW has diversified, international interests, derivative products offer **significant benefits** in the management of the financial risks to which the company is exposed. The board needs to determine the level of risk that it is prepared to accept in these areas so that an integrated set of guidelines can be established for the effective management of these issues.

(c) **Hedging interest rate risk**

The main techniques available to hedge this type of risk are as follows.

Forward rate agreements

A **forward rate agreement** (FRA) is an OTC contract to lend or borrow a given sum of money in the future at an interest rate that is agreed today. For currencies, the equivalent is the **forward contract**: an agreement to buy or sell a given amount of currency in the future at an exchange rate that is agreed today. These contracts can be used to **'fix' interest rates or exchange rates** on future transactions, thus **removing the risk of rate movements** in the intervening period.

Interest rate futures

These operate in a similar way to forward rate agreements. However, they are not negotiated directly with a bank but are **traded on the futures market**. Consequently, the terms, the amounts and the periods are **standardised**. For this reason, forward rate agreements are normally more appropriate than interest rate futures to non-financial companies such as QW.

Interest rate options

An interest rate option provides the **right to borrow or to lend a specified amount at a guaranteed rate of interest**. On the date of expiry of the option, or before, the buyer must decide whether or not to **exercise the right**. Thus in a borrowing situation, the option will only be exercised if market interest rates have risen above the option rate. Tailor made contracts can be purchased from major banks, while standardised contracts are traded in a similar way to interest rate futures. The cost of taking out an option is generally higher than for a forward rate agreement.

Interest rate swaps

These are transactions that exploit different interest rates in different markets for borrowing, to **reduce interest costs** for either fixed or floating rate loans. An interest rate swap is an arrangement whereby two companies, or a company and a bank, **swap interest rate commitments** with each other. In a sense, each simulates the other's borrowings, although each party to the swap retains its obligations to the original lenders. This means that the parties must accept counterparty risk.

The main benefits of a swap as compared with other hedging instruments are as follows.

- **Transaction** costs **are low**, being limited to legal fees

- They are **flexible**, since they can be arranged in any size, and they can be reversed if necessary

- Companies **with different credit ratings** can **borrow at the best cost in the market** that is most accessible to them and then swap this benefit with another company to reduce the mutual borrowing costs

- Swaps allow **capital restructuring** by changing the nature of interest commitments without the need to redeem debt or to issue new debt, thus reducing transaction costs

Mock Exams

ACCA

Paper F9

Financial Management

Mock Examination 1

Question Paper	
Time allowed	
Reading and Planning Writing	15 minutes 3 hours
ALL FOUR questions are compulsory and MUST be attempted	
During reading and planning time only the question paper may be annotated	

DO NOT OPEN THIS PAPER UNTIL YOU ARE READY TO START UNDER EXAMINATION CONDITIONS

Question 1

It is currently December 20X7. Phoenix Co, which manufactures building products, experienced a sharp increase in profits before interest and tax from the $25m level in 20X5-6 to $40m in 20X6-7 as the economy emerged from recession, and demand for new houses increased. The increase in profits has been entirely due to volume expansion, with margins remaining static. It still has substantial excess capacity and therefore no pressing need to invest, apart from routine replacements.

In the past, Phoenix has followed a rather conservative financial policy, with restricted dividend payouts and relatively low borrowing levels. It now faces the issue of how to utilise an unexpectedly sizeable cash surplus. Directors have made two main suggestions. One is to redeem the $10m secured loan stock issued to finance a capacity increase several years previously, the other is to increase the dividend payment by the same amount. Phoenix's present capital structure is shown below.

	$m
Issued share capital (25c par value)	70
Reserves	130
Payables falling due after more than one year:	
7% secured loan notes 20Y7	10

Further information

(i)   Phoenix has not used an overdraft during the two years.
(ii)   The rate of tax on company profits is 30%.
(iii)   The dividend paid by Phoenix in 20X5-6 was 1.50 cents per share.
(iv)   Sector averages currently stand as follows.

Dividend cover	2.6 times
Gearing (long-term debt/equity)	45%
Interest coverage	6.5 times

Required

(a)   Calculate the dividend payout ratios and dividend covers for *both* 20X5-6 *and* for the reporting year 20X6-7, if the dividend is raised as proposed.   **(7 marks)**

(b)   You have recently been hired to work as a financial strategist for Phoenix, reporting to the finance director. Using the information provided, write a report to your superior, which identifies and discusses the relative merits of the two proposals for utilising the cash surplus.   **(18 marks)**

(Total = 25 marks)

229

Question 2

(a)   Discuss:

(i)   The significance of trade payables in a firm's working capital cycle; and   **(4 marks)**

(ii)   The dangers of over-reliance on trade credit as a source of finance.   **(4 marks)**

(b)   Keswick Co traditionally follows a highly aggressive working capital policy, with no long-term borrowing.
Key details from its recently compiled accounts appear below.

	$m
Sales (all on credit)	10.00
Earnings before interest and tax (EBIT)	2.00
Interest payments for the year	0.50
Shareholders' funds (comprising $1m issued share capital, par value 25c, and $1m revenue reserves)	2.00
Receivables	0.40
Inventories	0.70
Trade payables	1.50
Bank overdraft	3.00

A major supplier, which accounts for 50% of Keswick's cost of sales, is highly concerned about Keswick's
policy of taking extended trade credit. The supplier offers Keswick the opportunity to pay for supplies within
15 days in return for a discount of 5% on the invoiced value.

Keswick holds no cash balances but is able to borrow on overdraft from its bank at 12%. Tax on corporate
profit is paid at 30%.

Required

Determine the costs and benefits to Keswick of making this arrangement with its supplier, and recommend
whether Keswick should accept the offer.

Your answer should include the effects on:

–   The working capital cycle
–   Interest coverage
–   Profits after tax
–   Earnings per share
–   Return on equity
–   Capital gearing   **(12 marks)**

(c)   Sellmoor Co is considering a proposal to change its credit policy from allowing its receivables a credit period
of 50 days, to either 40 days or 60 days, and supplied you with the following data.

Period of credit allowed to receivables	Annual turnover (all on credit)
Days	$'000
50 (current)	420
40	350 (estimated)
60	520 (estimated)

The average profit/volume ratio for the company is 22% and the cost of financing receivables is 12%.

Required

Compute and explain briefly what the effect on profit of each proposal by Sellmoor Co would be, if adopted.

(5 marks)

(Total = 25 marks)

Question 3

(a)   Briefly explain the main features of the following.

   (i)   Sale and leaseback
   (ii)   Hire purchase
   (iii)   Finance leases   **(6 marks)**

(b)   Howgill Co is the leasing subsidiary of a major commercial bank. It is approached by Clint Co, a company entirely financed by equity, which operates in the pharmaceutical industry, with a request to arrange a lease contract to acquire new computer-controlled manufacturing equipment to further automate its production line. The outlay involved is $20m. The equipment will have only a four-year operating life due to the fast rate of technical change in this industry, and no residual worth. The basic project has a positive net present value when operating cash flows are discounted at the shareholders' required rate of return.

Howgill would finance the purchase of the machinery by borrowing at a pre-tax annual rate of 14½%. The purchase would be completed on the final day of its accounting year, when it would also require the first of the annual rental payments. Howgill currently pays tax at 30%, 12 months after its financial year end. A writing-down allowance is available based on a 25% reducing balance.

Under the terms of the lease contract, Howgill would also provide maintenance services, valued by Clint at $750,000 pa. These would be supplied by Howgill's computer maintenance sub-division at no incremental cost as it currently has spare capacity which is expected to persist for the foreseeable future. Clint has the same financial year as Howgill, also pays tax at 30% and its own bank will lend at 17½% before tax.

Required

Calculate the minimum rental which Howgill would have to charge in order to just break even on the lease contract. You may assume that the rental is wholly tax-allowable as a business expense.

                                                                                                (6 marks)

(c)   Assume that Howgill does proceed with the contract and charges an annual rental of $7m. Calculate whether, on purely financial criteria, Clint should lease the asset or borrow in order to purchase it outright:

   (i)   Ignoring the benefit to Clint of the maintenance savings   **(6 marks)**
   (ii)   Allowing for the maintenance savings.   **(3 marks)**

(d)   Discuss the non-financial factors that may influence the decision whether to lease or buy.   **(4 marks)**

                                                                                    (Total = 25 marks)

Question 4

(a) KB Co has a paid-up ordinary share capital of $1,500,000 represented by 6 million shares of 25c each. It has no loan capital. Earnings after tax in the most recent year were $1,200,000. The P/E ratio of the company is 12.

The company is planning to make a large new investment which will cost $5,040,000, and is considering raising the necessary finance through a rights issue at 192c.

Required

(i) Calculate the current market price of KB Co's ordinary shares. **(2 marks)**

(ii) Calculate the theoretical ex-rights price, and state what factors in practice might invalidate your calculation. **(6 marks)**

(iii) Briefly explain what is meant by a deep-discounted rights issue, identifying the main reasons why a company might raise finance by this method. **(3 marks)**

(b) As an alternative to a rights issue, KB Co might raise the $5,040,000 required by means of an issue of convertible loan notes at par, with a coupon rate of 6%. The loan notes would be redeemable in seven years' time. Prior to redemption, the loan notes may be converted at a rate of 35 ordinary shares per $100 nominal.

Required

(i) Explain the term *conversion premium* and calculate the conversion premium at the date of issue implicit in the data given. **(4 marks)**

(ii) Identify the advantages to KB Co of issuing convertible loan notes instead of the rights issue to raise the necessary finance. **(5 marks)**

(iii) Explain why the market value of convertible loan notes is likely to be affected by the dividend policy of the issuing company. **(5 marks)**

(Total = 25 marks)

Answers

DO NOT TURN THIS PAGE UNTIL YOU HAVE
COMPLETED THE MOCK EXAM

A PLAN OF ATTACK

We've already established that you've been told to do it 101 times, so it is of course superfluous to tell you for the 102nd time to **Take a good look at the paper before diving in to answer questions.** You are going to remember aren't you; good!

Which order to do the questions

Having **looked through** the **paper in detail,** you need to have worked out the **order** in which to attempt the questions. You will probably have decided which question looks the easiest and started with that one. Answer plans will help you to decide how to approach each question.

The next step

You're probably thinking that you don't know where to begin or you could answer all of the questions in two hours!

Option 1 (Oh dear)

If you are challenged by this paper, do the **questions in the order of how well you think you can answer them.**

- **Question 1** is a mainly written question but there are some easy calculations to warm up with in part (a). Do a detailed answer plan for part (b) to help you get started.

- **Question 2** may look daunting but there are a number of parts where marks can be scored independent of your ability to do every section.

- **Question 3** is a leasing question which may again look daunting. You can however gain plenty of easy marks if you use a clear format, show all your workings and don't panic!

- **Question 4** requires you to be able to calculate share prices and conversion premium which may be tricky. There are some easy marks for straightforward explanations.

Option 2 (This one's definitely easier)

Are you **sure** it is? If you are then that's encouraging but don't forget to do answer plans to make sure you don't miss the point of the questions.

- Don't just concentrate on the calculations in **Question 1.** Make sure you also write full answers to the discussion parts and remember to use a report format.

- Don't just do a brain dump of everything you know in **Question 2.** Make sure you apply your discussions to the organisation in the question.

- Time management is going to be important in **Question 3** as there are a lot of calculations to get through.

- Work through **Question 4** slowly and carefully making sure you answer each part fully and accurately.

Once more for the road

You must must must **allocate your time** according to the marks for the question in total, and for the parts of the questions. And you must must must also **follow the requirements exactly.**

Finished with fifteen minutes to spare?

Looks like you slipped up on the time allocation. However if you have, make sure you don't waste the last few minutes; go back to **any parts of questions that you didn't finish** because you ran out of time.

Forget about it!

Forget about what? Excellent, you already have.

BPP
LEARNING MEDIA

Question 1

Marking scheme

		Marks	
(a)	Profit after tax calculation	3	
	Payout ratio	2	
	Dividend cover	2	
			7
(b)	Report format	2	
	Discussion of loan redemption proposal	8	
	Discussion of dividend proposal	8	
			18
			25

(a) **Dividend payout ratios and dividend covers**

Phoenix Co	20X5-6	20X7-9
	$m	$m
Profit before interest and tax	25.00	40.00
Less: interest: $10m × 7%	0.70	0.70
Profit before tax	24.30	39.30
Tax	7.29	11.79
After tax profit	17.01	27.51
Total dividend: 280m shares × 1.5c	4.20	
$4.2m + $10m		14.20
Pay-out ratio (dividend/after-tax profit)	24.7%	51.6%
Dividend cover (after-tax profit/dividend)	4.05	1.94 times

(b) To: Finance Director
     From: Financial Strategist
     Date: 15 December 20X7

Report on proposals for using cash surpluses

Under the terms of reference for this report I am required to evaluate two proposals for the use of the company's $10 million cash surplus:

- **Redeeming** the $10 million secured 7% **loan**
- **Increasing** the **dividend payout** by $10 million

Before making a final decision, however, other possible uses for the cash should be considered, including:

- **Placing the money on deposit** or in liquid investments
- **Capital investment** for organic growth
- **Acquisition** of other **businesses**
- **Share buyback**

These other alternatives are not specifically discussed in this report.

(i)   **Background**

The cash surplus has arisen because of a marked **expansion** in the **volume** of our business as the economy emerged from the recession. We should, however, bear in mind that ours is an industry which suffers from volatile fluctuations in demand and in future years we might suffer cash shortages.

(ii)   **Proposal to redeem the $10 million secured 7% loan**

If the loan is redeemed, eliminating future interest payments, then future **dividends** can be increased. Because share prices of quoted companies reflect expectations of future dividend payouts, the company's share price should increase.

Impact on shareholders

Thus, from the shareholders' point of view, the effect of the loan redemption can be seen as a sacrifice of a potentially large dividend now in return for an **increased 'ex div' share price**. Shareholders seeking capital gains as opposed to cash dividends (usually for tax reasons) will prefer this option.

Risk reduction

Eliminating debt also means that the shareholders will suffer less risk: the volatility of their earnings ('**financial risk**') will decrease and the chances of bankruptcy or financial distress are lessened.

Arguments against redemption of the loan

(1)   **Gearing levels**

The **company's gearing is very low** compared with the sector average. This implies that the bankruptcy risk mentioned above is not significant. Gearing (debt/shareholders funds) at present is $10m/$200m = 5% compared with the sector average of 45%, and interest coverage is $25m/$0.7m = 35.7 times at the moment compared with the sector average of 6.5 times.

(2)   **Taxation**

Loan interest is an **allowable expense** against tax on profits. The return on shareholders' investment is increased by this tax saving if loan finance is used. The benefits of this tax reduction (known as the '**tax shield**') will be lost if the loan is redeemed.

(3)   **Shareholder viewpoint**

If not properly explained to the market, the **loan repayment** may be **interpreted** by shareholders as a sign that there are difficult times ahead. This may cause the share price to fall, rather than rise.

Interest rate comparisons

An important point when deciding whether to redeem a fixed interest loan is its **interest rate compared** with **expected future market interest rates**. For example, if the loan is redeemable now *at par* but to borrow in future would cost more than 7% then redemption would probably be unwise.

However, if the loan notes are quoted with a market value, the price at which it can be purchased and cancelled will adjust to take account of this effect.

(iii) **Proposal to increase the equity dividend by $10 million**

This proposal is the extreme alternative to the previous one: a large dividend is paid immediately but future dividends cannot be as large as if the loan were repaid; hence there will be no increase in 'ex div' share price.

Views of shareholders

This proposal will be preferred by those shareholders who want a **large immediate cash distribution** and will not suffer any adverse tax consequences if it is received as a dividend. Such shareholders are often tax-exempt institutions. However, higher rate tax payers may regard the increased dividend as very unwelcome if they were looking for share price growth rather than a taxed dividend. These shareholders may sell their shares, assuming that the company had changed its dividend policy to one of high taxable dividend payouts.

Taxation

If the loan is not repaid, the advantage of the **tax shield** from loan interest is retained.

Dividend signalling

The main problem with the proposed increase in dividend is that it is **very large** in percentage terms (a 238% increase). Unless the reasons for the increase are carefully explained to the market, the wrong signals can be picked up. Some shareholders may assume that dividends in **future years** will continue to increase at the same rate, whereas others may assume the company has run out of investment ideas and is signalling an end to growth. It is best to avoid confusion of this sort, as it can have an adverse effect on the share price. Companies wishing to pay large increases in cash to shareholders have avoided this confusion either by announcing 'one-off' **special dividends** or by making **share buy-backs**.

Dividend management

Most finance directors tend to believe that dividend policy should be **managed** in such a way that dividends show a **steady rate of increase** over time, rather than just being a residual balancing figure after investment and financing decisions have been made. This positive management of dividend policy is said to increase investor confidence, though the matter is far from proved.

(iv) **Making the choice**

As stated at the outset, the choice is not a simple alternative between paying a $10 million dividend and repaying the $10 million loan. There are several alternatives which must be discussed carefully, each of which could merit a report longer than this one. The end result is likely to be a combination of several applications for the money. We cannot at this stage, therefore, make any recommendations.

Question 2

Text references. Working capital management is covered in Chapters 4, 5 and 6.

Top tips. In (a)(i) it is helpful to explain the components of working capital and their inter-relationships linking working capital with cash.

In (a)(ii) you should consider not only the direct costs and dangers of reliance on trade credit, but also some of the potential dangers that it entails in terms of threat to supplies of goods and the potential to obtain credit from new suppliers in the future.

It is possible to have negative working capital, so don't get distracted in (b) and make the mistake of adding payables to the other elements of working capital. The question leads you through what you have to do, and you shouldn't assume that there will be a significant change in every figure. The twist comes at the end with the increased capital gearing. Make sure you use the right figures in the calculation, distinguishing between the **changes** in figures (the extra interest charge for example) and the new totals.

Your discussion needs to stress that the gearing deterioration outweighs significantly any potential benefits. However as the company seems to be in good shape, its chances of obtaining long-term loan finance (and thus having a better **match** of funds) appear to be good.

In (c) the key elements are contribution and cost of receivables.

Marking scheme

			Marks
(a)	Up to 2 marks for each point		8
(b)	Working capital cycle	2	
	Interest cover	2	
	Profits after tax	2	
	Earnings per share	2	
	Return on equity	2	
	Capital gearing	2	
			12
(c)	Calculation	4	
	Explanation	1	
			5
			25

(a) (i) **Working capital**

The net working capital of a business can be defined as its current assets less its current liabilities. The management of working capital is concerned with ensuring that **sufficient liquid resources** are maintained within the business. For the majority of businesses, particularly manufacturing businesses, trade payables will form the major part of the current liabilities figure, and will be a significant element in the make-up of the working capital balance.

Trade credit period

It follows that the trade credit period taken will be a major determinant of the working capital requirement of the company. This is calculated (in days) as the total value of trade payables divided by the level of credit purchases times 365. The actual length of the period will depend partly on the credit terms offered by suppliers and partly on the decisions made by the company. For example, the company may choose to negotiate longer terms with its suppliers although this may be at the expense of any available settlement discounts.

Working capital cycle

The longer the payable days, the shorter the working capital cycle. This can be defined as the receivable days plus the inventory holding days less the payable days.

(ii) For many firms, trade payables provide a very important source of short-term credit. Since very few companies currently impose interest charges on overdue accounts, taking extended credit can appear to be a very cheap form of short-term finance. However, such a policy entails some risks and costs that are not immediately apparent, as follows.

   (1) If discounts are being forgone, the **effective cost** of this should be evaluated – it may be more beneficial to shorten the credit period and take the discounts.

   (2) If the company gains a reputation for slow payment this will **damage its credit references** and it may find it difficult to obtain credit from new suppliers in the future.

   (3) Suppliers who are having to wait for their money may seek recompense in other ways, for example by raising prices or by placing a lower priority on new orders. Such actions could do **damage** to both the **efficiency and profitability** of the company.

   (4) Suppliers may place the company **'on stop'** until the account is paid. This can jeopardise supplies of essential raw materials which in turn could cause production to stop: this will obviously provide the company with a high level of unwanted costs.

(b) **Working capital cycle**

Receivable days:	$0.4m × 365/$10m	14.6 days
Inventory holding days:	$0.7m × 365/($10m – $2m)	31.9 days
Payable days:	$1.5m × 365/($10m – $2m)	68.4 days
Working capital cycle		(21.9 days)

This is a remarkably short working capital cycle which suggests that Keswick is unusually efficient in its management of working capital. The effect of the proposal by the supplier would be to reduce the payable period for 50% of the purchases from 68.4 days to 15 days. The new payable days figure would therefore fall to:

(68.4 × 50%) + (15 × 50%) = 41.7 days

The working capital cycle will therefore rise to:

14.6 + 31.9 – 41.7 = 4.8 days

Interest coverage

Interest coverage can be defined as EBIT (earnings before interest and tax) divided by annual interest payments. The current figure for Keswick is four times ($2.0m/$0.5m) which for the majority of companies would be quite reasonable. The effect of the proposal made by the supplier will be to reduce the cost of sales, and therefore increase EBIT, but at the same time increase the level of interest since the company will have to finance the reduction in the working capital cycle. These elements can be calculated as follows.

Improvement in EBIT = (($10m – $2m) × 50%) × 5% = $0.2m

The net advanced payment to the supplier will be:

(($10m – $2m) × 50%) – discount ($0.2m) = $3.8m.

This must be financed for an additional 53.4 days (68.4 – 15). If this is financed using the overdraft, the interest rate to be paid will be 12%, generating additional interest of $3.8m × 12% × 53.4/365 = $66,700.

The interest coverage now becomes:

($2.0m + $0.2m)/($0.5m + $0.0667m) = 3.88 times

This represents only a very small reduction in the interest coverage.

Profits after tax

These will change as follows.

	Before	After
	$'000	$'000
Earnings before interest and tax	2,000	2,200
Interest	(500)	(566)
Taxable profit	1,500	1,634
Tax at 30%	450	490
Profit after tax	1,050	1,144

The proposal should give a small improvement in post-tax profit.

Earnings per share

Earnings attributable to equity have been calculated above (the profit after tax figure). The number of shares in issue is 4m ($1m/25c).

Existing EPS:	$1.050m/4m	=	26.3 cents
Projected EPS:	$1.144m/4m	=	28.6 cents

Thus, the EPS is also likely to improve if the proposals are adopted.

Return on equity

Return on shareholders' funds is calculated as profit attributable to equity divided by shareholders' funds. ($2m):

Existing:	$1.050m/$2m	=	52.5%
Projected:	$1.144m/$2m	=	57.2%

The return on equity will also rise if the proposals are adopted.

Capital gearing

Capital gearing is defined as prior charge capital (in this case the bank overdraft of $3m) divided by shareholders' funds ($2m). The existing level of gearing is therefore 150% ($3m/$2m).

If the proposals are adopted, the average level of the overdraft will rise by $3.8m × 53.4/365 = $556,000. The gearing level will therefore increase to 178% ($3.556m/$2m).

Summary

In summary, the effect of the proposal would be to give a **slight increase** in the **profitability** of Keswick, as measured by profit after tax, earnings per share and return on equity, but this would be at the expense of a **small reduction** in the **interest coverage**, a **lengthening** of the **working capital cycle**, and a significant increase in the level of **capital gearing**. It is this final item that gives the greatest cause for concern – to have such a high gearing level based totally on overdraft finance which is repayable on demand is a very dangerous position to be in. It is suggested that Keswick should either attempt to renegotiate its terms with the supplier to give a longer credit period than that being proposed, or alternatively seek to restructure its debt and to convert at least a part of the overdraft into more secure long-term borrowings.

(c) **Effect on profit levels**

The calculations show that the savings in financing costs resulting from a reduction in the credit period are more than outweighed by the associated **loss of contribution**. However, extending the credit period should increase the level of profits. The calculations also do not take into account the effect of the change in policy on the level of bad debts which could be expected to increase if the credit period is extended. An evaluation of this should be undertaken before any decisions are made.

Effect on profit levels of changing the credit period

	Credit period		
	50 days	40 days	60 days
	$	$	$
Turnover	420,000	350,000	520,000
Average receivables	57,534	38,356	85,479
Contribution (22%)	92,400	77,000	114,400
Cost of receivables (12%)	(6,904)	(4,603)	(10,257)
Profit	85,496	72,397	104,143
Increase/(decrease)	–	(13,099)	18,647

Question 3

Marking scheme

			Marks
(a)	Up to 2 marks for each explanation		6
(b)	Calculation of minimum rental		6
(c)	Lease or buy calculation	6	
	Effect of maintenance savings	3	
			9
(d)	1 mark for each factor		4
			25

(a) (i) **Sale and leaseback**

Sale and leaseback is an arrangement which is **similar to mortgaging**. A business which already owns an asset, for example a building or an item of equipment, agrees to sell the asset to a financial institution and then immediately to lease it back on terms specified in the agreement. The business has the **benefit of the funds from the sale** while retaining use of the asset, in return for regular payments to the financial institution.

Benefits of sale and leaseback

The principal benefit is that the company gains **immediate access to liquid funds**; however this is at the expense of the ability to profit from any capital appreciation (potentially significant in the case of property), and the capacity to borrow elsewhere may be reduced since the balance sheet value of assets will fall.

(ii) **Hire purchase**

Hire purchase (HP) is a form of **instalment credit** whereby the business purchases goods on credit and pays for them by instalments. The periodic payments include both an **interest element** on the initial price and a **capital repayment element**. The mechanics of the transaction are as follows.

(1) The **supplier** of the asset **sells** it to a **finance house**.

(2) The **supplier** of the asset **delivers** it to the **customer** who will be the user and the eventual owner.

(3) The hire purchase agreement is made between the **finance house** and the **customer**.

Benefits of hire purchase

At the end of the period, ownership of the asset passes to the user, who is also able to claim capital allowances on the basic purchase cost of the asset.

(iii) **Finance leases**

Finance leases are similar to HP contracts in that the asset is sold not to the user but to an intermediary who then leases the asset to the user in return for periodic payments. However, unlike with HP, **ownership** of the asset does not transfer to the user at the end of the lease period, but is retained by the purchaser. The **purchaser** (not the user) can **claim tax depreciation**, which may be passed on to the user in the form of a reduction in the periodic payments. A further difference is that although the user does not own the asset, entries **appear** in the **user's balance sheet** and income statement to reflect the capital element of the lease, the interest element of the payments, and the remaining lease commitment. This is to ensure that all forms of long-term debt are fully reflected in the balance sheet.

Primary and secondary periods

Many finance leases are structured into a '**primary period**' which covers the major part of the economic life of the asset, and a '**secondary period**' during which the user continues to lease the asset, but at a much lower (often only nominal) rate.

(b) **Cost to Howgill**

The cost to Howgill will be the purchase cost of the asset, less the present value of the tax allowable depreciation. Since there is no incremental cost to Howgill in providing the computer maintenance, the cost of this will be excluded from the calculations. The cash flows will be discounted at the after tax cost of borrowing: $14.5\% \times (1 - 0.3) = 10\%$ approx. The present value of the net-of-tax tax depreciation can now be found.

Year	0	1	2	3	4	5
	$'000	$'000	$'000	$'000	$'000	$'000
WDV at start of year	20,000	15,000	11,250	8,437	6,328	
WDV at end of year	15,000	11,250	8,437	6,328	–	
Depreciation	5,000	3,750	2,813	2,109	6,328	
30% tax saving on depreciation		1,500	1,125	844	633	1,898
Discount factor at 10%		0.909	0.826	0.751	0.683	0.621
PV of tax savings		1,364	929	634	432	1,178

Thus the NPV of the tax savings over the period is **$4,537,000**, say $4.5m approximately. Since the NPV of the tax savings amount to $4.5m, the effective net-of-tax cost of the machinery is **$15.5m** ($20m – $4.5m). Therefore for Howgill to break even, the present value of the after tax rental income must be at least $15.5m. The structure of the cash flows to Howgill will be as follows (R = annual pre-tax rental income).

BPP)))
LEARNING MEDIA

Year	0	1	2	3	4
Income	R	R	R	R	
Tax		0.3R	0.3R	0.3R	0.3R
Post tax income	R	0.7R	0.7R	0.7R	(0.3R)
10% discount factor	1.0	0.909	0.826	0.751	0.683
PV of income	R	0.636R	0.578R	0.526R	(0.205R)

NPV of after tax rental income = 2.535R

To break even: 2.535R = $15.5m*

   R = $6.11m

Thus the minimum annual rental required for Howgill to break even is $6,110,000 per annum.

(c)   (i)   **Lease or buy**

The approach is to calculate the net of tax present value of the two options available to Clint. The discount rate to be used will be the cost of borrowing net of tax. $17.5\% \times (1 - 0.3)$ = approximately 12%.

Purchasing outright

Year	0	1	2	3	4	5
	$'000	$'000	$'000	$'000	$'000	$'000
Initial outlay	20,000					
Tax savings on depreciation (above)		1,500	1,125	844	633	1,898
Net cash flow	(20,000)	1,500	1,125	844	633	1,898
Discount factor at 12%	1.000	0.893	0.797	0.712	0.636	0.567
PV of cash flow	(20,000)	1,340	897	601	403	1,076

Thus the NPV cost of purchasing outright is $15,683,000.

Leasing

Year	0	1	2	3	4
	$'000	$'000	$'000	$'000	$'000
Annual rental	(7,000)	(7,000)	(7,000)	(7,000)	
Tax savings (rental × 30%)		2,100	2,100	2,100	2,100
Net cash flow	(7,000)	(4,900)	(4,900)	(4,900)	2,100
Discount factor at 12%	1.000	0.893	0.797	0.712	0.636
PV of cash flow	(7,000)	(4,376)	(3,905)	(3,489)	1,336

Thus the NPV cost of leasing is **$17,434,000**. This is $1,751,000 more than the NPV cost of direct purchase over the life of the equipment, and direct purchase therefore appears more attractive on financial grounds.

(ii)   **Effect of additional maintenance costs**

The cost of purchase can be re-evaluated to take into account the additional maintenance costs that would be incurred of $750,000 per year. These costs are assumed to start in year 1, with the associated tax saving coming through in the subsequent year.

Year	0	1	2	3	4	5
	$'000	$'000	$'000	$'000	$'000	$'000
Initial outlay	(20,000)					
Tax savings on depreciation (above)		1,500	1,125	844	633	1,898
Maintenance costs		(750)	(750)	(750)	(750)	
Tax saving			225	225	225	225
Net cash flow	(20,000)	750	600	319	108	2,123
Discount factor at 12%	1.000	0.893	0.797	0.712	0.636	0.567
PV of cash flow	(20,000)	670	478	227	69	1,204

If the maintenance costs are taken into account, the NPV cost of purchase rises to **$17,352,000**, which is slightly less (by $30,000) than the cost of leasing. Although the decision is not reversed, the relative costs are marginal, and other factors should also be considered, for instance the reliability and availability of the different maintenance options.

(d) **Non-financial factors influencing the decision**

(i) The purchase option involves **three separate decisions** covering acquisition of the asset, financing and maintenance. The lease is one contract covering all three aspects and this is less risky.

(ii) The **flexibility** of the arrangements, for example the ability to exchange the asset after one or two years if technology changes.

(iii) The manner in which the **transactions are shown** in the company's accounts, for example whether asset on contract hire is capitalised.

(iv) If the asset is leased, the company does **not** have to **worry** about **the risks** involved in eventually selling it.

Question 4

Text references. Sources of finance are covered in Chapter 12, business valuations in Chapter 17.

Top tips. This question tests your knowledge of the theory surrounding rights issues and convertibles.

Part (a) (i) involves a simple calculation of share price using EPS and P/E ratios.

When considering in (a)(ii) the likely price following the rights issue, you should take into account stock market factors as well as the performance of the company. Does the market view the company rationally? Is the company competing for funds?

Don't forget in (a) (iii) that shares can never be issued below their nominal value; you need to mention this as it does limit the discounts on deep discounted issues.

In (b) (i) you are after a figure for how much loan notes you will need to purchase a single share on conversion.

(b) (ii) is a very good summary of the factors you should take into account when considering any new source of finance. One thing that will concern the business is how likely it is to obtain the funds it seeks, so don't forget to look at things from the finance provider's viewpoint.

The dividend valuation model is at the heart of the answer to (b) (iii).

Marking scheme

				Marks
(a)	(i)	Calculation of market value		2
	(ii)	Calculation of TERP	3	
		Explanation of factors	<u>3</u>	
				6
	(iii)	Explanation of deep-discounted rights issue	1	
		Reasons for use	<u>2</u>	
				3
(b)	(i)	Explanation	2	
		Calculation	<u>2</u>	
				4
	(ii)	1 mark per advantage		5
	(iii)	Explanation		<u>5</u>
				<u>25</u>

(a)   (i)   The **current market price** can be found by multiplying the earnings per share (EPS) by the price/earnings (P/E) ratio.

EPS is $1.2m/6m = 20 cents per share
P/E ratio is 12
Market price of shares is $12 \times 20c$ = **$2.40 per share**

      (ii)   In order to raise $5,040,000 at a price of 192 cents, the company will need to issue an additional 2,625,000 ($5,040,000/$1.92) shares.

Following the investment, the total number of shares in issue will be 8,625,000 (6,000,000 + 2,625,000).

At this point, the total value of the company will be:

$(6m \times \$2.40) + \$5,040,000 = \$19,440,000$

The **theoretical ex-rights price** will therefore be $19.44m/8.625m = **$2.25**.

Alternative solution

Theoretical ex-rights price

$$= \frac{1}{N+1}((N + \text{cum rights price}) + \text{issue price})$$

$$= \frac{1}{\left(\frac{6,000}{2,625}\right)+1} + \left(\left(\frac{6,000}{2,625} \times 2.40\right) + 1.92\right)$$

$= \$2.25$

Problems with calculations

(1)   The **costs of arranging the issue** have not been included in the calculations.

(2)   The **market view** of the **quality of the new investment** will affect the actual price of the company's shares.

(3)   If the **issue** is **not fully subscribed** and a significant number of shares remain with the underwriters, this will **depress the share price**.

(4)   The effect of the new investment on the **risk profile** of the company and the expected **future dividend stream** could also cause the share price to differ from that predicted.

(5)   The price of the shares depends not only on the financial performance of the company, but also on the **overall level of demand** in the stock market. If the market moves significantly following the announcement of the issue, this will affect the actual price at which the shares are traded.

(iii) Features of deep discounted rights issue

In a **deep-discounted** rights issue, the new shares are priced at a **large discount** to the current market price of the shares. The purpose of this is to ensure that the issue is well subscribed and that shares are not left with the underwriters, and thus this form of issue pricing is attractive when the stock market is particularly volatile. However, the shares cannot be issued at a price which is below their nominal value.

Disadvantage of deep discounted rights issue

The main drawback to this approach is that a **larger number of shares** will need to be **issued** in order to raise the required amount of finance, and this will lead to a larger dilution of earnings per share and dividends per share.

(b)   (i)   **Conversion premium**

The **conversion premium** is the **difference** between the **issue value** of the **notes** and the **conversion value** as at the date of issue. In other words it is the measure of the additional expense involved in buying shares via the convertible notes as compared with buying the shares on the open market immediately.

In this case, $100 loan notes can be converted into 35 ordinary shares. The **effective price** of these shares is therefore $2.86 ($100/35) per share.

The **current market price** of the shares is $2.40. The **conversion premium** is therefore $2.86 − $2.40 = **46 cents.** This can also be expressed in percentage terms as **19%** (0.46/2.40).

(ii)   **Advantages of issuing convertible loan notes**

(1)   **Convertibles** should be **cheaper than equity** because they offer greater security to the investor. This may make them particularly attractive in fast growing but high-risk companies.

(2)   **Issue costs** are **lower** for loan stock than for equity.

(3)   **Interest** on the **loan notes** is **tax deductible**, unlike dividends on ordinary shares.

(4)   There is **no immediate change** in the **existing structure** of control, although this will change over time as conversion rights are exercised.

(5)   There is no **immediate dilution** in **earnings** and **dividends per share**.

(iii)   **Dividend policy**

Dividend policy is one of the major factors which determines the share price. Under the **dividend valuation model**, the share price is held to be directly related both to the current dividend and to the expected future growth in dividends:

$$p_0 = \frac{d_0(1+g)}{(k_e - g)}$$

where: p_0 = market price of shares
d_0 = current level of dividend
k_e = required rate of return
g = growth in dividend

Impact of dividend growth

Thus it can be seen that dividend growth is important in determining the likely market value of the shares. As has already been discussed above, the market value of the shares is very important in determining the price of convertibles, and therefore the dividend policy of the company will have an important effect on the value of convertible notes.

ACCA

Paper F9

Financial Management

Mock Examination 2

Question Paper	
Time allowed	
Reading and Planning Writing	**15 minutes** **3 hours**
ALL FOUR questions are compulsory and MUST be attempted	
During reading and planning time only the question paper may be annotated	

DO NOT OPEN THIS PAPER UNTIL YOU ARE READY TO START UNDER EXAMINATION CONDITIONS

Question 1

Cavic Co services custom cars and provides its clients with a courtesy car while servicing is taking place. It has a fleet of 10 courtesy cars which it plans to replace in the near future. Each new courtesy car will cost $15,000. The trade-in value of each new car declines over time as follows:

Age of courtesy car (years)	1	2	3
Trade-in value ($/car)	11,250	9,000	6,200

Servicing and parts will cost $1,000 per courtesy car in the first year and this cost is expected to increase by 40% per year as each vehicle grows older. Cleaning the interior and exterior of each courtesy car to keep it up to the standard required by Cavic's clients will cost $500 per car in the first year and this cost is expected to increase by 25% per year.

Cavic Co has a cost of capital of 10%. Ignore taxation and inflation.

Required

(a) Using the equivalent annual cost method, calculate whether Cavic Co should replace its fleet after one year, two years, or three years. **(12 marks)**

(b) Discuss the causes of capital rationing for investment purposes. **(4 marks)**

(c) Explain how an organisation can determine the best way to invest available capital under capital rationing. Your answer should refer to the following issues:

    (i)   Single-period capital rationing;
    (ii)   Multi-period capital rationing;
    (iii)   Project divisibility;
    (iv)   The investment of surplus funds. **(9 marks)**

(Total = 25 marks)

Question 2

Extracts from the recent financial statements of Anjo Co are as follows:

INCOME STATEMENTS

	20X6	20X5
	$000	$000
Revenue	15,600	11,100
Cost of sales	9,300	6,600
Gross profit	6,300	4,500
Administration expenses	1,000	750
Profit before interest and tax	5,300	3,750
Interest	100	15
Profit before tax	5,200	3,735

BALANCE SHEET EXTRACTS

	20X6		20X7	
	$'000	$'000	$'000	$'000
Non-current assets		5,750		5,400
Current assets				
Inventories	3,000		1,300	
Receivables	3,800		1,850	
Cash	120		900	
		6,920		4,050
Current liabilities				
Trade payables	2,870		1,600	
Overdraft	1,000		150	
		(3,870)		(1,750)
Total assets less current liabilities		8,800		7,700

All sales were on credit. Anjo Co has no long-term debt. Credit purchases in each year were 95% of cost of sales. Anjo Co pays interest on its overdraft at an annual rate of 8%. Current sector averages are as follows:

Inventory days: 90 days   Receivable days: 60 days   Payable days: 80 days

Required

(a)   Calculate the following ratios for each year and comment on your findings.

   (i)   Inventory days
   (ii)   Receivable days
   (iii)   Payable days   **(6 marks)**

(b)   Calculate the length of the cash operating cycle (working capital cycle) for each year and explain its
       significance.   **(4 marks)**

(c)   Discuss the relationship between working capital management and business solvency, and explain the
       factors that influence the optimum cash level for a business.   **(7 marks)**

(d)   A factor has offered to take over sales ledger administration and debt collection for an annual fee of 0·5% of
       credit sales. A condition of the offer is that the factor will advance Anjo Co 80% of the face value of its
       receivables at an interest rate 1% above the current overdraft rate. The factor claims that it would reduce
       outstanding receivables by 30% and reduce administration expenses by 2% per year if its offer were
       accepted.

       Required

       Evaluate whether the factor's offer is financially acceptable, basing your answer on the financial information
       relating to 20X6.   **(8 marks)**
                                                                                           (Total = 25 marks)

Question 3

JER Co wishes to raise finance for a major investment project by means of a rights issue, and is proposing to issue shares on the basis of 1 for 5 at a price of $1.30 each. The following information relates to JER Co.

Current earnings: $1.5 million
Dividend paid (cents per share)
20X5:8
20X6:9
20X7:11
20X8:11
20X9:12

JER Co has 5 million ordinary shares in issue, with a market price of $1.60 each. JER Co has $1 million of irredeemable 12% debentures in issue, with a market price of $80 per $100 nominal value. It also has 500,000 15% preference shares in issue, with a nominal value per share of $1, and a market value of $1.45. The tax rate is 33%.

James Brown currently owns 10,000 shares in JER Co and is seeking advice on whether to not to take up the proposed rights.

Required

(a) Explain the difference between a rights issue and a scrip issue. Your answer should include comment on the reasons why companies make such issues and the effect of the issues on private investors. **(7 marks)**

(b) Calculate:

(i) The theoretical value of James Brown's shareholding if he takes up his rights
(ii) The theoretical value of James Brown's rights if he chooses to sell them **(4 marks)**

(c) Using only the information given above, and applying the dividend growth model formula, calculate the weighted average cost of capital of JER Co. **(8 marks)**

(d) Explain how a belief that the stock market operates with a strong level of efficiency might affect the behaviour of the finance directors of publicly quoted companies. **(6 marks)**

(Total = 25 marks)

Question 4

JetAWay is a 'low cost' airline providing airline services between 25 cities in the European Union. It now operates 40 aircraft and employs 7,500 people across the EU. The main areas of employment are in Aberdeen, where the company's headquarters and main aircraft service centre are located, Milan, which maintains the company's database services and most recently Selab, a new member of the EU. JetAWay recently opened a repair centre in Selab with the promise of connecting the main airport to 10 other European destinations.

Operations

JetAWay operates 275 different services every day ranging from 'commuter style' services, being cities with less than one hour flying time, to provision of holiday services. The 25 cities it serves are in 15 different countries with only 4 of these countries being in the Eurozone. JetAWay has to maintain staff in each country with salaries being paid in the local currency.

Customers make bookings using the Internet or JetAWay's call centre. All bookings are made in euros or the relevant local currency. However, tickets can be purchased from any of JetAWay's 15 national websites, and then funds are transferred via the Milan data centre to other locations as necessary. Currencies in some European countries which are not aligned to the euro still fluctuate significantly.

JetAWay has recognised has ordered 10 second-hand aircraft from an American airline which recently went into chapter 11 bankruptcy. The aircraft are only 3 years old and can seat 126 passengers each.

The aircraft will be available in three months' time at a cost of $40 million. JetAWay does not have any surplus funds. The following additional information is available:

	US $		UK £	
	Deposit rate	Borrowing rate	Deposit rate	Borrowing rate
	%	%	%	%
1 month	6.75	7.75	8.25	10.50
3 months	7.00	8.25	8.50	10.75

$/£ exchange rate ($=£1)

Spot	1.6625 – 1.6635
1 month forward	1.6565 – 1.6577
3 months forward	1.6445 – 1.6460

Required

(a) Explain the major types of foreign exchange risk (or currency risk) that JetAWay could be subject to regarding its European operations, noting the extent to which the company is affected by each risk.

(8 marks)

(b) JetAWay would like to hedge against exchange rate movements in the next three months. Calculate whether forward exchange contracts or the money markets should be used to hedge this risk. **(6 marks)**

(c) Explain the four-way equivalence model. **(4 marks)**

(d) Discuss the characteristics and benefits of interest rate swaps compared with other forms of interest rate management, including forward rate agreements and interest rate futures. **(7 marks)**

(Total = 25 marks)

Answers

**DO NOT TURN THIS PAGE UNTIL YOU HAVE
COMPLETED THE MOCK EXAM**

A PLAN OF ATTACK

We've already established that you've been told to do it 102 times, so it is of course superfluous to tell you for the 103rd time to **Take a good look at the paper before diving in to answer questions.** You are going to remember aren't you; good!

Which order to do the questions

Having **looked through** the **paper in detail,** you need to have worked out the **order** in which to attempt the questions. You will probably have decided which question looks the easiest and started with that one. Answer plans will help you to decide how to approach each question.

The next step

You're probably thinking that you don't know where to begin or you could answer all of the questions in two hours!

Option 1 (Oh dear)

If you are challenged by this paper, do the **questions in the order of how well you think you can answer them.**

- **Question 1** has 13 marks for explanations which can be written even if you struggle with the calculations in part (a).

- The calculations in parts (a) and (b) of **Question 2** are not too difficult if you can remember the formulae! Part (c) can be answered if you are struggling with the calculations in the other parts of the question.

- **Question 3** is a wide ranging share issue question which may look daunting. You can however gain marks in each part even if you cannot complete all of the calculations.

- **Question 4** concerns interest rate and exchange rate risks which you may find difficult. There are however plenty of marks available for some straightforward discussions and explanations.

Option 2 (This one's definitely easier)

Are you **sure** it is? If you are then that's encouraging but don't forget to do answer plans to make sure you don't miss the point of the questions.

- Don't just concentrate on the calculations in **Question 1.** Make sure you also write full answers to the discussion parts.

- Make sure you do full written explanations in **Question 2,** there are as many marks for discussion as for calculations.

- Time management is going to be important in **Question 3** as there are a lot of calculations to get through. Make sure you leave enough time for the written parts of the question which have equal marks.

- **Question 4** answers need to be sufficiently detailed and, in part (a), applied to the organisation in the question.

Once more for the road

You must must must **allocate your time** according to the marks for the question in total, and for the parts of the questions. And you must must must also **follow the requirements exactly.**

Finished with fifteen minutes to spare?

Looks like you slipped up on the time allocation. However if you have, make sure you don't waste the last few minutes; go back to **any parts of questions that you didn't finish** because you ran out of time.

Forget about it!

Forget about what? Excellent, you already have.

BPP ///
LEARNING MEDIA

Question 1

Text reference. Capital rationing is covered in Chapter 11.

Top tips. Parts (b) and (c) can be answered with no reference to the rest of the question. You might choose to do them first and to get these marks before doing the calculations in part (a).

In part (a) show your workings. This will ensure you earn good marks even if you make an arithmetic error.

Easy marks. Students are often tempted to spend more time on the numerical elements of a question.

Part (b) was straightforward and full marks should be attainable for making some obvious discussion points.

Again this is a question where a proforma approach could be used. Once you have your proforma for part (a) set out you should have been able to pick up some easy marks for costs and annuity factors.

There was a gift of a mark in part (a) for making a recommendation. Make a recommendation based on your calculations. As long as you recommend the lowest cost then the mark is yours!

For Part (c) make sure you cover all four elements covered in the question. In order to ensure this try to use separate sub-headings.

Marking scheme

			Marks
(a)	Servicing costs	1	
	Cleaning costs	1	
	Present values of total costs	1	
	Present values of trade-in values	2	
	Net present values of costs of each cycle	3	
	Annuity factors	1	
	Equivalent annual costs	2	
	Recommendation	1	
			12
(b)	Causes of capital rationing		4
(c)	Single-period and multi-period capital rationing	3-4	
	Project divisibility	3-4	
	Investment of surplus funds	2-3	
	Maximum		9
			25

Answer plan

This question has three parts.

It might be useful to sketch out an answer plan before you embark on this question so that you pick up the requirements of all parts of the question and don't just do a mind dump of all you know.

Step 1   For part (a)

- Set out the proformas for EAC calculations
- Show your workings
- Make and state your recommendation

Step 2 Part (b)

- State and explain the causes of capital rationing

Step 3 Part (c)

- Plan your answer before answering this part of the question
- Make sure you cover all parts of the question

(a) **Calculation of equivalent annual cost**

Year	1	2	3
Servicing costs (W1)	10,000	14,000	19,600
Cleaning costs (W2)	5,000	6,250	7,813
Total costs	15,000	20,250	27,413
Discount factors	0.909	0.826	0.751
Present values of costs	13,635	16,727	20,587

Replacement cycle (years)

	1	2	3
Cost of new vehicles	150,000	150,000	150,000
PV of Year 1 costs	13,635	13,635	13,635
PV of Year 2 costs		16,727	16,727
PV of Year 3 costs			20,587
Sum of PV of costs	163,635	180,362	200,949
Less:			
PV of trade-in value (W3)	102,263	74,340	46,562
Net PV of cost of cycle	61,372	106,022	154,387
Annuity factor	0.909	1.736	2.487
Equivalent annual cost	67,516	61,073	62,078

Replacement after two years is recommended, since this replacement cycle has the **lowest equivalent annual cost**.

Workings

1 **Servicing costs**

Year 1: $1,000 \times 10 = \$10,000$
Year 2: $10,000 \times 1.4 = \$14,000$
Year 3: $14,000 \times 1.4 = \$19,600$

2 **Cleaning costs**

Year 1: $500 \times 10 = \$5,000$
Year 2: $5,000 \times 1.25 = \$6,250$
Year 3: $6,250 \times 1.25 = \$7,813$

3 **PV of trade-in values**

Year 1: $11,250 \times 10 \times 0.909 = \$102,263$
Year 2 $9,000 \times 10 \times 0.826 = \$74,340$
Year 3: $6,200 \times 10 \times 0.751 = \$46,562$

(b) In order to invest in all projects with a positive net present value a company must be able to raise funds as and when it needs them: this is only possible in a **perfect capital market**. In practice capital markets are not perfect and the capital available for investment is likely to be **limited** or **rationed**. The causes of capital rationing may be external (hard capital rationing) or internal (soft capital rationing).

Soft capital rationing is more common than hard capital rationing. When a company cannot raise external finance even though it wishes to do so, this may be because providers of debt finance see the company as being **too risky**. In terms of **financial risk**, the company's gearing may be seen as too high, or its interest cover may be seen as too low. From a **business risk** point of view, lenders may be uncertain whether a company's future profits will be sufficient to meet increased future interest payments because its trading prospects are poor, or because they are seen as too variable.

When managers **impose restrictions** on the funds they are prepared to make available for capital investment, soft capital rationing is said to occur. One reason for soft capital rationing is that managers may not want to raise new external finance.

For example, they may not wish to raise new debt finance because they believe it would be unwise to commit the company to meeting future interest payments given the current economic outlook. They may not wish to issue new equity because the finance needed is insufficient to justify the **transaction costs** of a new issue, or because they wish to avoid **dilution of control**.

Another reason for soft capital rationing is that managers may prefer **slower organic growth**, where they can remain in control of the growth process, to the sudden growth arising from taking on one or more large investment projects.

A key reason for soft capital rationing is the desire by managers to make capital investments **compete** for funds, ie to create an internal market for investment funds. This competition for funds is likely to weed out weaker or marginal projects, thereby channelling funds to more robust investment projects with better chances of success and larger margins of safety, and reducing the risk and uncertainty associated with capital investment.

(c)   The net present value decision rule is to invest in all projects that have a **positive** net present value. By following this decision rule, managers will **maximise the value of a company** and therefore maximise the **wealth of ordinary shareholders**, which is a primary objective of financial management. Even when capital is rationed, it is still essential to be able to offer advice on which capital investment projects should be selected in order to secure the **maximum return** for the investing company, ie the maximum overall net present value.

Single-period and multi-period capital rationing

Capital may be rationed in more than one period, ie not only in the current period at the start of an investment project (single-period rationing), but in future periods as well (multi-period capital rationing). Selecting the best projects for investment in order to maximise overall net present value when faced with multi-period capital rationing calls for the use of **linear programming**. Here, the available capital investments are expressed as an **objective function**, subject to a series of constraints.

Project divisibility

The approach to solving single-period capital rationing problems depends on whether projects are **divisible** or not. A divisible project is one where a partial investment can be made in order to gain a pro rata net present value. For example, investing in a forest is a divisible project, since the amount of land purchased can be varied according to the funds available for investment (providing the seller agrees to a partial sale, of course). A non-divisible project is one where it is not possible to invest less than the full amount of capital. When building an oil refinery, for example, it is not possible to build only one part of the overall facility.

Where projects are divisible, the objective of maximising the net present value arising from invested funds can be achieved by **ranking projects** according to their profitability index and investing sequentially in order of decreasing profitability index, beginning with the highest, assuming that each project can be invested in only once, ie is non-repeatable.

The **profitability index** can be defined as net present value divided by initial investment. Ranking projects by profitability index is an example of **limiting factor analysis**. Because projects are divisible, there will be no investment funds left over: when investment funds are insufficient to for the next ranked project, part of the project can be taken on because it is divisible.

When projects are non-divisible, the objective of maximising the net present value arising from invested funds can be achieved by calculating the net present value arising from different combinations of projects. With this approach, there will usually be some surplus funds remaining from the funds initially available.

The investment of surplus funds

When investigating combinations of non-divisible projects in order to find the combination giving rise to the highest net present value, any **return from investing surplus funds is ignored**. The net present value analysis has been based on the company's average cost of capital and it is unlikely that surplus funds can be invested in order to earn a return as high as this.

Investment of surplus funds in, for example, the money markets would therefore be an investment project that would be rejected as having a negative net present value, or an internal rate of return less than the company's average cost of capital if using IRR to assess investments projects. However, it is **good working capital management** to ensure that liquid funds are invested to earn the highest available return, subject to any risk constraints, in order to increase overall profitability.

Question 2

Text reference. Working capital management is covered in Chapters 4, 5 and 6.

Top tips. Parts (c) can be answered with no reference to the rest of the question. You might choose to answer it first and to get these marks before doing the calculations in the rest of the question.

In parts (a) and (b) you were asked for calculations based on formulae you should have learnt. As a starting point for answering these types of questions write out the formula first and then slot in the numbers.

Where a question asks for a number of factors, as in part (c), then try to give as many factors as you can think of. Don't limit yourself to just a couple of points.

Note that there are two separate elements to part (b).

Easy marks. Part (a) and (b) were both very straightforward calculations followed by brief discussion parts. Note that there were as many marks for the discussion elements as the calculation.

Marking scheme

			Marks
(a)	Ratio calculations	3	
	Comment	3	
			6
(b)	Calculation of cash operating cycle	2	
	Significance of cash operating cycle	2	
			4
(c)	Working capital and business solvency	3-4	
	Factors influencing optimum cash level	4-5	
	Maximum		7
(d)	New level of receivables	1	
	Finance saving	1	
	Administration cost savings	1	
	Interest on advance form factor	2	
	Factor annual fee	1	
	Net benefit of factor's offer	1	
	Conclusion and discussion	1	
			8
			25

Answer plan

It might be useful to sketch out an answer plan for part (c) before you embark on this part of the question so that you pick up the requirements of the question and don't just do a mind dump of all you know with no reference to the question.

Step 1   For part (a)

- Calculate the ratios
- Comment on your findings

Step 2   Part (b)

- Calculate the length of the operating cycle
- Explain the significance

Step 3   Part (c)

- Discuss the relationship between capital management and business solvency
- Explain the factors that influence optimum cash levels

Step 4   Part (d)

- Number crunch – showing all your workings and assumptions
- State your conclusion

(a) **Inventory days**

$$\text{Inventory Days} = \frac{\text{Inventory level at year end}}{\text{Cost of sales}} \times 365$$

20X6: (3,000/9,300) × 365 = 118 days
20X5: (1,300/6,600) × 365 = 72 days

Sector average: 90 days

Receivable days

$$\text{Receivable Days} = \frac{\text{Receivables at year end}}{\text{Turnover}} \times 365$$

20X6: (3,800/15,600) × 365 = 89 days
20X5: (1,850/11,100) × 365 = 61 days

Sector average: 60 days

Payable days

$$\text{Payable Days} = \frac{\text{Trade payables at year end}}{\text{Cost of sales}} \times 365$$

20X6: (2,870/9,300 × 0.95) × 365 = 119 days
20X5: (1,600/6,600 × 0.95) × 365 = 93 days

Sector average: 80 days

Commentary

In each case, the ratio in 20X6 is **higher** than the ratio in 20X5, indicating that deterioration has occurred in the management of inventory, receivables and payables in 20X6.

Inventory days have increased by 46 days or 64%, moving from below the sector average to 28 days – one month – more than it. Given the rapid increase in turnover (40%) in 20X6, Anjo Co may be expecting a continuing increase in the future and may have built up inventories in preparation for this, ie inventory levels reflect future sales rather than past sales. Accounting statements from several previous years and sales forecasts for the next period would help to clarify this point.

Receivable days have increased by 28 days or 46% in 20X6 and are now 29 days above the sector average. It is possible that more generous credit terms have been offered in order to stimulate sales. The increased turnover does not appear to be due to offering lower prices, since both gross profit margin (40%) and net profit margin (34%) are unchanged.

Payable days. In 20X5, only management of payables was a cause for concern, with Anjo Co taking 13 more days on average to settle liabilities with trade payables than the sector. This has increased to 39 days more than the sector in 20X6. This could lead to difficulties between the company and its suppliers if it is exceeding the credit periods they have specified.

Anjo Co has no long-term debt and the balance sheet indicates an **increased reliance** on short-term finance, since cash has reduced by $780,000 or 87% and the overdraft has increased by $850,000 to $1 million. Perhaps the company should investigate whether it is **undercapitalised** (overtrading). It is unusual for a company of this size to have no long-term debt.

(b) Cash operating cycle = Inventory days + Receivable days – Payable days

Cash operating cycle (2005) = 72 + 61 – 93 = 40 days
Cash operating cycle (2006) = 118 + 89 – 119 = 88 days

BPP
LEARNING MEDIA

Significance

The cash operating cycle or working capital cycle gives the average time it takes for the company to receive payment from receivables after it has paid its trade payables. This represents the period of time for which receivables require financing. The cash operating cycle of Anjo Co has lengthened by 48 days in 20X6 compared with 20X5. This represents an increase in working capital requirement of approximately $15,600,000 × 48/365 = $2.05 million.

(c) The objectives of working capital management are **liquidity** and **profitability**, but there is a tension between these two objectives. Liquid funds, for example cash, earn no return and so will not increase profitability. Near-liquid funds, with short investment periods, earn a lower return than funds invested for a long period. Profitability is therefore decreased to the extent that liquid funds are needed.

The main reason that companies fail, though, is because they **run out of cash** and so good cash management is an essential part of good working capital management. Business solvency cannot be maintained if working capital management in the form of cash management is of a poor standard.

In order to **balance** the twin objectives of liquidity and profitability in terms of cash management, a company needs to decide on the **optimum** amount of cash to hold at any given time. There are several factors that can aid in determining the optimum cash balance:

First, it is important to note that cash management is a forward-looking activity, in that the optimum cash balance must reflect the expected need for cash in the next budget period, for example in the next month. The cash budget will indicate expected cash receipts over the next period, expected payments that need to be made, and any shortfall that is expected to arise due to the difference between receipts and payments. This is the **transactions need** for cash, since it is based on the amount of cash needed to meet future business transactions.

However, there may be a degree of **uncertainty** as to the timing of expected receipts. Receivables, for example, may not all pay on time and some may take extended credit, whether authorised or not. In order to guard against a possible shortfall of cash to meet future transactions, companies may keep a '**buffer inventory**' of cash by holding a cash reserve greater than called for by the transactions demand. This is the **precautionary demand** for cash and the optimum cash balance will reflect management's assessment of this demand.

Beyond this, a company may decide to hold additional cash in order to take advantage of any business opportunities that may arise, for example the possibility of taking over a rival company that has fallen on hard times. This is the **speculative demand** for cash and it may contribute to the optimum cash level for a given company, depending on that company's strategic plan.

(d)

	$000
Current receivables	3,800
Receivables under factor = 3,800 × 0.7	2,660
Reduction in receivables	1,140

	$000
Finance cost saving = 1,140 × 0.08	91.2
Administration cost saving = 1,000 × 0.02	20.0
Interest on advance = 2,660 × 0.8 × 0.01	(21.3)
Factor's annual fee = 15,600 × 0.005	(78.0)
Net benefit of accepting factor's offer	11.9

Although the terms of the factor's offer are financially acceptable, suggesting a net financial benefit of $11,900, this benefit is small compared with annual turnover of $15.6 million. Other benefits, such as the application of the factor's expertise to the receivable management of Anjo Co, might also be influential in the decision on whether to accept the offer.

Question 3

Text references. Sources of finance are covered in Chapter 12 and market efficiency in Chapter 18.

Top tips. A very good indication of the sort of question you might get in the exam, in terms of the calculations you may be asked to do and the balance between calculations and discussion.

Remember in (a) that on a rights issue, relative voting rights will only be unchanged if all current shareholders take up their rights, and they have to have the money to pay for the rights to do that. Also don't confuse scrip **issues** with scrip **dividends** (where shareholders are offered the choice of dividends in the form of shares or cash.)

In (b) (ii) remember you are calculating the value of the **rights**. A further adjustment (25/5) = 5c would be needed to calculate the value of the rights **to each share currently held.**

In (c) two alternative methods are given to calculate the rate of dividend growth. However the first method is superior if you can calculate the fourth roots of numbers. The methods of calculating the cost of debt and the cost of preference shares are identical; if the debt was redeemable however, you would have to carry out an internal rate of return calculation.

The best approach to (d) is to define strong form market efficiency first; points from the definition can be used to support your reasons as to the possible effects of the hypothesis on managers' behaviour.

Marking scheme

		Marks	
(a)	Rights issue explanation	2	
	Scrip issue explanation	2	
	Effect on private investors	3	
			7
(b)	Take up rights calculation	2	
	Sell rights calculation	2	
			4
(c)	Cost of equity	3	
	Cost of preference shares	1	
	Cost of debt	2	
	WACC	2	
			8
(d)	Explanation of strong form efficiency	3	
	Effect on behaviour	3	
			6
			25

(a)   **Rights issue**

A rights issue is a way of raising **new share capital** by means of an offer to existing shareholders enabling them to buy more shares, usually at a **price lower** than the **current market price**. Under a rights issue existing shareholders are invited to **subscribe cash** for new shares in proportion to their existing holdings.

Reasons for rights issue

A company may choose to make a rights issue for the following reasons:

(i)   Rights issues are **cheaper** than offers for sale to the general public. This is because:

      (1)   **No prospectus** is **required** (provided that the issue is for less than 10% of the class of shares concerned).

      (2)   **Administration** is **simpler**.

      (3)   The **costs** of **underwriting** will be **less**.

      The company will however need to **explain** clearly to shareholders the purpose for which the additional funds are required, and **demonstrate** that the **return on capital** will at least be **maintained**, and ideally enhanced as a result of the issue.

(ii)   Relative **voting rights** are **unaffected** if shareholders all take up their rights.

(iii)   Funds can be raised in this way for any type of **long term investment**, or to **reduce** the level of **capital gearing**.

Impact on private investor

The effects from the point of view of the **private investor** include:

(i)   He must decide whether to **take up** or **sell** the rights. If the market is efficient, he should be **no worse off** whether he decides to take up the rights or to sell them. However, if he were to do nothing then he would **forego** the **financial benefits** of the issue.

(ii)   If he decides to take up the rights he must have **additional funds** available to invest in the company. He must therefore decide if this is the **best use** of those funds, and also consider the effect of such an investment on the **risk/return profile** of his investment portfolio.

Scrip issue

A scrip issue (or bonus issue) is an issue of new shares to existing shareholders, by **converting equity reserves** into **issued share capital**. For example, a company with issued share capital of 10m $1 nominal value shares with a market price of $10 and reserves of $20m, could make a scrip issue of one for one. This would have the effect of doubling the number of shares in issue, and thus reducing the theoretical market price of the shares to $5.

Impact on company

The advantage to the company of a scrip issue is that it makes the **shares cheaper** and therefore **more marketable** on the Stock Exchange.

Impact on private investor

From the point of view of the investor, there should be **no change** as a result of a scrip issue. He is not required to subscribe additional capital, unlike the rights issue. Once the issue has taken place, he will own a **larger number of shares** in the company, but the overall value of his holding will be the same as it was before. However, in practice the **share price** may **rise slightly** as a result of improved marketability, and therefore he may experience a small capital gain.

(b)   (i)   Theoretical ex-rights price $= \dfrac{1}{N+1}((N \times \text{cum rights price}) + \text{issue price})$

$$= \dfrac{1}{5+1}((5 \times 1.60) + 1.30$$

$$= \$1.55 \text{ per share}$$

After the rights issue, James Brown will own 12,000 shares (10,000 + 2,000) at a price of $1.55. **The theoretical value** of **his holding** will therefore be $18,600.

(ii)   **Value of rights** per share   = Theoretical ex-rights price – Cost of taking up rights

= $1.55 – $1.30

= 25 cents per share

James Brown has the right to subscribe for an additional 2,000 shares. If he sells these rights he can expect to receive 2,000 × $0.25 = $500.

(c)   **The required return on equity using the dividend growth model**:

$$k_e = \frac{d_0(1+g)}{p_0} + g$$

Where d_0 =   Current level of dividends   =   12c per share

g   =   Rate of growth in dividends (see below)

p_0 =   Market price of shares   = $1.60 per share

'g' can be estimated over the four year period as $\left(\sqrt[4]{\frac{12}{8}}\right) - 1 = 0.1067$ ie 11%.

Alternatively, it can be approximated by finding the average annual rate of growth as follows:

Year	Div cents	Increase cents	Increase %
20X5	8		
20X6	9	1	12.5
20X7	11	2	22.2
20X8	11	0	0.0
20X9	12	1	9.1
			43.8

Over four years this gives an average rate of 11%.

The required rate of return can now be found:

$$k_e = \frac{12(1+0.11)}{160} + 0.11$$

= 19.3%

Cost of preference shares (k_{pref})

This can be found by dividing the preference dividend rate by the market price of the shares:

$$k_{pref} = \frac{15}{145}$$

= 10.3%

Although preference shares are included with prior charge capital, the dividend is not allowable for tax, and therefore no adjustment needs to be made for this.

Cost of debentures (k_{dnet})

The after tax cost of the debentures can be found using the following expression:

$$k_{dnet} = \frac{i(1-T)}{p_0}$$

where: i   =   rate of debenture interest

   p_0 =   market price of debentures

   T   =   rate of tax on profits

   k_{dnet} = $\dfrac{12(1-0.33)}{80}$

   k_{dnet} =   10.1%

Total market value of capital ($m)

$= (1.60 \times 5) + (1 \times 0.8) + (0.5 \times 1.45)$

$= \$m\ (8 + 0.8 + 0.725)$

$= \$9.525$ million

Weighted average cost of capital $= \dfrac{8(0.193) + 0.8(0.101) + 0.725(0.103)}{9.525}$

$= 17.8\%$

(d)   **Stock market efficiency**

An efficient stock market is one in which:

(i)   The prices of securities traded **reflect** all the **relevant information**, which is **available** to the buyers and sellers. Share prices **change quickly** to reflect all new information about future prospects.

(ii)   **No individual dominates** the market.

(iii)   **Transaction costs** of buying and selling are **not so high** as to **discourage trading** significantly.

Strong form efficiency

The efficient markets hypothesis exists in a number of forms, which relate to the nature of the information available to investors. Strong form efficiency means that share prices **reflect all information** available from:

(i)   Past price changes
(ii)   Public knowledge or anticipation
(iii)   Insider knowledge available to specialists or experts such as investment managers

Impact of strong form efficiency

If the stock market is believed to operate with strong level efficiency, this might affect the behaviour of the finance directors of publicly quoted companies in the following ways.

Managers are likely to be aware that **share prices** will **change quickly** to reflect decisions that they take. This means that all financial decisions are likely to be evaluated in the light of their **potential impact** on the **share price**. A contrary view is that management should concentrate simply on **maximising** the **net present value** of its investments and need not worry about the **effect** on **share prices** of financial results in the published accounts. **Investors** will make **allowances** for low profits or dividends in the current year if higher profits or dividends are expected in the future.

Question 4

Text reference. Foreign currency risk is covered in Chapter 19 and interest rate risk in Chapter 20.

Top tips. Make sure you apply your answer in part (a) to the specific circumstances of this company.

If you picked the wrong rate in (b), remember that the company needs to obtain dollars by buying them with pounds and the lower figures mean that it will get fewer dollars per pound (the customer always loses when it deals with the bank).

Part (c) is a textbook explanation and part (d) requires you to bring out that swaps are used for different reasons to other derivatives – as a means of borrowing on the best terms possible rather than trying to limit losses from foreign exchange dealings.

Marking scheme

			Marks
(a)	Up to 3 marks per risk discussed. To obtain high marks, must include discussion of company's circumstances		8
(b)	Forward market calculation	2	
	Money market calculation	3	
	Conclusion	1	6
(c)	Explanation of model		4
(d)	Swaps – must include advantages compared with other methods for maximum marks	4	
	Other methods	5	
	max		7
			25

(a) **Types of currency risk**

Economic risk

Economic risk refers to the effect of **exchange rate movements** on the international competitiveness of a company. For example, JetAWay provides airline services to many European countries. Movements in exchange rates will change the relative value of currencies. An appreciation of sterling against other European currencies will **erode the competitiveness** of the company where airline services are denoted in Sterling. Providing websites selling airline tickets in different currencies helps to alleviate this risk.

However, the fact that bookings can be made in any of JetAWay's web sites may cause problems. If JetAWay does not amend prices to reflect currency movements, this means that customers can '**shop around**' for the cheapest airfare from the 15 regional websites, paying in the site with the weakest currency. JetAWay needs to update its websites to **reflect currency movements** to ensure this does not happen.

Transaction risks

This is the risk of adverse exchange rate movements occurring in the **course of normal international trading transactions**. It arises when **export prices are fixed** in foreign currency terms or **imports are invoiced in other foreign currencies**.

For JetAWay, all sales are transferred to Milan and then to the regional locations for each JetAWay office. This exposes JetAWay to **currency risk** in respect of the euro against all non-euro countries. There will also be **transaction and conversion costs** for each currency movement. **Maintaining sales in local currencies** and **paying local expenditure** first before remitting surplus funds to Milan would help to limit this risk and transaction costs.

Translation risks

Translation risk arises from **differences in currencies** in which assets and liabilities are denominated. Where a company has different proportions of assets and liabilities denominated in different currencies, then exchange rate movements are likely to have varying effects on the value of those assets and liabilities.

In the case of JetAWay no information is available regarding the currencies in which assets and liabilities are denominated. It is possible that all assets are held in the UK accounts in which case the company would not be subject to translation risk.

(b) **Forward exchange market**

Cost of $40 million in 3 months = $40,000,000/1.6445 = £24,323,503

Money markets

US dollar deposit rate = 7%, so three month rate = 7/4 = 1.75%

To earn $40,000,000 in three months need to lend now:

40,000,000/1.0175 = $39,312,039

Purchase dollars now at spot rate of 1.6625

39,312,039/1.6625 = **£23,646,339**

Annual borrowing interest rate for 3 months = 10.75/4 = 2.6875%

Amount required = 23,646,339 × 1.026875 = £24,281,834

Conclusion – use money market to hedge risk.

(c) The **four-way equivalence model** states that in equilibrium, differences between forward and spot rates, differences in interest rates, expected differences in inflation rates and expected changes in spot rates are **equal** to one another.

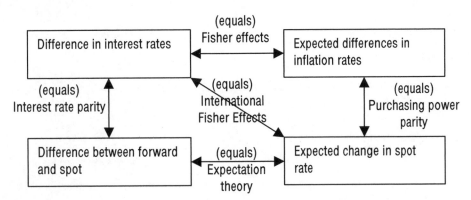

(d) **Hedging interest rate risk**

Interest rate risk can be hedged using the following techniques:

Forward rate agreements

This is an agreement that can be **purchased 'over the counter'** to lend or borrow a given sum of money in the future for an interest rate that is agreed now. In terms of currencies, this equates to a **forward contract** – that is an agreement to buy or sell a given amount of currency in the future at an exchange rate that is agreed today. Both types of contracts are used to **'fix' interest rates or exchange rates** on future transactions which removes the risk of rate movements in the intervening period.

Interest rate futures

Interest rate futures are similar to FRA's, although they are not available at a bank; they are **traded on the futures market**. The **terms, amounts and periods are standardised**. This means that forward rate agreements are more appropriate than interest rate futures for non-financial companies such as ReGen.

Interest rate options

An interest rate option gives the **right to borrow or lend a specified amount at a guaranteed rate of interest**. On or before the expiry of the option, the holder must decide whether or not to exercise the right to borrow or lend.

In a borrowing situation, the option will only be exercised if the **market interest rates** have **risen above the option rate**. Bespoke contracts can be obtained from major banks while standardised contracts are traded in a similar way to interest rate futures. Interest rate options tend to cost more than forward rate agreements.

Interest rate swaps

These are transactions which **exploit different interest** rates in different markets for borrowing, with the aim of reducing interest rate costs for fixed or floating loans. An interest rate swap is actually an agreement where two companies, or a bank and a company, swap interest rate commitments with each other. Each party effectively simulates the other's borrowings while maintaining their original obligation to their lender. Each party therefore accepts a counterparty risk.

The benefits of a swap compared to other hedging instruments include:

- **Low transaction costs** – legal fees only.

- **Flexibility** – swaps can be arranged in any size and reversed if necessary.

- **Companies with different credit ratings can borrow at the best cost** in the market that is accessible to each company, and then swap the benefit with another company with the aim of reducing mutual borrowing costs.

- Swaps can allow **capital restructuring** by changing the nature of interest commitments without the need to redeem old debt or issue new debt, which again reduces transaction costs.

ACCA

Paper F9

Financial Management

Mock Examination 3

Question Paper	
Time allowed	
Reading and Planning Writing	15 minutes 3 hours
ALL FOUR questions are compulsory and MUST be attempted	
During reading and planning time only the question paper may be annotated	

DO NOT OPEN THIS PAPER UNTIL YOU ARE READY TO START UNDER EXAMINATION CONDITIONS

ALL FOUR questions are compulsory and MUST be attempted

Question 1

Droxfol Co is a listed company that plans to spend $10m on expanding its existing business. It has been suggested that the money could be raised by issuing 9% loan notes redeemable in ten years' time. Current financial information on Droxfol Co is as follows.

Income statement information for the last year

	$000
Profit before interest and tax	7,000
Interest	(500)
Profit before tax	6,500
Tax	(1,950)
Profit for the period	4,550

Balance sheet for the last year	$000	$000
Non-current assets		20,000
Current assets		20,000
Total assets		40,000
Equity and liabilities		
Ordinary shares, par value $1	5,000	
Retained earnings	22,500	
Total equity		27,500
10% loan notes	5,000	
9% preference shares, par value $1	2,500	
Total non-current liabilities		7,500
Current liabilities		5,000
Total equity and liabilities		40,000

The current ex div ordinary share price is $4.50 per share. An ordinary dividend of 35 cents per share has just been paid and dividends are expected to increase by 4% per year for the foreseeable future. The current ex div preference share price is 76.2 cents. The loan notes are secured on the existing non-current assets of Droxfol Co and are redeemable at par in eight years' time. They have a current ex interest market price of $105 per $100 loan note. Droxfol Co pays tax on profits at an annual rate of 30%.

The expansion of business is expected to increase profit before interest and tax by 12% in the first year. Droxfol Co has no overdraft.

Average sector ratios:

Financial gearing: 45%   (prior charge capital divided by equity share capital on a book value basis)
Interest coverage ratio: 12 times

Required

(a)   Calculate the current weighted average cost of capital of Droxfol Co.   **(9 marks)**

(b)   Discuss whether financial management theory suggests that Droxfol Co can reduce its weighted average cost of capital to a minimum level.   **(8 marks)**

(c)   Evaluate and comment on the effects, after one year, of the loan note issue and the expansion of business on the following ratios:

(i)   Interest coverage ratio.
(ii)   Financial gearing.
(iii)   Earnings per share.

Assume that the dividend growth rate of 4% is unchanged.   **(8 marks)**

(Total = 25 marks)

Question 2

Nedwen Co is a UK-based company which has the following expected transactions.

One month: Expected receipt of $240,000
One month: Expected payment of $140,000
Three months: Expected receipts of $300,000

The finance manager has collected the following information:

Spot rate ($ per £):   1.7820 ± 0.0002
One month forward rate ($ per £):   1.7829 ± 0.0003
Three months forward rate ($ per £):   1.7846 ± 0.0004

Money market rates for Nedwen Co:

	Borrowing	Deposit
One year sterling interest rate:	4.9%	4.6
One year dollar interest rate:	5.4%	5.1

Assume that it is now 1 April.

Required

(a)   Discuss the differences between transaction risk, translation risk and economic risk.   **(6 marks)**

(b)   Explain how inflation rates can be used to forecast exchange rates.   **(6 marks)**

(c)   Calculate the expected sterling receipts in one month and in three months using the forward market.

(3 marks)

(d)   Calculate the expected sterling receipts in three months using a money-market hedge and recommend whether a forward market hedge or a money market hedge should be used.   **(5 marks)**

(e)   Discuss how sterling currency futures contracts could be used to hedge the three-month dollar receipt.

(5 marks)

(Total = 25 marks)

Question 3

Ulnad Co has annual sales revenue of $6 million and all sales are on 30 days' credit, although customers on average take ten days more than this to pay. Contribution represents 60% of sales and the company currently has no bad debts. Accounts receivable are financed by an overdraft at an annual interest rate of 7%.

Ulnad Co plans to offer an early settlement discount of 1.5% for payment within 15 days and to extend the maximum credit offered to 60 days. The company expects that these changes will increase annual credit sales by

5%, while also leading to additional incremental costs equal to 0.5% of turnover. The discount is expected to be taken by 30% of customers, with the remaining customers taking an average of 60 days to pay.

Required

(a)   Evaluate whether the proposed changes in credit policy will increase the profitability of Ulnad Co.

(6 marks)

(b)   Renpec Co, a subsidiary of Ulnad Co, has set a minimum cash account balance of $7,500. The average cost to the company of making deposits or selling investments is $18 per transaction and the standard deviation of its cash flows was $1,000 per day during the last year. The average interest rate on investments is 5.11%.

Determine the spread, the upper limit and the return point for the cash account of Renpec Co using the Miller-Orr model and explain the relevance of these values for the cash management of the company.

(6 marks)

(c)   Identify and explain the key areas of accounts receivable management.   **(6 marks)**

(d)   Discuss the key factors to be considered when formulating a working capital funding policy.

(7 marks)

(Total = 25 marks)

Question 4

Trecor Co plans to buy a new machine to meet expected demand for a new product, Product T. This machine will cost $250,000 and last for four years, at the end of which time it will be sold for $5,000. Trecor Co expects demand for Product T to be as follows:

Year	1	2	3	4
Demand (units)	35,000	40,000	50,000	25,000

The selling price for Product T is expected to be $12.00 per unit and the variable cost of production is expected to be $7.80 per unit. Incremental annual fixed production overheads of $25,000 per year will be incurred. Selling price and costs are all in current price terms.

Selling price and costs are expected to increase as follows:

	Increase
Selling price of Product T:	3% per year
Variable cost of production:	4% per year
Fixed production overheads:	6% per year

Other information

Trecor Co has a real cost of capital of 5.7% and pays tax at an annual rate of 30% one year in arrears. It can claim capital allowances on a 25% reducing balance basis. General inflation is expected to be 5% per year.

Trecor Co has a target return on capital employed of 20%. Depreciation is charged on a straight-line basis over the life of an asset.

Required

(a)   Calculate the net present value of buying the new machine and comment on your findings (work to the nearest $1,000).   **(13 marks)**

(b)   Calculate the before-tax return on capital employed (accounting rate of return) based on the average investment and comment on your findings.   **(5 marks)**

(c)   Discuss the strengths and weaknesses of internal rate of return in appraising capital investments.   **(7 marks)**

(Total = 25 marks)

Answers

DO NOT TURN THIS PAGE UNTIL YOU HAVE COMPLETED THE MOCK EXAM

A PLAN OF ATTACK

We've already established that you've been told to do it 103 times, so it is of course superfluous to tell you for the 104th time to **Take a good look at the paper before diving in to answer questions.** You are going to remember aren't you; good!

Which order to do the questions

Having **looked through** the **paper in detail,** you need to have worked out the **order** in which to attempt the questions. You will probably have decided which question looks the easiest and started with that one. Answer plans will help you to decide how to approach each question.

The next step

You're probably thinking that you don't know where to begin or you could answer all of the questions in two hours!

Option 1 (Oh dear)

If you are challenged by this paper, do the **questions in the order of how well you think you can answer them.**

*   **Question 1** has some straightforward calculations if you have practised them, and you can answer part (b) even if you haven't completed the calculations.

*   You may not like this part of the syllabus but there are easy marks available in each part of **Question 2.**

*   **Question 3** does have some hard calculations but there are some easy marks available for use of the Miller-Orr formula in part (b). You do not need to do the calculations correctly to be able to write the explanations in parts (c) and (d).

*   **Question 4** requires you to be able to do an investment appraisal with inflation and taxation. This may be daunting but use a proforma layout and move on if you get stuck.

Option 2 (This one's definitely easier)

Are you **sure** it is? If you are then that's encouraging but don't forget to do answer plans to make sure you don't miss the point of the questions.

*   Don't just concentrate on the calculations in **Question 1.** Make sure you also write full answers to the discussion and comment parts.

*   **Question 2** requires you to demonstrate your understanding of the numbers rather than just do calculations.

*   **Question 3** requires a logical approach to the calculations with clear workings. Make sure your explanations are sufficiently detailed and not just a list of points.

*   **Question 4** needs a clear layout and workings to make life easier for the marker. Make sure you write full discussions in the written parts of the question.

Once more for the road

You must must must **allocate your time** according to the marks for the question in total, and for the parts of the questions. And you must must must also **follow the requirements exactly.**

Finished with fifteen minutes to spare?

Looks like you slipped up on the time allocation. However if you have, make sure you don't waste the last few minutes; go back to **any parts of questions that you didn't finish** because you ran out of time.

Forget about it!

Forget about what? Excellent, you already have.

Question 1

Marking scheme

			Marks
(a)	Calculation of market values	2	
	Calculation of cost of equity	2	
	Calculation of cost of preference shares	1	
	Calculation of cost of debt	2	
	Calculation of WACC	2	
			9
(b)	Relative costs of equity and debt	1	
	Discussion of theories of capital structure	7-8	
	Conclusion	1	
	Maximum		8
(c)	Analysis of interest coverage ratio	2-3	
	Analysis of financial gearing	2-3	
	Analysis of earnings per share	2-3	
	Comment	2-3	
	Maximum		8
			25

(a) **Weighted average cost of capital**

Market values	$ million
Equity (5m × $4.50)	22.500
Preference shares (2.5m × $0.762)	1.905
10% loan notes (5m × (105/100))	5.250
	29.655

Cost of equity using dividend growth model $= \dfrac{D_0(1+g)}{P_0} + g$

$$= \frac{35(1+0.04)}{450} + 0.04$$

$$= 12.09\%$$

Cost of preference shares $= \dfrac{D}{P_0} = \dfrac{9}{76.2} = 11.81\%$

Cost of debt:

Year		Cash flow $	Discount factor 10%	PV $	Discount factor 5%	PV $
0	Market value	(105)	1.000	(105)	1.000	(105)
1 – 8	After tax interest	7	5.335	37.34	6.463	45.24
8	Redemption	100	0.467	46.70	0.677	67.70
				(20.96)		7.94

Using interpolation, cost of debt $= a + \left(\dfrac{NPV_a}{NPV_a - NPV_b} \right)(b - a)\%$

$$= 5 + \left(\dfrac{7.94}{7.94 + 20.96} \times 5 \right)$$

$$= 6.37\%$$

WACC $= [(12.09\% \times 22.5) + (11.81\% \times 1.905) + (6.37\% \times 5.25)]/29.655 = 11.05\%$

(b)   **Sources of finance**

The sources of long-term finance for Droxfol Co are ordinary shares, preference shares and loan notes and the rate of return expected by investors depends on the **relative risks** of each type of finance. Equity is the most risky and therefore has the highest cost of capital and the loan notes are the least risky with the lowest cost of capital.

Therefore, if we ignore taxation, the weighted average cost of capital would be expected to decrease if equity is replaced by debt.

Traditional view

In the **traditional view** of capital structure, ordinary shareholders are relatively **indifferent** to the addition of small amounts of debt so the WACC falls as a company gears up.

However, as equity is replaced by debt and gearing increases, **financial risk** will increase so the cost of equity will rise and this will offset the effect of cheaper debt.

The before-tax cost of debt will also increase at high levels of gearing due to the risk of bankruptcy and this **bankruptcy risk** will further increase the cost of equity.

A company can therefore gear up using debt and reduce its WACC to a **minimum**. When the WACC is minimised, the **market value** of the company, equal to the present value of its cash flows, will be maximised.

Beyond this minimum point, the WACC will increase due to the effect of increasing financial and bankruptcy risk.

Modigliani and Miller

In contrast to this traditional view, **Modigliani and Miller**, assuming a perfect market and ignoring tax, demonstrated that the WACC remained constant as a company increased its gearing. They argued that the increase in the cost of equity due to financial risk **exactly balanced** the decrease in WACC caused by the lower before-tax cost of debt.

In a perfect capital market, there is no bankruptcy risk so the WACC and therefore the market value of the company is constant at all gearing levels. The market value of a company depends on its **business risk** only. This means that Droxfol Co cannot reduce its WACC to a minimum.

However, corporate tax does exist and interest payments on debt reduce tax liability, so it could be argued that WACC falls as gearing increases and Droxfol Co could reduce its WACC to a minimum by taking on as much debt as possible.

The assumption of a perfect capital market is unrealistic and so bankruptcy risk and other costs of servicing debt will increase as gearing increases and this will offset the value of the tax shield.

Conclusion

In conclusion, Droxfol Co should be able to reduce its WACC by gearing up, but the minimum WACC achievable may be hard to determine.

(c) (i) **Interest coverage ratio**

Current interest coverage ratio = 7,000/500 = 14 times
Increased profit before interest and tax = $7,000 \times 1.12$ = \$7.84m
Increased interest payment = \$0.5m + (\$10m $\times$ 9%) = \$1.4m
Interest coverage ratio after one year = 7.84/1.4 = 5.6 times

The current interest coverage of Droxfol Co is higher than the sector average of 12 times and can be considered quite safe. However, after the new issue of loan notes, the interest coverage ratio falls to less than half of the sector average and could indicate that Droxfol Co may find it difficult to meet the interest payments.

(ii) **Financial gearing**

$$\text{Financial gearing} = \frac{\text{Prior charge capital}}{\text{Equity share capital}}$$

$$\text{Current financial gearing at book values} = \frac{5,000 + 2,500}{5,000 + 22,500} \times 100 = 27.3\%$$

Ordinary dividend after one year = $0.35 \times 5m \times 1.04$ = \$1.82 million

Preference dividend = $2,500 \times 0.09$ = \$225,000

INCOME STATEMENT AFTER ONE YEAR

	$'000	$'000
Profit before interest and tax		7,840
Interest		(1,400)
Profit before tax		6,440
Income tax expense		(1,932)
Profit for the period		4,508
Preference dividends	225	
Ordinary dividends	1,820	
		(2,045)
Retained earnings		2,463

$$\text{Financial gearing after one year} = \frac{5,000 + 10,000 + 2,500}{5,000 + 22,500 + 2,463} = 58.4\%$$

The current financial gearing of Droxfol Co is around 40% ((45 – 27.3)/45) less than the sector average. After the loan note issue, it is predicted to be 30% ((58.4 – 45)/45) more than the sector average. This increase in, and level of, financial gearing may be of concern to investors and the stock market. However, if the company continues to grow at 12% per annum, financial gearing will gradually reduce as the proportion of debt to equity falls.

(iii) **Earnings per share (EPS)**

$$EPS = \frac{\text{Profit attributable to ordinary shareholders}}{\text{Number of ordinary shares}}$$

$$\text{Current EPS} = \frac{4,550 - 225}{5,000} = 0.865 = 86.5 \text{ cents per share}$$

$$\text{EPS after one year} = \frac{4,508 - 225}{5,000} = 0.857 = 85.7 \text{ cents per share}$$

Any decrease in EPS tends to be disliked by investors as it is seen as a key ratio. However, this decrease is relatively small and the expected future growth in earnings should quickly reverse it.

In conclusion, the issue of new debt is likely to have a **negative impact** on the company's financial position at least in the short-term.

Droxfol Co will also need to consider whether it has sufficient non-current asset **security** for a new debt issue as the existing loan notes are already secured on the existing assets. The new loan notes may need to be secured on any new non-current assets bought which may not be sufficient.

The company must also consider the future **redemption** of the loan notes. The existing loan notes are due to be redeemed in eight years' time and an additional need for re-financing only two years later may cause difficulties. They may need to consider a **longer maturity** for the new loan notes.

In view of this, Droxfol Co should also consider an **equity issue** and compare its potential impact on the company's financial position.

Question 2

Text references. Foreign currency risk is covered in Chapter 19.

Top tips. In part (a), using numerical examples will help you to discuss the differences between the different types of risk.

The purchasing power parity formula relating inflation rates to exchange rates is on the formula sheet so you simply need to be able explain what it means in part (b).

Parts (c) and (d) are standard hedging calculations that you should be able to do if you have practised the methods.

Easy marks. There are five parts to this question, each with a relatively small mark allocation so you should be able to pick up marks on some parts, even if you find this part of the syllabus challenging.

Marking scheme

			Marks
(a)	Transaction risk	2	
	Translation risk	2	
	Economic risk	2	
			6
(b)	Discussion of purchasing power parity	4-5	
	Discussion of interest rate parity	1-2	
	Maximum		6
(c)	Netting	1	
	Sterling value of 3-month receipt	1	
	Sterling value of 1-year receipt	1	
			3

(d)	Evaluation of money market hedge		4	
	Comment		1	
				5
(e)	Definition of currency futures contract		1-2	
	Initial margin and variation margin		1-2	
	Buying and selling of contracts		1-2	
	Hedging the three-month receipt		1-2	
		Maximum		5
				25

(a) **Transaction risk**

This is the risk of adverse exchange rate movements occurring in the course of **normal international trading transactions**. This arises when the prices of imports or exports are fixed in foreign currency terms and there is movement in the exchange rate between the date when the price is agreed and the date when the cash is paid or received in settlement.

For example, a sale worth $3,000 when the exchange rate is $1.7820 per £ has an expected sterling value of £1,684. If the dollar has **depreciated** against sterling to $1.8500 per £ when the transaction is settled, the sterling receipt will have fallen to £1,622.

Transaction risk therefore affects cash flows so companies often choose to **hedge** or protect themselves against transaction risk.

Translation risk

This is the risk that the organisation will make exchange losses when the accounting results of its foreign branches or subsidiaries are **translated** into the home currency. Translation losses can result, for example, from restating the book value of a foreign subsidiary's assets at the exchange rate on the balance sheet date.

For example, an asset is valued on a balance sheet at $14 million and was acquired when the exchange rate was $1.79 per £. One year later, the exchange rate has moved to $1.84 per £ and the balance sheet value of the asset has changed from $7.82 million to $7.61 million, resulting in an **unrealised** (paper) **loss** of $0.21 million.

Translation risk does not affect cash flows so does not **directly** affect shareholder wealth. However, **investors** may be influenced by the changing values of assets and liabilities so a company may choose to hedge translation risk through, for example **matching the currency of assets and liabilities**. For example an asset denominated in euros would be financed by a euro loan.

Economic risk

This refers to the effect of exchange rate movements on the **international competitiveness** of a company. For example, a UK company might use raw materials which are priced in US dollars, but export its products mainly within the EU. A depreciation of sterling against the dollar or an appreciation of sterling against other EU currencies will both erode the competitiveness of the company. Economic exposure can be difficult to avoid, although **diversification of the supplier and customer base** across different countries will reduce this kind of exposure to risk.

(b) **Purchasing power parity theory**

Purchasing power parity theory states that the exchange rate between two currencies is the same in equilibrium when the purchasing power of currency is the same in each country.

The theory predicts that the exchange value of foreign currency depends on the relative purchasing power of each currency in its own country and that **spot exchange rates will vary over time according to relative price changes.**

Formally, purchasing power parity can be expressed in the following formula.

$$F_0 = S_0 \times \frac{(1+i_c)}{(1+i_b)}$$

Where F_0 = expected spot rate
  S_0 = current spot rate
  i_c = expected inflation rate in country c
  i_b = expected inflation rate in country b

This relationship has been found to hold true in the longer term and so tends to be used for forecasting exchange rates a number of years into the future, rather than for forecasting less than one year ahead.

For shorter periods, forward rates can be calculated using **interest rate parity theory**, which suggests that changes in exchange rates reflect differences between interest rates in different countries.

(c) **Forward market**

Net receipt in one month = $(240,000 – 140,000) = $100,000
Nedwen Co needs to sell $s at an exchange rate of 1.7829 + 0.0003 = $1.7832 per £
Sterling value of net receipt = $100,000/1.7832 = £56,079

Receipt in three months = $300,000
Nedwen Co needs to sell $s at an exchange rate of 1.7846 + 0.0004 = $1.7850 per £
Sterling value of receipt = $300,000/1.7850 = £168,067

(d) **Money market hedge**

Expected receipt after three months = $300,000

$ interest rate over three months = 5.4/4 = 1.35%

$s to borrow now in order to have $300,000 liability after three months = $300,000/1.0135 = $296,004

Spot rate for selling $s = 1.7820 + 0.0002 = $1.7822 per £

Sterling deposit from borrowed s at spot = $296,004/1.7822 = £166,089

Sterling interest rate over three months = 4.6/4 = 1.15%

Value in three months of sterling deposit = £166,089 × 1.0115 = $167,999

In conclusion, the forward market is marginally preferable to the money market hedge for the $ receipt expected after three months.

(e) A **currency futures contract** is a standardised contract for the sale or purchase at a set future date of a set quantity of currency.

A **future** represents a commitment to an additional transaction in the future **that limits the risk** of existing commitments.

It is traded on a **futures market** and **settlement** takes place in three-monthly cycles ending in March, June, September and December.

The **contract price** is the price at which the futures contract can be bought or sold. For all currency futures the contract price is in US dollars. The contract price is the figure which is traded on the futures exchange. It changes continuously and is the basis for computing gains or losses.

When a currency futures contract is bought or sold, the buyer or seller is required to deposit a sum of money with the exchange. This is called the **initial margin**. If losses are incurred as exchange rates and therefore currency futures prices change, the buyer or seller may be called on to deposit additional funds with the exchange. This is the **variation margin.** In the same way profits are credited to the margin account on a **daily basis**.

Most currency futures contracts are **closed out** before their settlement dates by undertaking the **opposite** transaction to the initial futures transaction. For example, if the initial transaction is buying currency futures, it is closed out by selling currency futures. A gain made on the futures transaction will **offset** a loss made on the currency markets and vice versa.

Nedwen Co expects to receive $300,000 in three months' time and would want to hedge against an **appreciation** (strengthening) in sterling as this would reduce the sterling receipt. This could be achieved by **selling** sterling futures contracts. As it is now 1st April, Nedwen would sell June futures contracts. In June, Nedwen would **buy** the same number of futures and exchange the $300,000 receipt on the currency market.

Question 3

Text references. Working capital management is covered in Chapters 4, 5 and 6.

Top tips. In part (a), think logically about the change in costs as a result of the credit policy and set out your workings clearly. In part (b) don't forget to explain your findings as well as do the calculation. Parts (c) and (d) require full explanations so don't just simply write a list of points.

Easy marks. There are 4 easy marks available in part (b) for simply using the Miller-Orr formulae given to you in the exam. If you have learnt the subject matter in for parts (c) and (d), they should be straightforward explanations.

Marking scheme

			Marks
(a)	Increase in financing cost	2	
	Incremental costs	1	
	Cost of discount	1	
	Contribution from increased sales	1	
	Conclusion	1	
			6
(b)	Calculation of spread	2	
	Calculation of upper limit	1	
	Calculation of return point	1	
	Explanation of findings	2	
			6
(c)	Policy formulation	1-2	
	Credit analysis	1-2	
	Credit control	1-2	
	Collection of amounts due	1-2	
	Maximum		6
(d)	Analysis of assets	1-2	
	Short-term and long-term debt	2-3	
	Discussion of policies	2-3	
	Other factors	1-2	
	Maximum		7
			25

(a) **Evaluation of change in credit policy**

Current average collections period = 30 + 10 = 40 days

Current accounts receivable = $6m × 40/365 = $657,534

Average collection period under new policy = (30% × 15 days) + (70% × 60 days) = 46.5 days

New level of credit sales = $6m × 1.05 = $6.3m

Accounts receivable after policy change = $6.3m × 46.5/365 = $802,603

Increase in financing cost = $(802,603 – 657,534) × 7% = $10,155

	$
Increase in financing cost	10,155
Incremental costs ($6.3m × 0.5%)	31,500
Cost of discount (30% × $6.3m × 1.5%)	28,350
Increase in costs	70,005
Contribution from increased sales ($6m × 5% × 60%)	180,000
Net benefit of policy change	109,995

The proposed policy will therefore increase the profitability of Ulnad Co.

(b) **Determination of spread**

Daily interest rate = 5.11/365 = 0.014% per day

Variance of cash flows = 1,000 × 1,000 = $1,000,000 per day

Transaction cost = $18 per transaction

$$\text{Spread} = 3 \times ((0.75 \times \text{transaction cost} \times \text{variance})/\text{interest rate})^{1/3}$$
$$= 3 \times ((0.75 \times 18 \times 1,000,000)/0.00014)1/3 = 3 \times 4,585.7 = \$13,757$$

Lower limit = $7,500

Upper limit = $(7,500 + 13,757) = $21,257

Return point = 7,500 + (13,757/3) = $12,086

Relevance of the values

The Miller-Orr model takes account of **uncertainty** in relation to cash flows. The cash balance of Renpec Co is allowed to vary between the lower and upper **limits** calculated by the model.

If the cash balance reaches an **upper limit** the firm **buys sufficient securities** to return the cash balance to a normal level (called the 'return point'). When the cash balance reaches a lower limit, the firm sells securities to bring the balance back to the return point.

The Miller-Orr model therefore helps Renpec Co to decrease the risk of running out of cash, while avoiding the loss of profit caused by having unnecessarily high cash balances.

(c) **Key areas of accounts receivable management**

There are four key areas of accounts receivable management.

(i) **Formulation of policy**

A **framework** needs to be established within which the management of accounts receivable in an organisation takes place. Elements of the framework to be considered include establishing the **terms of trade** such as the period of credit offered and **early settlement discounts.** The organisation must also consider whether to **charge interest** on overdue accounts. Laid-down procedures will be needed for granting credit to new customers and determining what to do when accounts become overdue.

(ii) **Assessment of creditworthiness**

Information relating to a new customer needs to be analysed. The information may come from bank references, trade references or credit reference agency reports.

The greater the amount of credit being granted and the possibility of repeat business, the more credit analysis is needed.

(iii) Credit control

Accounts receivable' payment records must be **monitored** continually. This depends on successful sales ledger administration.

Credit monitoring can be simplified by a system of **in-house credit ratings**. For example, a company could have five credit-risk categories for its customers. These credit categories or ratings could be used to decide either individual credit limits for customers within that category or the frequency of the credit review.

A **customer's payment record** and the **accounts receivable aged analysis** should be examined regularly, as a matter of course. Breaches of the credit limit, or attempted breaches of it, should be brought immediately to the attention of the credit controller.

(iv) Collection of amounts due

A company needs to have in place agreed procedures for dealing with overdue accounts. Examples include instituting reminders or final demands, chasing payment by telephone or making a personal approach. If this does not work, the company could refuse to grant any more credit to the customer, hire a specialist debt collecting agency or, as a last resort, take legal action.

The overall **debt collection policy** of the firm should be such that the administrative costs and other costs incurred in debt collection do not exceed the benefits from incurring those costs.

(d) Formulating a working capital funding policy

In order to understand working capital financing decisions, assets can be divided into three different types.

Non-current (fixed) assets are long-term assets from which an organisation expects to derive benefit over a number of periods. For example, buildings or machinery.

Permanent current assets are the amount required to meet long-term minimum needs and sustain normal trading activity. For example, inventory and the average level of accounts receivable.

Fluctuating current assets are the current assets which vary according to normal business activity. For example due to seasonal variations.

Fluctuating current assets together with **permanent** current assets form part of the working capital of the business, which may be financed by either long-term funding (including equity capital) or by current liabilities (short-term funding).

Short-term sources of funding are usually **cheaper** and **more flexible** than long-term ones. However short-term sources are **riskier** for the borrower as interest rates are more volatile in the short term and they may not be renewed.

The matching principle suggests that long-term finance should be used for long-term assets. A **balance** between risk and return might be best achieved by a **moderate approach** to working capital funding. This is a policy of **maturity matching** in which long-term funds finance permanent assets while short-term funds finance non-permanent assets. This means that the maturity of the funds **matches** the maturity of the assets.

A **conservative approach** to financing working capital involves all non-current assets and permanent current assets, as well as part of the fluctuating current assets, being financed by long-term funding. This is less risky and less profitable than a matching policy. At times when fluctuating current assets are low, there will be **surplus cash** which the company will be able to invest in marketable securities.

Finally, an organisation may adopt an **aggressive approach** to financing working capital. Not only are fluctuating current assets all financed out of short-term sources, but so are some of the permanent current assets. This policy represents an **increased risk** of liquidity and cash flow problems, although potential returns will be increased if short-term financing can be obtained more cheaply than long-term finance.

Other factors that influence a working capital funding policy include **previous management attitudes to risk**; this will determine whether there is a preference for a conservative, aggressive or moderate approach. Secondly, **previous funding decisions** will determine the current position being considered in policy formulation. Finally, the **size of the organisation** will influence its ability to access different sources of finance. For example, a small company may have to adopt an aggressive working capital funding policy because it cannot raise additional long-term finance.

Question 4

Text references. Investment appraisal is covered in Chapters 7, 8 and 9.

Top tips. In part (a), set out your workings clearly to gain the maximum number of marks for your workings. Do as much of the NPV calculation as you possibly can, as marks are awarded for each stage. Make an assumption and carry on if you get stuck on any part. Nominal cash flows are used so the nominal discount rate must be calculated and used.

Remember to deduct depreciation from the cash flows in part (b) to calculate accounting profit.

Write a full answer with clearly made and well supported arguments in part (c). Don't just list the strengths and weaknesses.

Easy marks. Part (b) is a straightforward relatively simple calculation. Part (c) is a standard textbook discussion and you should be able to gain most of the marks.

Marking scheme

			Marks
(a)	Discount rate	1	
	Inflated sales revenue	2	
	Inflated variable cost	1	
	Inflated fixed production overheads	1	
	Taxation	2	
	Capital allowance tax benefits	3	
	Discount factors	1	
	Net present value	1	
	Comment	1	
			13
(b)	Calculation of average annual accounting profit	2	
	Calculation of average investment	2	
	Calculation of return on capital employed	1	
			5
(c)	Strengths of IRR	2-3	
	Weaknesses of IRR	5-6	
	Maximum		7
			25

BPP
LEARNING MEDIA

(a) **Calculation of NPV**

Nominal discount rate:

$(1 + i) = (1 + r)(1 + h) = 1.057 \times 1.05 = 1.10985$

$i = 11\%$

	1	2	3	4	5
	$'000	$'000	$'000	$'000	$'000
Sales (W1)	433	509	656	338	
Variable cost (W2)	284	338	439	228	
Contribution	149	171	217	110	
Fixed production overheads	27	28	30	32	
Net cash flow	122	143	187	78	
Tax		(37)	(43)	(56)	(23)
CA tax benefits (W3)		19	14	11	30
After-tax cash flow	122	125	158	33	7
Disposal				5	
After-tax cash flow	122	125	158	38	7
Discount factors	0.901	0.812	0.731	0.659	0.593
Present values	110	102	115	25	4

	$
PV of benefits	356,000
Investment	250,000
NPV	106,000

Workings

1

Year	1	2	3	4
Demand (units)	35,000	40,000	50,000	25,000
Selling price ($/unit)	12.36	12.73	13.11	13.51
Sales ($/year)	432,600	509,200	655,500	337,750

2

Year	1	2	3	4
Demand (units)	35,000	40,000	50,000	25,000
Variable cost ($/unit)	8.11	8.44	8.77	9.12
Sales ($/year)	283,850	337,600	438,500	228,000

3

	Capital allowances		**Tax benefits**	
		$		$
1	$250,000 \times 0.25 =$	62,500	$62,500 \times 0.3 =$	18,750
2	$62,500 \times 0.75 =$	46,875	$46,875 \times 0.3 =$	14,063
3	$46,875 \times 0.75 =$	35,156	$25,156 \times 0.3 =$	10,547
4	By difference	100,469	$100,469 \times 0.3 =$	30,141
	$250,000 - 5,000 =$	245,000		73,501

(b) **Calculation of before-tax return on capital employed (ROCE)**

Cash flow before tax = 122 + 143 + 187 +78 = $530,000

Total depreciation = (250,000 – 5,000) = $245,000

Average annual accounting profit = (530 – 245)/4 = $71,250

Average investment = (250,000 + 5,000)/2 = $127,500

ROCE = 71,250/127,500 × 100 = 56%

The target ROCE is 20% and the expected ROCE is significantly higher than this so the purchase of the machine can be recommended.

(c) **Strengths of IRR**

The main advantage of the IRR method is that the information it provides is **more easily understood** by managers than NPV, especially non-financial managers. It gives a **relative measure** of the value of a proposed investment in the form of a percentage which can be compared with the company's cost of capital or the rates of interest and inflation.

IRR is a **discounted cash flow method** and so takes account of the **time value** of money: the concept that $1 received today is not equal to $1 received in the future.

IRR considers cash flows over the **whole** of the project life and is sensitive to both the amount and the **timing** of cash flows.

Weaknesses of IRR

IRR ignores the **relative sizes** of investments. It therefore does not measure the absolute increase in company value, and therefore shareholder wealth, which will be created by an investment.

Where cash flow patterns are **non-conventional**, for example cash flows change from positive to negative during the life of the project, there may be **several IRRs** which decision makers must be aware of to avoid making the wrong decision. When **discount rates** are **expected to differ** over the life of the project, such **variations** can be incorporated easily into **NPV** calculations, but not into IRR calculations.

Mutually exclusive projects are two or more projects from which only one can be chosen. Examples include the choice of a factory location or the choice of just one of a number of machines. The IRR and NPV methods can, however, give **conflicting rankings** as to which project should be given priority. Where there is a conflict, NPV always offers the **technically correct investment advice.**

Despite the advantages of the NPV method over the IRR method, the **IRR method** is **widely used** in practice.

Pilot Paper
ACCA model answers

Pilot Paper F9   Answers
Financial Management

1   (a)   Calculation of weighted average cost of capital (WACC)

Market values
Market value of equity = 5m x 4.50 = $22.5 million
Market value of preference shares = 2.5m x .0762 = $1.905 million
Market value of 10% loan notes = 5m x (105/ 100) = $5.25 million
Total market value = 22.5m + 1.905m + 5.25m = $29.655 million

Cost of equity using dividend growth model = [(35 x 1.04)/ 450] + 0.04 = 12.08%

Cost of preference shares = 100 x 9/ 76.2 = 11.81%

Annual after-tax interest payment = 10 x 0.7 = $7

Year	Cash flow	$	10% DF	PV ($)	5% DF	PV ($)
0	market value	(105)	1.000	(105)	1.000	(105)
1–8	interest	7	5.335	37.34	6.463	45.24
8	redemption	100	0.467	46.70	0.677	67.70
				(20.96)		7.94

Using interpolation, after-tax cost of loan notes = 5 + [(5 x 7.94)/ (7.94 + 20.96)] = 6.37%

WACC = [(12.08 x 22.5) + (11.81 x 1.905) + (6.37 x 5.25)]/ 29.655 = 11.05%

(b)   Droxfol Co has long-term finance provided by ordinary shares, preference shares and loan notes. The rate of return required by each source of finance depends on its risk from an investor point of view, with equity (ordinary shares) being seen as the most risky and debt (in this case loan notes) seen as the least risky. Ignoring taxation, the weighted average cost of capital (WACC) would therefore be expected to decrease as equity is replaced by debt, since debt is cheaper than equity, i.e. the cost of debt is less than the cost of equity.

However, financial risk increases as equity is replaced by debt and so the cost of equity will increase as a company gears up, offsetting the effect of cheaper debt. At low and moderate levels of gearing, the before-tax cost of debt will be constant, but it will increase at high levels of gearing due to the possibility of bankruptcy. At high levels of gearing, the cost of equity will increase to reflect bankruptcy risk in addition to financial risk.

In the traditional view of capital structure, ordinary shareholders are relatively indifferent to the addition of small amounts of debt in terms of increasing financial risk and so the WACC falls as a company gears up. As gearing up continues, the cost of equity increases to include a financial risk premium and the WACC reaches a minimum value. Beyond this minimum point, the WACC increases due to the effect of increasing financial risk on the cost of equity and, at higher levels of gearing, due to the effect of increasing bankruptcy risk on both the cost of equity and the cost of debt. On this traditional view, therefore, Droxfol Co can gear up using debt and reduce its WACC to a minimum, at which point its market value (the present value of future corporate cash flows) will be maximised.

In contrast to the traditional view, continuing to ignore taxation but assuming a perfect capital market, Miller and Modigliani demonstrated that the WACC remained constant as a company geared up, with the increase in the cost of equity due to financial risk exactly balancing the decrease in the WACC caused by the lower before-tax cost of debt. Since in a prefect capital market the possibility of bankruptcy risk does not arise, the WACC is constant at all gearing levels and the market value of the company is also constant. Miller and Modigliani showed, therefore, that the market value of a company depends on its business risk alone, and not on its financial risk. On this view, therefore, Droxfol Co cannot reduce its WACC to a minimum.

When corporate tax was admitted into the analysis of Miller and Modigliani, a different picture emerged. The interest payments on debt reduced tax liability, which meant that the WACC fell as gearing increased, due to the tax shield given to profits. On this view, Droxfol Co could reduce its WACC to a minimum by taking on as much debt as possible.

However, a perfect capital market is not available in the real world and at high levels of gearing the tax shield offered by interest payments is more than offset by the effects of bankruptcy risk and other costs associated with the need to service large amounts of debt. Droxfol Co should therefore be able to reduce its WACC by gearing up, although it may be difficult to determine whether it has reached a capital structure giving a minimum WACC.

(c)   (i)   Interest coverage ratio
Current interest coverage ratio = 7,000/ 500 = 14 times
Increased profit before interest and tax = 7,000 x 1.12 = $7.84m
Increased interest payment = (10m x 0.09) + 0.5m = $1.4m
Interest coverage ratio after one year = 7.84/ 1.4 = 5.6 times

The current interest coverage of Droxfol Co is higher than the sector average and can be regarded as quiet safe. Following the new loan note issue, however, interest coverage is less than half of the sector average, perhaps indicating that Droxfol Co may not find it easy to meet its interest payments.

(ii) Financial gearing

This ratio is defined here as prior charge capital/equity share capital on a book value basis

Current financial gearing = 100 x (5,000 + 2,500)/ (5,000 + 22,500) = 27%

Ordinary dividend after one year = 0.35 x 5m x 1.04 = $1.82 million

Total preference dividend = 2,500 x 0.09 = $225,000

Income statement after one year

	$000	$000
Profit before interest and tax		7,840
Interest		(1,400)
Profit before tax		6,440
Income tax expense		(1,932)
Profit for the period		4,508
Preference dividends	225	
Ordinary dividends	1,820	
		(2,045)
Retained earnings		2,463

Financial gearing after one year = 100 x (15,000 + 2,500)/ (5,000 + 22,500 + 2,463) = 58%

The current financial gearing of Droxfol Co is 40% less (in relative terms) than the sector average and after the new loan note issue it is 29% more (in relative terms). This level of financial gearing may be a cause of concern for investors and the stock market. Continued annual growth of 12%, however, will reduce financial gearing over time.

(iii) Earnings per share

Current earnings per share = 100 x (4,550 – 225)/ 5,000 = 86.5 cents

Earnings per share after one year = 100 x (4,508 - 225)/ 5,000 = 85.7 cents

Earnings per share is seen as a key accounting ratio by investors and the stock market, and the decrease will not be welcomed. However, the decrease is quiet small and future growth in earnings should quickly eliminate it.

The analysis indicates that an issue of new debt has a negative effect on the company's financial position, at least initially. There are further difficulties in considering a new issue of debt. The existing non-current assets are security for the existing 10% loan notes and may not available for securing new debt, which would then need to be secured on any new non-current assets purchased. These are likely to be lower in value than the new debt and so there may be insufficient security for a new loan note issue. Redemption or refinancing would also pose a problem, with Droxfol Co needing to redeem or refinance $10 million of debt after both eight years and ten years. Ten years may therefore be too short a maturity for the new debt issue.

An equity issue should be considered and compared to an issue of debt. This could be in the form of a rights issue or an issue to new equity investors.

2 **(a)** **Transaction risk**

This is the risk arising on short-term foreign currency transactions that the actual income or cost may be different from the income or cost expected when the transaction was agreed. For example, a sale worth $10,000 when the exchange rate is $1.79 per £ has an expected sterling value is $5,587. If the dollar has depreciated against sterling to $1.84 per £ when the transaction is settled, the sterling receipt will have fallen to $5,435. Transaction risk therefore affects cash flows and for this reason most companies choose to hedge or protect themselves against transaction risk.

Translation risk

This risk arises on consolidation of financial statements prior to reporting financial results and for this reason is also known as accounting exposure. Consider an asset worth €14 million, acquired when the exchange rate was €1.4 per $. One year later, when financial statements are being prepared, the exchange rate has moved to €1.5 per $ and the balance sheet value of the asset has changed from $10 million to $9.3 million, resulting an unrealised (paper) loss of $0.7 million. Translation risk does not involve cash flows and so does not directly affect shareholder wealth. However, investor perception may be affected by the changing values of assets and liabilities, and so a company may choose to hedge translation risk through, for example, matching the currency of assets and liabilities (eg a euro-denominated asset financed by a euro-denominated loan).

Economic risk

Transaction risk is seen as the short-term manifestation of economic risk, which could be defined as the risk of the present value of a company's expected future cash flows being affected by exchange rate movements over time. It is difficult to measure economic risk, although its effects can be described, and it is also difficult to hedge against it.

(b) The law of one price suggests that identical goods selling in different countries should sell at the same price, and that exchange rates relate these identical values. This leads on to purchasing power parity theory, which suggests that changes in exchange rates over time must reflect relative changes in inflation between two countries. If purchasing power parity holds true, the expected spot rate (S_f) can be forecast from the current spot rate (S_0) by multiplying by the ratio of expected inflation rates (($1 + i_f$)/ ($1 + i_{UK}$)) in the two counties being considered. In formula form: $S_f = S_0 (1 + i_f)/ (1 + i_{UK})$.

This relationship has been found to hold in the longer-term rather than the shorter-term and so tends to be used for forecasting exchange rates several years in the future, rather than for periods of less than one year. For shorter periods, forward rates can be calculated using interest rate parity theory, which suggests that changes in exchange rates reflect differences between interest rates between countries.

(c) Forward market evaluation

Net receipt in 1 month = 240,000 – 140,000 = $100,000
Nedwen Co needs to sell dollars at an exchange rate of 1.7829 + 0.003 = $1.7832 per £
Sterling value of net receipt = 100,000/ 1.7832 = $56,079

Receipt in 3 months = $300,000
Nedwen Co needs to sell dollars at an exchange rate of 1.7846 + 0.004 = $1.7850 per £
Sterling value of receipt in 3 months = 300,000/ 1.7850 = $168,067

(d) Evaluation of money-market hedge

Expected receipt after 3 months = $300,000
Dollar interest rate over three months = 5.4/ 4 = 1.35%
Dollars to borrow now to have $300,000 liability after 3 months = 300,000/ 1.0135 = $296,004
Spot rate for selling dollars = 1.7820 + 0.0002 = $1.7822 per £
Sterling deposit from borrowed dollars at spot = 296,004/ 1.7822 = $166,089
Sterling interest rate over three months = 4.6/ 4 = 1.15%
Value in 3 months of sterling deposit = 166,089 x 1.0115 = $167,999

The forward market is marginally preferable to the money market hedge for the dollar receipt expected after 3 months.

(e) A currency futures contract is a standardised contract for the buying or selling of a specified quantity of foreign currency. It is traded on a futures exchange and settlement takes place in three-monthly cycles ending in March, June, September and December, ie a company can buy or sell September futures, December futures and so on. The price of a currency futures contract is the exchange rate for the currencies specified in the contract.

When a currency futures contract is bought or sold, the buyer or seller is required to deposit a sum of money with the exchange, called initial margin. If losses are incurred as exchange rates and hence the prices of currency futures contracts change, the buyer or seller may be called on to deposit additional funds (variation margin) with the exchange. Equally, profits are credited to the margin account on a daily basis as the contract is 'marked to market'.

Most currency futures contracts are closed out before their settlement dates by undertaking the opposite transaction to the initial futures transaction, ie if buying currency futures was the initial transaction, it is closed out by selling currency futures. A gain made on the futures transactions will offset a loss made on the currency markets and vice versa.

Nedwen Co expects to receive $300,000 in three months' time and so is concerned that sterling may appreciate (strengthen) against the dollar, since this would result in a lower sterling receipt. The company can hedge the receipt by selling sterling futures contracts and since it is 1 April, would sell June futures contracts. In June, Nedwen Co would buy the same number of futures it sold in April and sell the $300,000 it received on the currency market.

3 (a) Evaluation of change in credit policy

Current average collection period = 30 + 10 = 40 days
Current accounts receivable = 6m x 40/ 365 = $657,534
Average collection period under new policy = (0.3 x 15) + (0.7 x 60) = 46.5 days
New level of credit sales = $6.3 million
Accounts receivable after policy change = 6.3 x 46.5/ 365 = $802,603
Increase in financing cost = (802,603 – 657,534) x 0.07 = $10,155

	$
Increase in financing cost	10,155
Incremental costs = 6.3m x 0.005 =	31,500
Cost of discount = 6.3m x 0.015 x 0.3 =	28,350
Increase in costs	70,005
Contribution from increased sales = 6m x 0.05 x 0.6 =	180,000
Net benefit of policy change	109,995

The proposed policy change will increase the profitability of Ulnad Co

(b) Determination of spread:
Daily interest rate = 5.11/ 365 = 0.014% per day
Variance of cash flows = 1,000 x 1,000 = $1,000,000 per day
Transaction cost = $18 per transaction

Spread = 3 x ((0.75 x transaction cost x variance)/interest rate)$^{1/3}$
= 3 x ((0.75 x 18 x 1,000,000)/ 0.00014)1/3 = 3 x 4,585.7 = $13,757

Lower limit (set by Renpec Co) = $7,500
Upper limit = 7,500 + 13,757 = $21,257
Return point = 7,500 + (13,757/ 3) = $12,086

The Miller-Orr model takes account of uncertainty in relation to receipts and payment. The cash balance of Renpec Co is allowed to vary between the lower and upper limits calculated by the model. If the lower limit is reached, an amount of cash equal to the difference between the return point and the lower limit is raised by selling short-term investments. If the upper limit is reached an amount of cash equal to the difference between the upper limit and the return point is used to buy short-term investments. The model therefore helps Renpec Co to decrease the risk of running out of cash, while avoiding the loss of profit caused by having unnecessarily high cash balances.

(c) There are four key areas of accounts receivable management: policy formulation, credit analysis, credit control and collection of amounts due.

Policy formulation

This is concerned with establishing the framework within which management of accounts receivable in an individual company takes place. The elements to be considered include establishing terms of trade, such as period of credit offered and early settlement discounts: deciding whether to charge interest on overdue accounts; determining procedures to be followed when granting credit to new customers; establishing procedures to be followed when accounts become overdue, and so on.

Credit analysis

Assessment of creditworthiness depends on the analysis of information relating to the new customer. This information is often generated by a third party and includes bank references, trade references and credit reference agency reports. The depth of credit analysis depends on the amount of credit being granted, as well as the possibility of repeat business.

Credit control

Once credit has been granted, it is important to review outstanding accounts on a regular basis so overdue accounts can be identified. This can be done, for example, by an aged receivables analysis. It is also important to ensure that administrative procedures are timely and robust, for example sending out invoices and statements of account, communicating with customers by telephone or e-mail, and maintaining account records.

Collection of amounts due

Ideally, all customers will settle within the agreed terms of trade. If this does not happen, a company needs to have in place agreed procedures for dealing with overdue accounts. These could cover logged telephone calls, personal visits, charging interest on outstanding amounts, refusing to grant further credit and, as a last resort, legal action. With any action, potential benefit should always exceed expected cost.

(d) When considering how working capital is financed, it is useful to divide assets into non-current assets, permanent current assets and fluctuating current assets. Permanent current assets represent the core level of working capital investment needed to support a given level of sales. As sales increase, this core level of working capital also increases. Fluctuating current assets represent the changes in working capital that arise in the normal course of business operations, for example when some accounts receivable are settled later than expected, or when inventory moves more slowly than planned.

The matching principle suggests that long-term finance should be used for long-term assets. Under a matching working capital funding policy, therefore, long-term finance is used for both permanent current assets and non-current assets. Short-term finance is used to cover the short-term changes in current assets represented by fluctuating current assets.

Long-term debt has a higher cost than short-term debt in normal circumstances, for example because lenders require higher compensation for lending for longer periods, or because the risk of default increases with longer lending periods. However, long-term debt is more secure from a company point of view than short-term debt since, provided interest payments are made when due and the requirements of restrictive covenants are met, terms are fixed to maturity. Short-term debt is riskier than long-term debt because, for example, an overdraft is repayable on demand and short-term debt may be renewed on less favourable terms.

A conservative working capital funding policy will use a higher proportion of long-term finance than a matching policy, thereby financing some of the fluctuating current assets from a long-term source. This will be less risky and less profitable than a matching policy, and will give rise to occasional short-term cash surpluses.

An aggressive working capital funding policy will use a lower proportion of long-term finance than a matching policy, financing some of the permanent current assets from a short-term source such as an overdraft. This will be more risky and more profitable than a matching policy.

Other factors that influence a working capital funding policy include management attitudes to risk, previous funding decisions, and organisation size. Management attitudes to risk will determine whether there is a preference for a conservative, an aggressive or a matching approach. Previous funding decisions will determine the current position being considered in policy formulation. The size of the organisation will influence its ability to access different sources of finance. A small company, for example, may be forced to adopt an aggressive working capital funding policy because it is unable to raise additional long-term finance, whether equity of debt.

4 (a) Calculation of NPV

Nominal discount rate using Fisher effect: 1.057 x 1.05 = 1.1098 ie 11%

Year	1	2	3	4	5
	$000	$000	$000	$000	$000
Sales (W1)	433	509	656	338	
Variable cost (W2)	284	338	439	228	
Contribution	149	171	217	110	
Fixed production overheads	27	28	30	32	
Net cash flow	122	143	187	78	
Tax		(37)	(43)	(56)	(23)
CA tax benefits (W3)		19	14	11	30
After-tax cash flow	122	125	158	33	7
Disposal				5	
After-tax cash flow	122	125	158	38	7
Discount factors	0.901	0.812	0.731	0.659	0.593
Present values	110	102	115	25	4

	$
PV of benefits	356,000
Investment	250,000
NPV	106,000

Since the NPV is positive, the purchase of the machine is acceptable on financial grounds.

Workings

(W1) Year	1	2	3	4
Demand (units)	35,000	40,000	50,000	25,000
Selling price ($/unit)	12.36	12.73	13.11	13.51
Sales ($/year)	432,600	509,200	655,500	337,750

(W2) Year	1	2	3	4
Demand (units)	35,000	40,000	50,000	25,000
Variable cost ($/unit)	8.11	8.44	8.77	9.12
Variable cost ($/year)	283,850	337,600	438,500	228,000

(W3) Year	Capital allowances			Tax benefits	
1	250,000 x 0.25 =	62,500	62,500 x 0.3 =		18,750
2	62,500 x 0.75 =	46,875	46,875 x 0.3 =		14,063
3	46,875 x 0.75 =	35,156	25,156 x 0.3 =		10,547
4	By difference	100,469	100,469 x 0.3 =		30,141
	250,000 – 5.000 =	245,000			73,501

(b) Calculation of before-tax return on capital employed

Total net before-tax cash flow = 122 + 143 + 187 + 78 = $530,000
Total depreciation = 250,000 – 5,000 = $245,000
Average annual accounting profit = (530 – 245)/ 4 = $71,250

Average investment = (250,000 + 5,000)/ 2 = $127,500

Return on capital employed = 100 x 71,250/ 127,500 = 56%

Given the target return on capital employed of Trecor Co is 20% and the ROCE of the investment is 56%, the purchase of the machine is recommended.

(c) One of the strengths of internal rate of return (IRR) as a method of appraising capital investments is that it is a discounted cash flow (DCF) method and so takes account of the time value of money. It also considers cash flows over the whole of the project life and is sensitive to both the amount and the timing of cash flows. It is preferred by some as it offers a relative measure of the value of a proposed investment, ie the method calculates a percentage that can be compared with the company's cost of capital, and with economic variables such as inflation rates and interest rates.

IRR has several weaknesses as a method of appraising capital investments. Since it is a relative measurement of investment worth, it does not measure the absolute increase in company value (and therefore shareholder wealth), which can be found using the net present value (NPV) method. A further problem arises when evaluating non-conventional projects (where cash flows change from positive to negative during the life of the project). IRR may offer as many IRR values as there are changes in the value of cash flows, giving rise to evaluation difficulties. There is a potential conflict between IRR and NPV in the evaluation of mutually exclusive projects, where the two methods can offer conflicting advice as which of two projects is preferable. Where there is conflict, NPV always offers the correct investment advice: IRR does not, although the advice offered can be amended by considering the IRR of the incremental project. There are therefore a number of reasons why IRR can be seen as an inferior investment appraisal method compared to its DCF alternative, NPV.

Review Form & Free Prize Draw – Paper F9 Financial Management (4/07)

All original review forms from the entire BPP range, completed with genuine comments, will be entered into one of two draws on 31 July 2007 and 31 January 2008. The names on the first four forms picked out on each occasion will be sent a cheque for £50.

Name: _____   Address: _____

_____

_____

How have you used this Kit?
(Tick one box only)

☐ Home study (book only)

☐ On a course: college _____

☐ With 'correspondence' package

☐ Other _____

Why did you decide to purchase this Kit?
(Tick one box only)

☐ Have used the complementary Study text

☐ Have used other BPP products in the past

☐ Recommendation by friend/colleague

☐ Recommendation by a lecturer at college

☐ Saw advertising

☐ Other _____

During the past six months do you recall seeing/receiving any of the following?
(Tick as many boxes as are relevant)

☐ Our advertisement in *Student Accountant*

☐ Our advertisement in *Pass*

☐ Our advertisement in *PQ*

☐ Our brochure with a letter through the post

☐ Our website www.bpp.com

Which (if any) aspects of our advertising do you find useful?
(Tick as many boxes as are relevant)

☐ Prices and publication dates of new editions .

☐ Information on product content

☐ Facility to order books off-the-page

☐ None of the above

Which BPP products have you used?

Text	☐	Success CD	☐	Learn Online	☐
Kit	☑	i-Learn	☐	Home Study Package	☐
Passcard	☐	i-Pass	☐	Home Study PLUS	☐

Your ratings, comments and suggestions would be appreciated on the following areas.

	Very useful	Useful	Not useful
Passing ACCA exams	☐	☐	☐
Passing F6	☐	☐	☐
Planning your question practice	☐	☐	☐
Questions	☐	☐	☐
Top Tips etc in answers	☐	☐	☐
Content and structure of answers	☐	☐	☐
'Plan of attack' in mock exams	☐	☐	☐
Mock exam answers			

Overall opinion of this Kit   Excellent ☐   Good ☐   Adequate ☐   Poor ☐

Do you intend to continue using BPP products?   Yes ☐   No ☐

The BPP author of this edition can be e-mailed at: juiletgood@bpp.com

Please return this form to: Nick Weller, ACCA Publishing Manager, BPP Learning Media Ltd, FREEPOST, London, W12 8BR

Review Form & Free Prize Draw (continued)

TELL US WHAT YOU THINK

Please note any further comments and suggestions/errors below.

Free Prize Draw Rules

1 Closing date for 31 July 2007 draw is 30 June 2007. Closing date for 31 January 2008 draw is 31 December 2007.

2 Restricted to entries with UK and Eire addresses only. BPP employees, their families and business associates are excluded.

3 No purchase necessary. Entry forms are available upon request from BPP Learning Media Ltd. No more than one entry per title, per person. Draw restricted to persons aged 16 and over.

4 Winners will be notified by post and receive their cheques not later than 6 weeks after the relevant draw date.

5 The decision of the promoter in all matters is final and binding. No correspondence will be entered into.